VISUAL QUICKSTART GUIDE

FIREWORKS 2

FOR WINDOWS AND MACINTOSH

Sandee Cohen

Peachpit Press

macromedia®
PRESS

Visual QuickStart Guide
Fireworks 2 for Windows and Macintosh
Copyright © 1999 by Sandee Cohen

Peachpit Press
1249 Eighth Street
Berkeley, CA 94710
800 283-9444 • 510 524 2178
fax 510 524 2221
Find us on the Web at http://www.peachpit.com

Published by Peachpit Press in association with Macromedia, Inc.
Peachpit Press is a division of Addison Wesley Longman.

Notice of Liability
The information in this book is distributed on an "as is" basis, without warranty. Although every precaution has been taken in the preparation of this book, neither the author nor Peachpit Press shall have any liability to any person or entity with respect to any loss or damage caused or alleged to be caused directly or indirectly by the instructions contained in this book or by the computer software and hardware products described herein.

Trademarks
Many of the designations used by manufacturers and sellers to distinguish their products are claimed as trademarks. Where those designations appear in this book, and Peachpit Press was aware of a trademark claim, the designations appear as requested by the owner of the trademark. All other product names and services identified throughout this book are used in editorial fashion only and for the benefit of such companies. No such use, or the use of any trade name, is intended to convey endorsement or other affiliation with the book.

Fireworks is a registered trademark of Macromedia Inc.
Visual QuickStart Guide is a trademark of Peachpit Press, a division of Addison Wesley Longman.

Development Editor: Marjorie Baer
Copy Editor: Nancy Dunn
Technical Reviewer: Joanne Watkins
Production Coordinator: Kate Reber
Compositor & Interior Design: Sandee Cohen
Cover Design: The Visual Group
Indexer: Steve Rath

ISBN 0-201-35458-6

0 9 8 7 6 5 4 3 2 1

Printed and bound in the United States of America

DEDICATED TO

Anyone who has ever been baffled by a
computer program. I hope my books
make it easier.

THANKS TO

Nancy Ruenzel, publisher of Peachpit Press.

Marjorie Baer, my project editor at Peachpit Press.

Nancy Dunn, who is more than a copy editor; she is a great friend.

Kate Reber of Peachpit Press, who made the production process the smoothest ever.

The staff of Peachpit Press, all of whom make me proud to be a Peachpit author.

Lynda Weinman, who has again written a foreword. Check out her Fireworks instructional video (www.lynda.com).

Steve Rath, who does the best index in the business.

Diana Smedley of Macromedia, who made me feel like a part of the gang.

Doug Benson and David Morris of Macromedia, who gave me the behind-the-scenes info.

Mark Haynes of Macromedia, who provides the best support in the Fireworks newsgroup (http://forums/macromedia.com/macromedia.fireworks).

Joanne Watkins of Macromedia, who again did the technical editing.

Joe Lowery, author of the *Fireworks 2 Bible.* Joe has been a great resource, and I'm thrilled that readers will now have his book to graduate to after they read mine.

Fireworks beta list participants, too numerous to name, who all gave me great insight into features and techniques.

Ray Villarosa, who created special artwork for the Introduction that shows off all of Fireworks' graphics capabilities.

Robert Ransick and the staff of the New School for Social Research Computer Instruction Center.

Sharon Steuer, author of the *Illustrator 8 Wow! Book,* who helped me during more than one late-night panic attack.

Pixel, my cat, who thinks chapter 12 is all about her.

Colophon

This book was created using Fireworks for illustrations, QuarkXPress 4 for layout, Ambrosia SW Snapz Pro and Snagit for screen shots. The computers used were a Power Macintosh 8500, a PowerBook G3, and a Monorail 166LS. The fonts used were Minion and Futura from Adobe and two specialty fonts created using Macromedia Fontographer.

FOREWORD

When Fireworks 1.0 was released, it was the first program of its kind. Its power rested in the fact that it used vectors and bitmaps within one program to achieve a balance between editable images and Web bitmap file formats. Though it was a breakthrough product, Fireworks was challenging to learn because of its novel approach to a variety of Web graphics problems. Without Sandee Cohen's first edition, I, and many others, would have had a much harder time learning the product.

One of the great strengths of Fireworks is its ability to create complicated buttons and graphical navigation elements. Because of its vector-based creation tools, it is actually much easier to create the large quantity of graphics often required for a Web site. Changing your mind about color, size, or appearance is usually just a single click away. This is untrue of most bitmap editing programs, which rely on layers and fixed pixels.

Fireworks 2.0 is a quantum leap from the prior version. Like most software upgrades, its newfound strengths and features carry a steeper learning curve. Thankfully, Sandee is at it again with this second edition of her wonderful book. Without her, few of us would figure out all the great new features and depth of this remarkable upgrade.

The new version of Fireworks offers enhanced color control, with the ability to lock, shift, and more easily identify Web-safe colors. One of the program's biggest strengths—the ability to create JavaScript rollovers—has been enhanced to allow multiple events and behaviors, plus improved compatibility with Dreamweaver, FrontPage, and other HTML editors. The animation features have been improved to offer instant browser previews and the ability to preview within the creation tools. While the improvements are numerous, so are the changes!

If your goal is to get up and running quickly, which is essential in the fast-paced world of Web development, then you've come to the right book. I highly recommend this second edition if you want to use Fireworks to its best advantage. Thanks again Sandee, for providing this invaluable guide to an invaluable product!

Lynda Weinman

Author and educator
http://www.lynda.com

TABLE OF CONTENTS

Foreword . . . . **v**

Introduction **1**

Chapter 1:   **Fireworks Basics** **5**

Minimum System requirements (Mac) 6
Check memory (Mac) 6
Check hard disk space (Mac) 6
Minimum System requirements (Win) 7
Check memory (Win) 7
Check hard disk space (Win) 7
Install Fireworks (Mac) 8
Install Fireworks (Win) 8
Launch Fireworks (Mac) 8
Launch Fireworks (Win) 8
Layers panel 9
Frames panel 9
Stroke panel 9
Fill panel 10
Effect panel 10
Color Mixer 11
Swatches panel 11
Color Well Swatches panel 11
Options panel 12
Info panel 12
Object panel 12
URL Manager panel 13
Behaviors panel 13
Find & Replace panel 13
Styles panel 14
Project Log panel 14
View controls 14
Working with interface elements 15
Working with pop-up sliders 15
Panel tabs 16
Main toolbar (Win) 16
Modify toolbar (Win) 16
Text Editor 17
Toolbox .18

Chapter 2:   **Document Setup** **19**

Create a new document 20
Change the image size 21
Change the canvas size numerically 22
Change the canvas color visually 22
Change the canvas color 23
Open a document as untitled 23

Display the document rulers 24
Change the zero point 24
Create guides 25
Position guides 25
Edit guides 26
View the document grid 26
Edit the document grid 27
Use the magnification commands 27
Use the Zoom tool 28
Change the display options 29
Use the Grabber tool .30

Chapter 3: **Colors** **31**
Use the Color Mixer .32
Define RGB colors 32
Define hexadecimal colors 33
Define CMY colors 34
Define HSB colors 35
Define Grayscale colors 36
Use the Swatches panel 36
Choose the Web 216 palette swatches 37
Choose the Macintosh System swatches 37
Choose the Windows System swatches 38
Choose the Grayscale swatches 38
Add colors to the Swatches panel 38
Delete colors from the Swatches panel 39
Delete all colors from the Swatches panel 39
Sort the swatches by color 39
Save colors in the Swatches panel 40
Load colors to the Swatches panel 40
Work with the default colors 40
Change the default colors 41
Sample colors with the Eyedropper 41
Fill objects with the Paint Bucket 41
Use the Info panel 42

Chapter 4: **Path Tools** **43**
Rectangle 44
Rounded-corner rectangle 45
Ellipse 45
Polygon 46
Star 47
Elements of paths 48
Straight path segment 48
Curved path segment .49
Corner curve 49
Retract the handle into a point 50
Extend a handle out from a point 50
Open path 51
Closed path 51
Line 51
Draw with the Brush .52
Draw straight segments with the Brush 52

Modify a brush path 53
Draw with the Pencil 54
Anti-alias pencil lines 54
Use the Auto Erase 55
Add points to a path 56
Delete points from a path 56

Chapter 5: **Selecting Paths** **57**
Pointer tool 58
Marquee selected objects 58
Add or subtract objects from a selection 59
Subselection tool 59
Select Behind tool 60
Select menu commands 60
Mouse Highlight 61
Preview drag 61
Group selected objects .62
Ungroup objects 62
Select objects within groups 62
Nested groups 63
Subselect command 63
Superselect command .63
Control the highlight of selected objects 64
Change the highlight color 64

Chapter 6: **Working with Objects.** **65**
Move an object by eye .66
Move an object numerically 66
Copy and paste an object 66
Clone an object 67
Duplicate an object 67
Copy an object as you move it 67
Drag and drop an object 67
Scale an object 68
Skew an object 69
Distort an object 70
Rotate an object 71
Move an object in the transformation mode 71
Transform menu commands 72
Numeric Transform dialog box 72
Scale attributes options 73
Auto-crop images option 73
Freeform tool options .74
Freefrom tool in the Push mode 75
Freeform tool in the Pull mode 75
Reshape Area tool options 76
Reshape Area tool 77
Eraser tool 77
Union command 78
Intersect command 78
Punch command 79
Crop objects command 79

Simplify a path 80
Expand a path 80
Inset a path 81
Align menu commands 82
Align pop-up list (Win) 82
Send objects to the front or back of a layer 83
Move objects forward or backward in a layer 83
Work with the Layers panel 84
Use the Layers panel menu 85
Use Single Layer Editing 86
Move an object between layers 86

Chapter 7:   **Fills. 87**
Apply a solid color fill 88
Apply the None fill setting 88
Change the edges of a fill 89
Apply a Web dither fill 89
Apply a gradient fill .90
Edit the colors of a gradient fill 91
Save a gradient 92
Delete a gradient fill .92
Change the appearance of a gradient 93
Apply a pattern fill 94
Add patterns 94
Apply textures to a fill 95
Add textures 95
Change the object transparency 96
Join command 96
Split command 96
Mask Group 97
Release a Mask Group 97
Select objects within a mask 98
Move objects within a mask 98
Change the object blending mode 98
Normal blending mode 99
Multiply blending mode 99
Screen blending mode 99
Darken blending mode 99
Lighten blending mode 99
Difference blending mode 100
Hue blending mode 100
Saturation blending mode 100
Color blending mode 100
Luminosity blending mode 101
Invert blending mode 101
Tint blending mode 101
Erase blending mode 101
Paste attributes from one object to another 102

Chapter 8:   **Strokes 103**
View the Stroke panel 103
Apply a basic brush stroke 103
Change the stroke attributes 105

Apply textures to a stroke 106
Use the Pencil tool 106
Save Brush panel settings 107
Create a natural brush stroke 107
Use the Path Scrubber tool 108
Create your own strokes 109
Change the position of a stroke on a path 110
Change how the fill meets a stroke 110

Chapter 9: Effects **111**
View the Effect panel .112
Apply a bevel effect 112
Change the color of a bevel 113
Using the Button menu 113
Drop Shadow effect 114
Emboss effect 115
Change the appearance of the embossing 115
Glow effect 116
Save an effect 117
Apply multiple effects 117

Chapter 10: Text **119**
Text tool 120
Text Editor 120
Reopen the Text Editor 120
Set the font 121
Set the point size 121
Add electronic styling 121
Apply different text attributes 121
Kern the text 122
Set the range kerning .122
Set the leading 123
Add a baseline shift 123
Change the horizontal scale 124
Set the horizontal alignment 124
Set the vertical alignment 125
Reverse the text flow .125
Modify text inside a text block 126
Transform text in a text block 127
Set the object properties for a text block 127
Attach text to a path .128
Change the alignment of text on a path 128
Change the text offset along a path 129
Change the orientation of text on a path 129
Reverse the direction of text on a path 130
Apply path attributes to text 130
Convert text to paths .130

Chapter 11: Automation Features **131**
Understanding styles .132
Define an object style .132
Define a text style 133
Apply styles to objects 133
Export styles 134

Import styles 134
Edit styles 135
Change style views 135
Reset styles 135
Delete styles 135
Find and Replace Commands 136
Set the Find & Replace location 136
Find and replace text attributes 137
Find and replace font attributes 138
Find and replace color attributes 139
Find and replace URL attributes 140
Understanding the Project Log 141
Add or delete files to the Project Log 141
Export files from the Project Log 141
Batch Processing Changes 142
Set the files for batch processing 142
Bath Replace options .143
Bath Export options .143
Backup Original File options 144
Batch process settings as a script 144
Run a Script 144

Chapter 12:   Working with Pixels. 145
Switch to the image-editing features 146
Switch back to vector drawing 146
Import pixel-based images 147
Crop image objects 147
Combine or convert objects 148
Work with an empty image 148
Marquee tools 149
Change the Marquee tool constraints 149
Change the Marquee tool edges 150
Lasso tools 150
Magic Wand 151
Deselect a selected area 151
Change the shape of selections 152
Selection commands .152
Similar command 153
Feather an existing selection 153
Rubber Stamp options 154
Use the Rubber Stamp tool 155
Eraser options 156
Eyedropper 157
Paint Bucket options .158
Use the Paint Bucket .158

Chapter 13:   Xtras 159
Apply Xtras to vector objects 160
Blur and Blur more 160
Gaussian Blur 161
Sharpen and Sharpen More 162
Unsharp Mask 163
Invert 164
Find Edges 164

Mask using the Convert to Alpha Xtra 165
PhotoOptics filters 166
CSI GradTone 166
CSI HueSlider 167
CSI MonoChrome 167
CSI PhotoFilter 167
CSI Negative 168
CSI Noise 168
CSI PseudoColor 168
CSI Levels 169
Reapply Xtras quickly 169
Add Xtras from other companies 169
Increase the area around an image 170

Chapter 14: **Importing** **171**
Open a scanned image 172
Import scans as image objects 172
Open Photoshop files with layer masks 173
Open vector artwork .174
Set the size of imported vector artwork 174
Set which pages of vector artwork to open 175
Set the layers of opened vector artwork 175
Render imported vector art into pixel images 176
Set the edge of opened vector artwork 176
Set additional folders for textures or patterns 177

Chapter 15: **Basic Exporting** **179**
Export an image 180
Open the Export Preview window 181
Change the Preview area views 181
GIF or JPEG? 182
Choose a file format .182
GIF Web 216 palette options 183
GIF Adaptive palette options 184
Other palette options 184
WebSnap Adaptive palette options 185
Control colors in a GIF palette 186
Use the Color Export menu 187
Save a palette 187
Load a palette 187
JPEG options 188
Sharpen the edges of a JPEG image 189
Create images that appear gradually 189
Compare export settings 190
Create a transparent GIF (by color table) 191
Create a transparent GIF (in image) 191
Choose the matte color 192
Save export settings .192
Use saved export settings 192
Exporting other file formats 193
Export defaults 193
Export options for batch processing 194
Scale an exported image 194

Export a portion of an image 195
Export Area tool in the Export Preview 195
Export a portion of an image numerically 196
Export Again command 196
Export Wizard 197
Export Size Wizard 197
Export Special command 198

Chapter 16:   Hotspots and URLs 199
Rectangular or circular hotspot 200
Polygon hotspot 200
Show and hide hotspot objects 200
Convert objects into hotspots 201
Move and modify hotspot objects 201
Convert hotspot shapes 201
Apply a single URL link 202
Work with the history list 202
Apply no link to a hotspot 203
Set the hotspot options 203
Import links 204
Create a URL library .204
Add the history list to a Library 205
Add a new URL link to a Library 205
Delete URL links 205
Edit URL links 206
Document Properties .206

Chapter 17:   Slices 207
Why Slices? (Part One) 208
Slice using ruler guides 208
Create slice objects 209
Show and hide slice objects and slice guides 209
Slice options 210
Link for a slice object 210
Alt text, target or slice display 210
Why Slices? (Part Two) 211
Slice export options .211
Text slice 212
Document Properties slice options 213
Table shims 213
Auto-naming conventions 214
Custom name for slices 214
Work with both slice and hotspot objects 215
Exporting HTML code for slices 215
Set the Web browser and preview a file 216
Copy HTML code into Web pages 216
Why Slices? (Part Three) 216

Chapter 18:   Behaviors 217
Rollover states 218
Create the frames for a simple rollover 219
Duplicate Frame dialog box 219

Frame States 220
Modify the frame of a rollover 220
Share across frames 220
Assign a simple rollover behavior 221
Create multiple rollovers 222
Edit a behavior 222
Delete a behavior 222
Display Status Message behavior 223
Elements of a swap-image behavior 224
Frames for the area to be changed 224
Define area to be changed 225
Define area that triggers the change 225
Swap-Image behavior 226
Toggle group 227
Export files with behaviors 228

Chapter 19:   **Animations 229**
Animation basics 230
Open the Frames panel 230
Distribute objects onto frames 230
Control frames in the Layers panel 230
Show a layer across frames 231
Copy objects onto frames 231
Animating with imported artwork 232
Distribute vector layers onto frames 232
Distribute pages onto frames 232
Tweening with symbols and instances 233
Create a symbol 233
Copy and paste an instance from a symbol 233
Option/Alt-drag an instance from a symbol 233
Modify symbols and instances 234
Move both the symbol and instances 234
Move only the symbol 233
Change the opacity of the symbol only 234
Create motion by tweening 235
Tween appearances 236
Alter tweened images 237
Break the link between a symbol and its instance 237
Add objects to the symbol 238
Find the symbol an instance is based on 238
Delete the instances based on a symbol 238
Turn on onion skinning 239
Customize onion skinning 239
Multi-frame editing .240
Preview animation 240
Animation export controls 241
Set duration of a frame 241
Transition of the frames 242
Set the number of times the animation plays 242
Preview animations with Export Preview 243
Specify which frames to export 243

Appendix A: **Defaults.** **245**

Textures 246
Patterns 248
Gradients 250
Brushes 251
Effects 254

Appendix B: **Keyboard Shortcuts** **255**

Windows Keyboard Shortcuts 256
Macintosh Keyboard Shortcuts 258
Toolbox Keyboard Shortcuts 260

Appendix C: **Regular Expressions.** **261**

Regular expressions table 262

Index **263**

INTRODUCTION

Welcome to Macromedia Fireworks 2. In less than one year, Fireworks has become a very important tool in the creation of graphics for the Web. Using Fireworks, students have been able to create extremely sophisticated graphics without having to learn complicated code. Now, with this second version of Fireworks, the program is even more powerful and sophisticated. It has been very exciting to revise my original book. So many new features have added more pages to the book. And yet, some of the original features have been made much simpler and easier to understand. Just as Fireworks has evolved, so has this Visual Quickstart Guide.

What You Can Create with Fireworks

Fireworks was specially designed to create graphics to be used on the World Wide Web. Fireworks gives you one tool that does it all, from start to finish. All your Web graphic elements—text, photos, buttons, banners, animations, and interface elements—can be created, modified, optimized, and output from one Fireworks file. As the artwork at the end of this introduction shows, Fireworks has all the tools you need to create sophisticated graphics. This makes Fireworks a complete Web graphics solution.

How This Book Is Organized

The first two chapters provide overviews of the program. The next dozen chapters cover all the tools and techniques for creating graphics from within Fireworks. This is where you learn to create artwork and add special effects. Chapter 15 covers exporting artwork out of Fireworks in various formats. Since exporting, converting file formats, and optimizing Web graphics are so important, you can easily start right away with that chapter. The final chapters cover advanced features such as rollovers and animations.

Using This Book

If you have used any of the Visual QuickStart Guides, you will find this book very similar. Each of the chapters consists of numbered steps that deal with a specific technique or feature of the program. As you work through the steps, you gain an understanding of the technique or feature. The illustrations help you judge if you are following the steps correctly.

Instructions

Using a book such as this you will find works better once you understand the terms I am using. This is especially important since some other computer books use terms differently. Therefore, here are the terms I use in the book and explanations of what they mean.

Click refers to pressing down and releasing the mouse button on the Macintosh, or the left mouse button on Windows. You must release the mouse button or it is not a click. *Press* means to hold down the mouse button, or a keyboard key.

Press and drag means to hold the mouse button down and then move the mouse. In later chapters, I use the shorthand term *drag;* just remember that you have to press and hold as you drag the mouse.

Menu Commands

Fireworks has menu commands that you follow to open dialog boxes, change artwork, and initiate certain actions. These menu commands are listed in bold type. The typical direction to choose a menu command might be written as **Modify** > **Arrange** > **Bring to Front**. This means that you should first choose the Modify menu, then choose the Arrange submenu, and then choose the Bring to Front command.

Keyboard Shortcuts

Most of the menu commands for Fireworks have keyboard shortcuts that help you work faster. For instance, instead of choosing New from the File menu, it is faster and easier to use the keyboard shortcut.

The modifier keys useds in keyboard shortcuts are sometimes listed in different orders by different software companies or authors. For example, I always list the Command or Ctrl keys first, then the Option or Alt key, and then the Shift key. Other people may list the Shift key first. The order that you press those modifier keys is not important. However, it is very important that you always add the last key (the letter or number key) after you are holding the other keys.

The keyboard shortcuts for the menu commands are listed in Appendix B. There are several reasons for not including those shortcuts right in the book. Most importantly, many of the keyboard shortcuts for the Macintosh platform differ from those for the Windows platform. This means that the shortcut for **File** > **Save As** would have appeared in the text as Command-Shift-S/Ctrl-Shift-S. Rather than clutter the exercises, the shortcuts are listed in Appendix B separated by platform.

Learning Keyboard Shortcuts

While keyboard shortcuts help you work faster, you really do not have to start using them right away. In fact, you will most likely learn more about Fireworks by using the menus. As you look for one command, you may see another feature that you would like to explore.

Once you feel comfortable working with Fireworks, you can start adding keyboard shortcuts to your repertoire. My suggestion is to look at which menu commands you use a lot. Then each day choose one of those shortcuts. For instance, if you import a lot of art from other programs, you might decide to learn the shortcut for the Import command. For the rest of that day use the Import shortcut every time you import art. Even if you have to look at the menu to refresh your memory, still use the keyboard shortcut to actually open the Import dialog box. By the end of the day you will have memorized the Import shortcut. The next day you can learn a new one.

Cross-Platform Issues

One of the great strengths of Fireworks is that it is almost identical on both the Macintosh and Windows platforms. In fact,

at first glance it is hard to tell which platform you are working on. However, because there are some differences between the platforms, there are some things you should keep in mind.

Modifier Keys

Modifier keys are always listed with the Macintosh key first and then the Windows key second. So a direction to hold the Command/Ctrl key as you drag means to hold the Command key on the Macintosh platform or the Ctrl key on the Windows platform. When the key is the same on both computers, such as the Shift key, only one key is listed.

Generally the Command key on the Macintosh (sometimes called the Apple key) corresponds to the Ctrl key on Windows. The Option key on the Macintosh corresponds to the Alt key on Windows. The Control key on the Macintosh does not have an equivalent on Windows. Notice that the Control key for the Macintosh is always spelled out while the Ctrl key for Windows is not.

Platform-Specific Features

A few times in the book, I have written separate exercises for the Macintosh and Windows platforms. These exercises are indicated by (Mac) and (Win).

Most of the time this is because the procedures are so different that they need to be written separately. Some features exist only on one platform. Those features are then labeled as to their platform.

Learning Fireworks

I sincerely hope this book can give you the quick start you need to use Fireworks. There are things a book can't do; sometimes it helps to watch and listen to an instructor. Fortunately, the author and instructor, Lynda Weinman has produced a two-hour video that shows you how to use Fireworks 2 image editing, optimization, animation, and JavaScript capabilities. It is available at http://store.lynda.com. Lynda was one of the pioneers in Web graphics. Having her video is not just a way to understand Fireworks, but it is also great training in designing Web graphics. Finally, if you need the most complete reference book—a bible—you should look at *The Fireworks Bible* by Joseph W. Lowery. Joe's book goes far beyond the scope of this QuickStart Guide.

If you have been working with Web graphics for some time, then all you need to do is learn the specific features of Fireworks. However, if you are new to the Web, you may need some background information on Web graphics. I have tried to provide some in each of the Fireworks chapters. You may want to read some additional material. Some of the books I like are *Designing Web Graphics.2* by Lynda Weinman, and *The Non-Designer's Web Book* by Robin Williams and John Tollett.

Just remember to have fun!

Sandee Cohen

(SandeeC@aol.com)
April 1999

An example of the types of artwork you can create using Fireworks. (Artwork courtesy of the illustrator and designer Ray Villarosa, industrial@earthlink.net)

FIREWORKS BASICS 1

Before you can start working with Fireworks, there are a few preliminary things you need to cover. For instance, you should be familiar with the controls in the document window and with the onscreen elements. This way you will be able to quickly find the panels referred to in the later chapters.

In this chapter you will learn

The system requirements.

How to install Fireworks.

How to launch Fireworks.

The elements of the various panels.

The elements of the View Controls.

How to work with the interface elements.

How to work with the pop-up slider controls.

How to work with the panel tabs.

The elements of the Main toolbar.

The elements of the Modify toolbar.

The elements of the Text Editor.

The elements of and keyboard shortcuts for the Toolbox.

Minimum System Requirements (Mac)

There are certain minimum requirements
of your computer and operating
system you need to have for Fireworks to
perform correctly.

- System 7.5.5 or higher

- Adobe Type Manager 4 or higher to use
  Type 1 fonts

- Power Macintosh processor required
  (Power Macintosh 604/120 MHz or
  greater, 603e/180 MHz or greater, or G3
  recommended)

- 24 MB of application RAM with virtual
  memory on (32 MB or more with
  virtual memory off recommended)

- 60 MB of available hard disk space
  (100 MB or more recommended)

- CD-ROM drive

- Mouse or digitizing tablet

- 640×480 resolution, 256-color
  monitor required (1024×768
  resolution, millions-of-colors monitor
  recommended)

❶ *The Macintosh* **Memory** *display.*

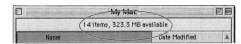

❷ *The Macintosh* **Hard Disk space** *display.*

To check memory (Mac):

Choose About This Computer from the
Apple menu **❶**.

To check hard disk space (Mac):

Open the hard disk and read the available
space at the top of the window **❷**.

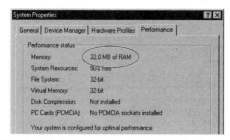

❸ *The Windows* **System Properties** *display.*

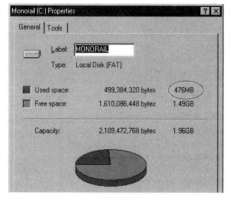

❹ *The Windows* **Hard Disk Properties** *display.*

Minimum System Requirements (Win)

There are certain minimum requirements of your computer and operating system you need to have for Fireworks to perform correctly.

- Windows 95 or Windows NT 4 (with Service Pack 3) or later
- Adobe Type Manager 4 or higher to use Type 1 fonts
- Intel Pentium 120 MHz processor required (Pentium 166 MHz with MMX recommended)
- 32 MB of system RAM on Windows 95 (40 MB or more recommended on Windows NT)
- 60 MB of available hard disk space (100 MB or more recommended)
- CD-ROM drive
- Mouse or digitizing tablet
- 640×480 resolution, 256-color monitor required (1024×768 resolution, millions-of-colors monitor recommended)

To check memory (Win):

Choose System from the Control Panels directory ❸.

To check hard disk space (Win):

1. Select the hard disk, usually named a letter such as C.
2. Click with the right mouse button and then choose Properties from the contextual menu ❹.

System Requirements (Win)

Once you have confirmed that your system meets the minimum requirements for running Fireworks, you can then install the application.

To install Fireworks (Mac):

1. Disable any virus-protection software.
2. Insert the Fireworks CD-ROM in the CD-ROM drive.
3. Double-click the Fireworks installer ❺.
4. Follow the instructions that appear.
5. After installation, restart the Macintosh.

To install Fireworks (Win):

1. Insert the Fireworks CD-ROM in the CD-ROM drive.
2. Follow the instructions that appear ❻.
3. After installation, restart the computer.

Once you have installed Fireworks, you can then launch the application.

To launch Fireworks (Mac):

Open the folder that contains the Fireworks application and then double-click the Fireworks application icon ❼.

To launch Fireworks (Win):

Use the Start menu ❽ to navigate to the Fireworks folder and then choose the Fireworks application.

Fireworks Installer

❺ *The* **Fireworks installer** *for the Macintosh.*

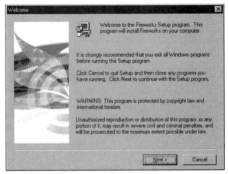

❻ *The opening screen for the Fireworks installer for Windows.*

Fireworks

❼ *The Fireworks application icon.*

❽ *The Fireworks application in the Start menu.*

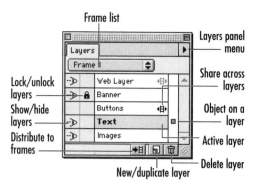

Frame list

Layers panel menu

Share across layers

Object on a layer

Active layer

Delete layer

Lock/unlock layers

Show/hide layers

Distribute to frames

New/duplicate layer

❾ *The elements of the* **Layers panel.**

Once you have launched Fireworks, you see the various Fireworks onscreen elements. These elements can be closed, opened, resized, or rearranged to suit your own work habits.

Elements of the Layers Panel

The Layers panel **❾** allows you to control the order in which objects appear onscreen. *(For more information on the Layers panel, see Chapter 6, "Working With Objects.")*

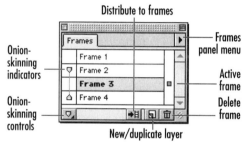

Distribute to frames

Frames panel menu

Active frame

Delete frame

Onion-skinning indicators

Onion-skinning controls

New/duplicate layer

❿ *The elements of the* **Frames panel.**

Elements of the Frames Panel

The Frames panel **❿** controls the elements used for creating animations. *(For more information on the Frames panel, see Chapter 19, "Animations.")*

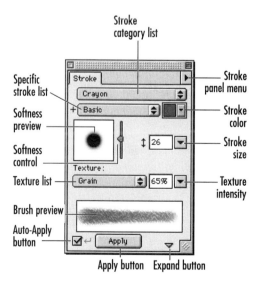

Stroke category list

Stroke panel menu

Stroke color

Stroke size

Texture intensity

Specific stroke list

Softness preview

Softness control

Texture list

Brush preview

Auto-Apply button

Apply button   Expand button

⓫ *The elements of the* **Stroke panel.**

Elements of the Stroke Panel

The Stroke panel **⓫** controls the look of the brush stroke that is applied to the edge of an object. *(For more information on strokes, see Chapter 8, "Strokes.")*

TIP The Expand button, found on the Stroke, Fill, and Effects panels, lets you show or hide the preview area to create shorter panels.

Layers Panel; Frames Panel; Stroke Panel

Elements of the Fill Panel

The Fill panel ⑫ controls the effect that is applied to the area inside an object. *(For more information on working with fills, see Chapter 7, "Fills.")*

Elements of the Effect Panel

The Effect panel ⑬ controls the additional effects that can be added to an object. *(For more information on Effects, see Chapter 9, "Effects.")*

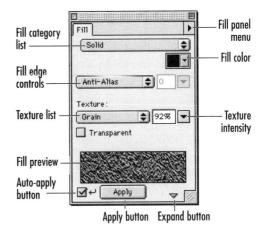

Fill category list — Fill panel menu — Fill color — Fill edge controls — Texture list — Texture intensity — Fill preview — Auto-apply button — Apply button — Expand button

⑫ *The elements of the* **Fill** *panel.*

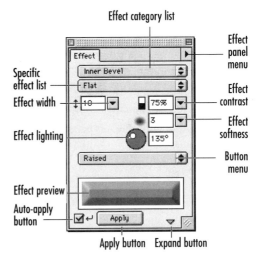

Effect category list — Specific effect list — Effect panel menu — Effect width — Effect contrast — Effect softness — Effect lighting — Button menu — Effect preview — Auto-apply button — Apply button — Expand button

⑬ *The elements of the* **Effect** *panel.*

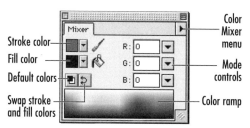

Stroke color
Fill color
Default colors
Swap stroke and fill colors

Color Mixer menu
Mode controls
Color ramp

⑭ *The elements of the* **Color Mixer.**

Elements of the Color Mixer Panel

The Color Mixer **⑭** allows you to define colors according to five different modes: RGB, Hexadecimal, HSB, CMY, or Grayscale. *(For more information on the color modes, see Chapter 3, "Colors.")*

Elements of the Swatches Panel

The Swatches panel **⑮** lets you work with preset palettes of color or store your own sets of colors.

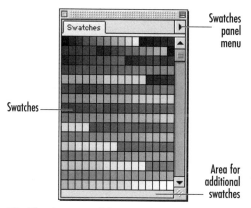

Swatches panel menu

Swatches

Area for additional swatches

⑮ *The elements of the* **Swatches panel** *as a floating panel.*

Elements of the Color Well Swatches Panel

Rather than repeatedly going to the Color Mixer or Swatches panel to apply colors, you can use the Color Well, located in the Toolbox and other panels and dialog boxes. When you click on the small control next to the Color Well, the Swatches panel appears **⑯**. This allows you to choose a swatch or access the eyedropper to apply a color. The None button lets you remove a fill or stroke from an object.

Color Well control
Color dialog button
None button
Eyedropper
#FFFFFF
Color label
Swatches

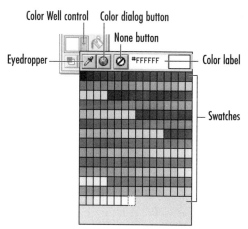

⑯ *Elements of the* **Color Well Swatches Panel.**

Elements of the Options Panel

The Options panel ❶ displays any options for working with the currently selected tool. These options change depending on the tool selected.

Name of selected tool

Tool controls

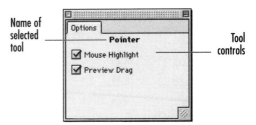

❶ *The elements of the* **Options panel.**

Elements of the Info Panel

The Info panel ❶ provides feedback as to the color and position of selected objects. *(For more information on using the Info panel, see page 42.)*

Info panel menu

Dimensions of selected object

Upper-left corner of object

Color beneath cursor

Cursor position

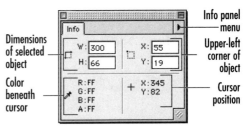

❶ *The elements of the* **Info panel.**

Elements of the Object Panel

The Object panel ❶ controls the opacity of objects and how they interact with other objects on the page. *(For more information on using the Object panel, see page 96, and pages 98–101.)*

Object panel menu

Opacity

Blending mode

Stroke controls

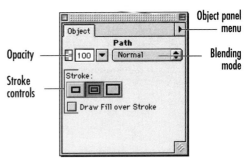

❶ *The elements of the* **Object panel.**

Choose URL Library   Add new URL   Delete URL   Add current   URL Manager
URL   panel menu

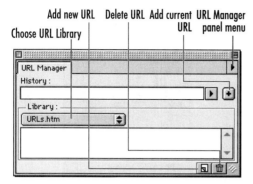

⑳ *The elements of the* **URL Manager** *panel.*

Add   Remove   Behavior
Action   Action   panel menu

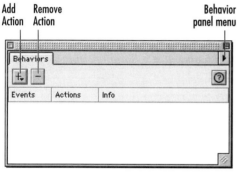

㉑ *The elements of the* **Behaviors** *panel.*

Find & Replace
menu

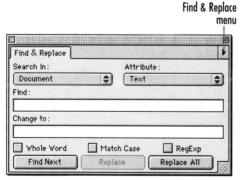

㉒ *The elements of the* **Find & Replace** *panel.*

Elements of the URL Manager Panel

The URL Manager panel **⑳** allows you to add URL links to areas on the page. *(For more information on adding links to areas of your Web graphics, see Chapter 16, "Hotspots and URLs," and Chapter 17, "Slices.")*

Elements of the Behaviors Panel

The Behaviors panel **㉑** allows you to assign JavaScript to elements such as rollovers and image maps. *(For more information on working with Behaviors, see Chapter 18, "Behaviors.")*

Elements of the Find & Replace Panel

The Find & Replace panel **㉒** allows you to make changes in text and graphic elements. *(For more information on working with the Find & Replace panel, see Chapter 11, "Automation Features.")*

URL Manager Panel; Behaviors Panel; Find & Replace Panel

Elements of the Styles Panel

The Styles panel ❷❸ allows you to save the settings for an object's appearance and then apply them quickly to other objects. *(For more information on working with styles, see Chapter 11, "Automation Features.")*

Elements of the Project Log Panel

The Project Log panel ❷❹ allows you to list a series of files you are currently working on and apply changes to all the files in the list. *(For more information on working with with Project Log, see Chapter 11, "Automation Features.")*

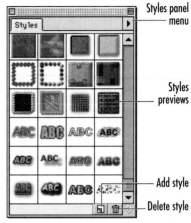

Styles panel menu

Styles previews

Add style

Delete style

❷❸ *The elements of the* **Styles** *panel.*

Elements of the View Controls

The View Controls ❷❺ are part of the document window. They let you change the magnification and display of your page. The frame controls let you preview animations.

In the Windows version of Fireworks, the View Controls ❷❻ either can be fixed to the edge of the application window or positioned as a floating panel. *(For more information on using the View Controls, see page 27 and page 240.)*

Project Log Description   Project Log panel menu

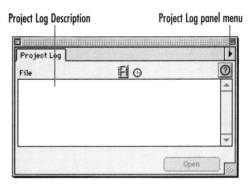

❷❹ *The elements of the* **Project Log** *panel.*

Magnification   Display   Page Preview

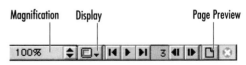

❷❺ *The Macintosh* **View Controls** *toolbar.*

Magnification   Display   Page Preview

❷❻ *The Windows* **View Controls** *toolbar.*

Click a tab   Click a box

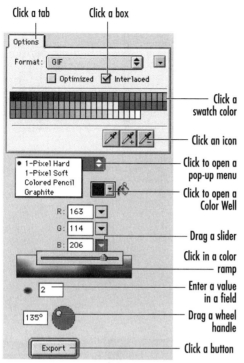

Click a
swatch color

Click an icon

Click to open a
pop-up menu

Click to open a
Color Well

Drag a slider

Click in a color
ramp

Enter a value
in a field

Drag a wheel
handle

Click a button

27 *The composite dialog box shows the* **interface elements** *and how you control them.*

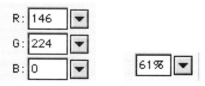

28 *Slider controls in the closed positions.*

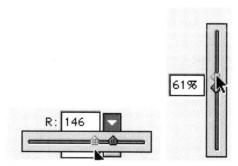

29 *Press the triangular arrow to open a slider and then drag to change the setting.*

Working with the Interface Elements

You set many of the Fireworks features using panels and dialog boxes. Though the panels and dialog boxes differ in function and layout, they all use similar interface devices that you adjust to control the settings **27**.

Working with Pop-Up Sliders

Most elements of the Fireworks interface will look familiar to you if you have used a Mac or Windows program before.

One interface element is fairly new to graphics applications: the pop-up slider. It is a slider control that does not look like a slider control at first glance. When closed, the slider collapses into a small triangle control **28**.

Press the triangle to reveal the slider control **29**. Then drag the small pointer to change the amount in the field. When you release the mouse button, the slider collapses and the amount is entered in the field.

TIP You don't need to use the slider control to change the values. You can also enter the amount in the field for that slider.

Interface Elements; Pop-up Sliders

Panel Tabs

The panel tabs allow you to group any
Fireworks panel with the other panels.

To group panels:

1. Drag a panel by its tab onto another
   panel to group the panels together **30**.

2. Drag a panel by its tab out of a
   grouping to separate the panels.

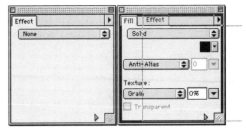

30 Drag the tab of a panel *to group or
ungroup the panels.*

Elements of the Main Toolbar (Win)

The Main toolbar **31** gives you easy access
to the most commonly used commands.
You can fix the Main toolbar to the sides of
the application window or position it as a
floating panel.

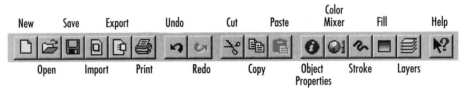

31 *The elements of the* **Main toolbar.**

Elements of the Modify toolbar (Win)

The Modify toolbar **32** provides easy access
to the most commonly used modification
commands. You can fix the Modify toolbar
to the sides of the application window or
position it as a floating panel.

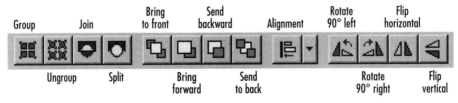

32 *The elements of the* **Modify toolbar.**

Elements of the Text Editor

The Text Editor ㉝ lets you enter and format text. *(For more information on working with text, see Chapter 10, "Text.")*

Leading   Baseline Shift   Point size   Color Well   Alignment

Font list

Kerning

Horizontal scale

Text preview

Preview controls

Text style

Text flow

Horizontal or vertical text

㉝ *The elements of the* **Text Editor.**

Text Editor

Toolbox Elements and Keyboard Shortcuts

Fireworks has 35 different tools. You can choose the tools by clicking the tool in the Toolbox ❸❹ or by pressing the group.

You can also access the tools by pressing the keyboard shortcut (shown in the parentheses). The tool shortcuts do not need modifiers such as Command or Ctrl.

TIP In the Windows, the Toolbox can be fixed to the side of the window or positioned as a floating panel.

TIP When tools share the same keyboard shortcut, press the key several times to rotate through the different tools.

Each of the tools can be set for icon cursors or precision cursors ❸❺.

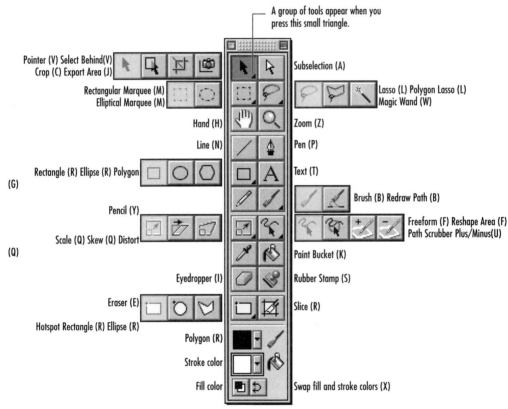

❸❹ *The tools in the* **Toolbox** *and their keyboard shortcuts (in parentheses).*

❸❺ *Pressing the Caps Lock key changes the icon cursor to a precision cursor. The precision cursors can also be set in the Preferences.*

DOCUMENT SETUP 2

O nce you have launched Fireworks, you can begin work. You can start by creating a new Fireworks document or you can open an existing document. You can also open scanned images from other programs. Once you have a document open, there are various controls that affect how the document is displayed and how you work in the document.

In this chapter you will learn how to

Create a new document.

Change the image size.

Change the canvas size.

Change the canvas color.

Open existing documents as untitled.

Display the document rulers.

Change the zero point.

Create guides.

Position guides.

Edit guides.

View the document grid.

Edit the document grid.

Use the magnification commands.

Use the Zoom tool.

Change the display options.

Use the Grabber tool.

New Document

When you start a new document, you must make certain decisions about the document that affect the final output.

To create a new document:

1. Choose **File** > **New**. This opens the New Document dialog box **❶**.

2. Use the height and width fields to set the size of the document.

TIP Use the pop-up list to change the unit of measurement from pixels to inches or centimeters.

3. Use the resolution field to set the number of points per inch for the graphics of the document.

TIP Most Web graphics are saved at 72 pixels per inch. Print graphics usually need higher resolutions.

4. Set the canvas color of the document, by choosing white, transparent, or custom.

5. If you choose custom, click the color well to open the color picker, where you can set your color.

6. Click OK to create the new document, which appears in an untitled document window **❷**.

TIP Press the Document Info Display button to see a representation of the size of the document as well as a read-out of the document's size and resolution **❸**.

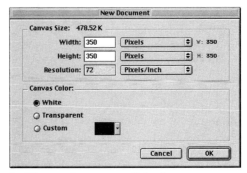

❶ *The* **New Document** *dialog box.*

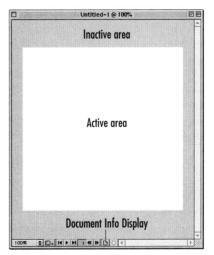

❷ *The* **document window.**

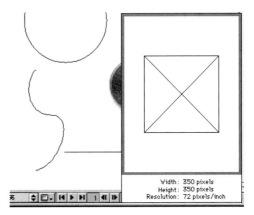

❸ *The* **document info display area.**

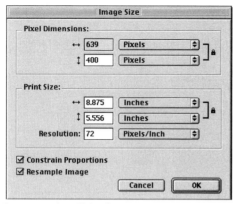

❹ Image size *dialog box.*

❺ *The effects of* **resampling an image** *to increase its size and resolution. Notice the blurry edges in the resampled image.*

Once you have created a document, you can change the size of the image. This stretches or compacts the pixels in the image. You can also resample or change the number of pixels per inch.

To change the image size:

1. Choose **Modify**>**Document**>**Image Size** to open the Image Size dialog box **❹**.

2. Use the Pixel Dimensions height and width fields to change the absolute number of pixels in the document.

TIP The Pixel Dimensions fields are not available if Resample Image is turned off.

3. Use the Print Size height and width fieds to change the display size of the image.

TIP Press the pop-up control to change the size of the document by a percentage.

4. Use the Resolution field to change the image size by increasing or reducing the number of pixels per inch.

TIP Scanned images may become slightly blurred if the resolution or size of the image is increased by more than 50% **❺**. (There is no problem reducing the size of the image or resolution.)

If this is not acceptable, you may need to rescan the image at the higher resolution or larger size. *(For more information on working with scanned images, see Chapter 12, "Working With Pixels.")*

Change Image Size

You can keep the size of the image constant while changing the area of the background. This adds space to or deletes space from the canvas outside the image area. There are two ways to do this: numerically, using the Canvas Size dialog box; and visually, using the Crop tool.

To change the canvas size numerically:

1. Choose **Modify** > **Document** > **Canvas Size** to open the Canvas Size dialog box **❻**.

2. Enter new amounts in the New Size height and width fields.

TIP Use the current size as a reference.

3. Click the squares in the anchor area to determine where the canvas will be added to or subtracted from.

4. Click OK.

TIP If you reduce the size of your document, objects in the clipped areas are not lost. Although they are not visible, you can move them back into the active area, where they reappear.

To change the canvas size visually:

1. Choose the Crop tool from the toolbox **❼**.

2. Drag with the Crop tool to create the handles **❽** that define the area that you want to crop.

3. Double-click inside the crop area to apply the crop.

   or

   Double-click outside the crop area or choose a new tool to continue without applying the crop.

TIP The Crop handles can be extended outside the current canvas area to increase the size of the canvas.

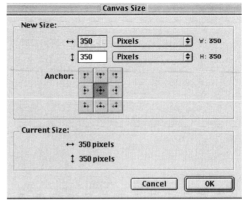

❻ Canvas size *dialog box.*

❼ *The* **Crop tool** *in the Toolbox.*

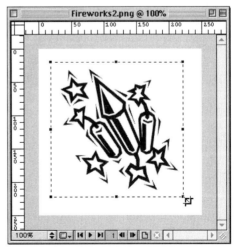

❽ *The* **Crop tool handles** *define the final canvas size after cropping.*

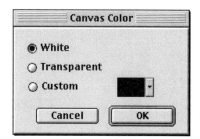

❾ *The* **Canvas Color** *dialog box.*

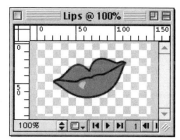

❿ *The* **checkerboard grid** *indicates a transparent background.*

The canvas color is the color automatically applied behind all the images in a document. You can change the canvas color at any time while you work on a document.

To change the canvas color:

1. Choose **Modify** > **Document** > **Canvas Color** to open the Canvas Color dialog box **❾**.

2. Click white, transparent, or custom.

TIP The transparent background is designated by a gray-and-white checkerboard **❿**.

3. If you choose custom, click the Color Well to open the Swatches panel to choose a specific color.

When you open an existing document, Fireworks lets you protect the original file by opening it as an untitled document.

To open a document as untitled:

1. Choose **File** > **Open** and navigate to find the original version of the file.

2. Click Open as "Untitled" and then click Open. The document opens in an unsaved, untitled version.

3. Make any changes and save the document as you would any other file.

If you want to work precisely in your document, you need to work with the rulers.

To display the document rulers:

Choose **View > Rulers**. The rulers appear at the top and left sides of the document ⓫. The rulers are displayed in the unit of pixels.

TIP Two lines appear on the rulers that track your position as you move around the document.

Fireworks uses the upper-left corner of a document as its *zero point*, or the point where the rulers start. You can change the zero point for a document. This can help you position items on the page.

To change the zero point:

1. Drag the zero-point crosshairs onto the page ⓬.

2. Double-click the zero-point crosshairs in the corner of the document window to reset the zero point to the upper-left corner.

Vertical ruler   Horizontal ruler

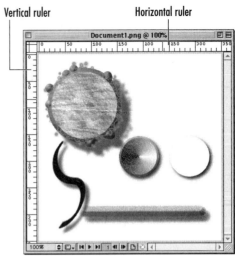

⓫ *The rulers in the document window.*

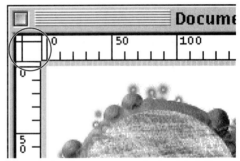

⓬ **Drag the zero-point crosshairs** (*circled*) *onto the page to set the new zero point.*

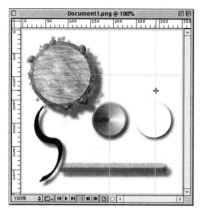

⑬ **Dragging a guide** *from the ruler onto the active area.*

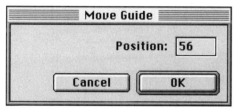

⑭ *The* **Move Guide** *dialog box.*

The rulers also let you add guides that you can use to align objects.

To create guides:

1. Drag from the left ruler to create a vertical guide **⑬**. Release the mouse button to place the guide.

2. Drag from the top ruler to create a horizontal guide. Release the mouse button to place the guide.

3. Repeat to add as many horizontal or vertical guides as you need.

To position guides:

Drag an existing guide to move it to a new position.

or

Double-click the guide to open the Move Guide dialog box **⑭** and enter the exact position of the guide.

TIP Use **View > Guide Options > Snap To Guides** to have objects automatically snap, or align, to the guides.

There are several ways you can edit or control the look of guides.

To edit guides:

1. Choose **View**>**Guide Options**>**Edit Guides** to open the Guides dialog box ⓯–⓰.

2. Click the color box to open the color picker and choose a new color to make the guides look more or less obvious.

3. Click Show Guides to show or hide the guides.

4. Click Snap to Guides to turn on or off the snap-to-guides feature.

5. Click Lock Guides to keep the guides from being moved.

TIP You can also lock the guides by choosing **View** > **Guide Options** > **Lock Guides**.

6. Click Clear All to delete all the guides from the document.

7. Click OK to apply the changes.

TIP (Mac) Click the Grid tab to switch from editing the guides to editing the grid *(see the steps below)*.

⓯ *The* **Guides (Win)** *dialog box.*

⓰ *The* **Grids and Guides (Mac)** *dialog box in the Guides mode.*

In addition to guides, Fireworks has a grid, which you can use to align objects.

To view the document grid:

Choose **View**>**Grid** to display the document grid ⓱. You can use the document grid to arrange your images into certain areas or to make sure objects are aligned or are the same size.

TIP You can use **View**>**Grid Options**> **Snap to Grid** to have objects automatically snap, or align, to the grid.

TIP When Snap to Grid is turned on, objects snap to the grid even if the grid is not visible.

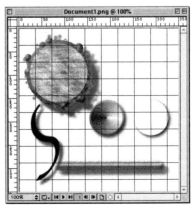

⓱ *The* **document grid** *shown over the art.*

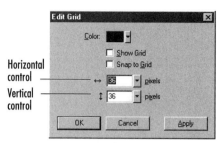

⓲ *The* **Edit Grid (Win)** *dialog box.*

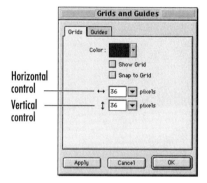

⓳ *The* **Grids and Guides (Mac)** *dialog box in the Grid mode.*

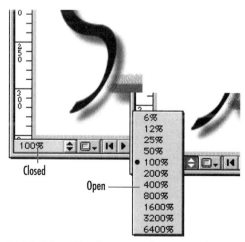

⓴ *The* **Magnification control menu** *at the bottom of the document window.*

You can also change the size of the grid. This makes it easy to create objects all the same size or shape.

To edit the document grid:

1. Choose **View > Grid Options > Edit Grid** to open the Grids and Guides dialog box **⓲–⓳**.

2. Click the color box to open the color picker and choose a new color for the grid.

3. Use the horizontal control slider or type in the field to increase or decrease the horizontal spacing.

4. Use the vertical control slider or type in the field to increase or decrease the vertical spacing.

5. Click Snap to Grid to turn on or off the snap-to-grid feature.

6. Click Show Grid to show or hide the document grid.

You may need to zoom in or out to see specific areas or the big picture.

To use the magnification commands:

To zoom to a specific magnification, use the magnification control **⓴**.

or

Choose **View > Magnification** and then choose a specific magnification.

or

Choose **View > Zoom In** or **View > Zoom Out** to jump to a specific magnification.

or

Choose **View > Fit Selection** to display the object selected.

or

Choose **View > Fit All** to display the entire document.

You can use the Zoom tool to jump to a specific magnification and position.

To use the Zoom tool:

1. Click the Zoom tool in the Toolbox **21**.

2. Click the Zoom tool on the area you want to zoom in on. Click as many times as you need to get as close as necessary to the area you want to see.

   or

   Drag the Zoom tool diagonally across the area you want to see. Release the mouse button to zoom in **22–23**.

TIP Press Command/Ctrl and Spacebar to access the Zoom tool without leaving the tool that is currently selected.

TIP Press the Option/Alt key while in the Zoom tool to zoom out from objects. The icon changes from a plus sign (+) to a minus sign (–).

21 *The* **Zoom tool** *in the toolbox.*

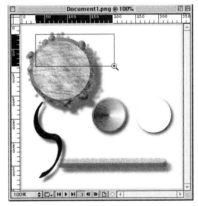

22 *Use the* **Zoom tool** *to zoom in on a specific area by dragging a marquee around that area. The line indicates the area being selected.*

23 *After dragging, the selected area fills the window.*

Zoom Tool

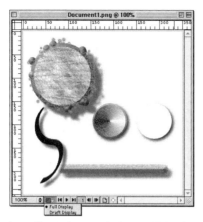

㉔ *The* **Full Display** *mode shows all the fills, brushes, and effects for the objects.*

Fireworks lets you work in two different display modes. The Full Display mode **㉔** shows all the objects in the document with their fills, brushes, and effects.

The Draft Display mode **㉕** shows only the paths for all the unselected objects. Only the selected object displays its fill, brush, or effect.

To change the display options:

1. Press the Display mode control at the bottom of the document window **㉖**.
2. Choose between Full Display or Draft Display.

   or

   Choose **View**>**Full Display** to switch beetween the two display modes.

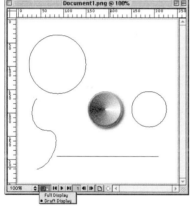

㉕ *The* **Draft Display** *mode shows only the paths for the unselected objects. The selected object shows its fills, brushes, or effects.*

Display mode control

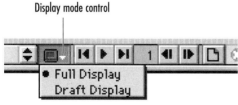

㉖ *The* Display mode choices.

If you have used a computer for any type of program, you should be familiar with the scroll bars of a window that let you see areas of the document that are outside the view of the window. Fireworks also has a Grabber tool that lets you move around the window without using the scroll bars.

To use the Grabber tool:

1. Choose the Grabber tool in the toolbox **㉗**

2. Position the Grabber tool inside the document window and drag **㉘**. This reveals the areas of the image that were previous hidden.

TIP Hold the spacebar to access the Grabber tool without leaving the tool that is currently selected.

㉗ *The* **Grabber tool** *in the toolbox.*

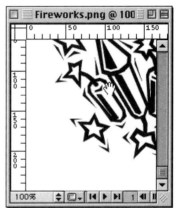

㉘ *The* **Grabber tool** *allows you to move an image within the document window.*

COLORS 3

Because Fireworks was developed to create graphics for display on the World Wide Web, it has special features for working with Web-safe colors. These let you create graphics that do not shift color when viewed by different Web browsers. However, you are not limited to just Web colors. Fireworks also lets you define colors using several other color systems.

In this chapter you will learn how to

Use the Color Mixer.

Define RGB colors.

Define hexadecimal colors.

Define CMY colors.

Define HSB colors.

Define Grayscale colors.

Use the Swatches panel.

Choose the Web 216 palette swatches.

Choose the Macintosh System swatches.

Choose the Windows System swatches.

Choose the Grayscale swatches.

Add colors to the Swatches panel.

Delete colors from the Swatches panel.

Sort the swatches by color.

Save colors in the Swatches panel.

Load colors to the Swatches panel.

Use the default colors.

Use the Eyedropper to sample colors.

Use the Paint Bucket to fill with colors.

Use the Info panel color information.

Two panels control color in Fireworks. The first, the Color Mixer, lets you define your own colors to use in your document.

To use the Color Mixer:

1. If you do not see the Color Mixer, choose **Window** > **Color Mixer**.

   or

   Click the title bar of the Color Mixer panel to bring it in front of any other onscreen elements.

2. Use the Mode menu to choose from the five different color modes **❶**.

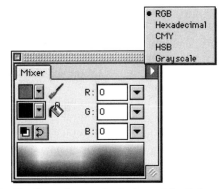

❶ *The* **five color mode choices** *of the Color Mixer.*

Because the Web is viewed on computer monitors or television screens, one of the most common ways of defining colors for Web graphics is to use the RGB (red, green, blue) color system, also called *additive* color. This is the system used in computer monitors. *(See the color insert for a diagram of how additive colors can be mixed.)* In the additive color system, all three colors combine to create white. Each of the RGB components is given a number between 0 and 255. So, for example, a yellow color could have the RGB values of R: 250, G: 243, and B: 117.

To define RGB colors:

1. Make sure the Color Mixer mode is set to RGB.

2. To choose the R (red) component, drag the slider or enter a value in the R field. Do the same for the G (green) component and the B (blue) component **❷**.

   or

   Click anywhere along the RGB color ramp at the bottom of the Color Mixer to choose colors by eye, rather than by numeric values.

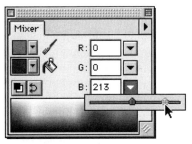

❷ **Drag the slider** *to set the value for one of the RGB color components. The RGB colors are set with numbers from 0 to 255.*

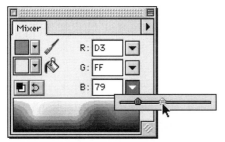

❸ **Hexadecimal colors** *use combinations of letters and numbers to define colors.*

Text, links, and background colors of Web graphics are defined for the Web by using a color system called *hexadecimal*. Instead of numbers from 0 to 255, the hexadecimal system uses combinations of letters and numbers. So the yellow in the previous exercise would be defined in hexadecimal as R: FA, G: F3, B: 75.

To define hexadecimal colors:

1. Make sure the Color Mixer mode is set to Hexadecimal.

2. To choose the R (red) component, drag the slider or enter a value in the R (red) field. Do the same for the G (green) component and the B (blue) component ❸.

   or

   Click in the color ramp at the bottom of the Color Mixer to choose colors by eye, rather than by numbers.

   TIP The color ramp in the hexadecimal mode limits you to working with the 216 Web-safe colors *(see page 37)*.

   TIP The hexadecimal system uses one or two-digit combinations of the following characters: 0, 1, 2, 3, 4, 5, 6, 7, 8, 9, A, B, C, D, E, F. Other characters are ignored.

   TIP You can also use the hexadecimal codes from your Fireworks graphics as part of the HTML code for your Web pages.

For more information on hexadecimal codes, see *HTML for the World Wide Web: Visual QuickStart Guide* by Elizabeth Castro or *The Non-Designer's Web Book* by Robin Williams and John Tollett, both published by Peachpit Press, or *Coloring Web Graphics.2* by Lynda Weinman, published by New Riders Publishing.

Hexadecimal Colors

You can also define colors using pure CMY, or cyan, magenta, and yellow colors. This is a *subtractive* color system, in which all three colors combine to create black. *(See the color insert for a diagram of how subtractive colors can be mixed.)* Like the RGB system, the CMY components are defined using numbers from 0 to 255. If you have worked primarily in print, you may find it easier to mix colors using the CMY mode.

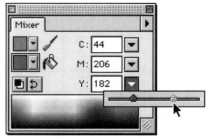

❹ **CMY colors** *use the numbers from 0 to 255 to set the amount of each color component.*

To define CMY colors:

1. Make sure the Color Mixer mode is set to CMY.

2. To choose the C (cyan) component, drag the slider or enter a value in the C (cyan) field. Do the same for the M (magenta) component and the Y (yellow) component **❹**.

   or

   Click anywhere along the CMY color ramp at the bottom of the Color Mixer to choose colors by eye, rather than by numeric values.

TIP The pure CMY colors are not the same as the CMYK colors used in printing. Theoretically (and in Fireworks), combining the three pure CMY colors produces black. In actual printing, combining the three CMY inks produces a muddy brown-black, so an extra black printing plate is added to create real black.

CMY Colors

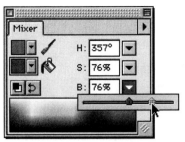

❺ **HSB colors** *use a combination of degrees around the color wheel for hue and percentages of saturation and brightness to define colors.*

You can also define colors using the classic HSB or hue, saturation, and brightness system. Hue uses the principle of arranging colors in a wheel. Changing the colors from 0 to 360° moves through the entire color spectrum. Saturation uses percentage values, where 100% is a totally saturated color. Lower saturation values create pastel versions of a color. Brightness uses percentage values, where 100% is a color with no darkness or black. The lower the brightness percentage, the more darkness or black is added to the color.

To define HSB colors:

1. Make sure the Color Mixer mode is set to HSB.

2. To choose the H (hue) component, drag the slider or enter a degree value in the H (hue) field ❺.

3. To choose the S (saturation) component, drag the slider or enter a percentage value in the S (saturation) field. Do the same for the B (brightness) component.

   or

   Click anywhere along the HSB color ramp at the bottom of the Color Mixer to choose colors by eye, rather than by numeric values.

HSB Colors

While Fireworks graphics are exported in RGB or indexed colors, you may need to match colors used in grayscale images. So the Color Mixer also lets you define colors using values of a single black (K) color plate.

To define Grayscale colors:

1. Make sure the Color Mixer mode is set to Grayscale.

2. To choose the K (black) component, drag the slider or enter a value in the K (black) field **⊙**.

   or

   Click anywhere along the grayscale color ramp at the bottom of the Color Mixer to choose colors by eye, rather than by numeric values.

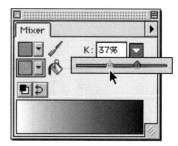

⊙ **Grayscale colors** *use percentages of black to define colors.*

The second panel for working with colors is the Swatches panel. The Swatches panel lets you access preset palettes of swatches.

To use the Swatches panel:

1. If you do not see the Swatches panel, choose **Window>Swatches panel**.

   or

   If the Swatches panel is behind another panel, click the title bar of the Swatches panel to bring it in front of any other onscreen elements.

2. Use the Swatches panel menu to access the Swatches commands **⊙**.

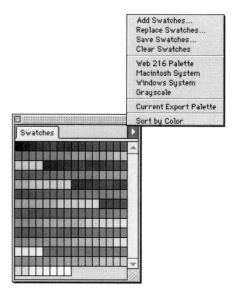

⊙ *The Swatches panel menu.*

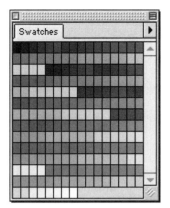

❽ *The* 216 **Web-safe colors** *in the Swatches panel. (See the color insert for the color version of this illustration.)*

One of the most important considerations in creating Web graphics is using *Web-safe colors*. Web-safe colors are those that can be displayed predictably by different Web browsers as well as different computer systems. There are 216 Web-safe colors. Limiting your Fireworks graphics to only those 216 colors ensures that the colors of your document do not shift or change when they are displayed on different monitors using different browsers. You access the 216 Web-safe colors via the Swatches panel.

To choose the Web 216 palette swatches:

Open the Swatches panel menu and choose Web 216 Palette. The color swatches appear in the panel ❽.

You can also limit your colors to those found in the Macintosh operating system. To do so, you can choose the Macintosh System colors.

To choose the Macintosh System swatches:

Open the Swatches panel menu and choose Macintosh System. The 256 color swatches appear in the panel ❾.

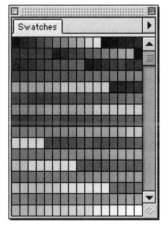

❾ *The* Macintosh System colors *in the Swatches panel. (See the color insert for the color version of this illustration.)*

Just as you can pick colors using the Macintosh System colors, you can also pick colors using the Windows System colors.

To choose the Windows System swatches:

Open the Swatches panel menu and choose Windows System. The 256 color swatches appear in the panel **⑩**.

You can also limit your colors to grayscale colors. This is done by choosing the Grayscale swatches.

To choose the Grayscale swatches:

Open the Swatches panel menu and choose Grayscale. The 256 grayscale color swatches appear in the panel **⑪**.

You can use the Swatches panel to store colors that you create in the Color Mixer. This makes it easy to maintain a consistent look in all your graphics.

To add colors to the Swatches panel:

1. Use the Color Mixer to define a color that you want to store.
2. Move the mouse over to the gray area at the end of the Swatches panel where there are no swatches. A paint bucket cursor appears **⑫**.
3. Click the mouse button. The new color appears in its own color swatch.

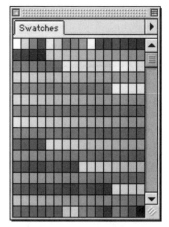

⑩ *The* **Windows System colors** *in the Swatches panel. (See the color insert for the color version of this illustration.)*

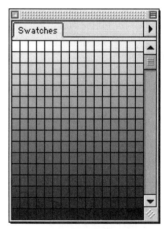

⑪ *The* **Grayscale colors** *in the Swatches panel.*

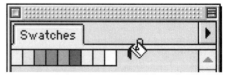

⑫ *The* **paint bucket cursor** *indicates you can store a color in the Swatches panel.*

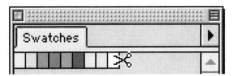

⓭ *The Command/Ctrl key displays the* **scissors cursor,** *which allows you to delete a color from the Swatches panel.*

Before

After

⓮ *The Swatches panel before and after* **sorting** *the colors.*

You can also delete colors from the Swatches panel.

To delete colors from the Swatches panel:

1. Move the cursor over the swatch for the color you want to delete.
2. Hold the Command/Ctrl key. A scissors cursor appears **⓭**.
3. Click to delete the color from the Swatches panel.

You can also delete all the colors from the Swatches panel at once.

To delete all the colors from the Swatches panel:

Open the Swatches panel menu and choose Clear Swatches.

If you keep adding colors to the Swatches panel, you may want to arrange the swatches so that similar colors are grouped together. To do so, you use the Sort by Color command.

To sort the swatches by color:

Open the Swatches panel menu and choose Sort by Color. The various color swatches in the panel automatically sort, first by hue and then from light to dark **⓮**.

Delete Swatches; Sort Swatches

Once you have created a custom Swatches panel with your own colors, you can save that Swatches panel to use at other times.

To save colors in the Swatches panel:

1. Open the Swatches panel menu and choose Save Swatches.

2. Give the file a name and then save the file. The saved file can be loaded into the Swatches panel at any time.

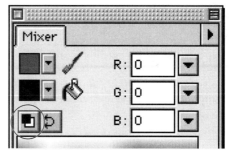

⓯ *Click the* **default colors icon** *(circled) in the Color Mixer to reset the brush and fill colors to their default setting.*

To load colors to the Swatches panel:

Open the Swatches panel menu and choose Replace Swatches. Then open a saved Swatches panel file. This replaces the current set of swatches with those from the saved file.

or

Open the Swatches panel menu and choose Add Swatches. Then open a saved Swatches panel file. This adds the new swatches to those already in the Swatches panel.

TIP The Fireworks Swatches panel can also load swatches created in Adobe Photoshop.

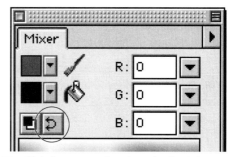

⓰ *Click the* **swap colors icon** *in the Color Mixer to reverse the brush and fill colors.*

Fireworks has a set of default colors for the brush and fill colors. These default colors can be accessed easily and changed to suit your needs.

To work with the default colors:

1. Click the default colors icon **⓯** in either the Toolbox or the Color Mixer to set the brush and fill colors to their default settings.

2. Click the swap colors icon **⓰** in either the Toolbox or the Color Mixer to reverse the brush and fill colors.

Save Swatches; Load Swatches; Default Colors

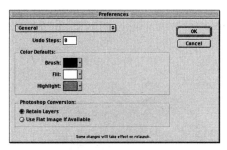

⑰ *The* **Preferences** *dialog box.*

⑱ *The* **Eyedropper** *in the Toolbox.*

⑲ *The Eyedropper sampling for a* **Fill color.**

⑳ *The Eyedropper sampling for a* **Stroke color.**

㉑ *The* **Paint Bucket** *in the Toolbox.*

To change the default colors:

1. Choose **File** > **Preferences** to open the Preferences dialog box ⑰.
2. Click the color box for the Brush or Fill Color Defaults.
3. Use the color picker to choose a new default color.
4. Click OK to apply the changes.

The Eyedropper tool lets you pick colors from objects or images *(see page 157).*

To sample colors with the Eyedropper:

1. Choose the Eyedropper in the Toolbox ⑱.
2. Position the Eyedropper over the color you want to sample.
3. Click. The color appears as either the Fill or Brush color.

TIP When the Fill color is chosen *(see page 88),* the Eyedropper shows a black dot next to it ⑲.

TIP When the Stroke color is chosen in the Toolbox *(see page 104),* the Eyedropper shows a curved line next to it ⑳.

The Paint Bucket lets you drop fills onto objects whether or not they are selected.

To fill objects with the Paint Bucket

1. Choose the Paint Bucket in the Toolbox ㉑.
2. Click an object. The object fills with the currently selected Fill color. *(For more information on working with fills, see Chapter 7, "Fills.")*

Eyedropper; Paint Bucket

As you are working, you may want to know the exact composition of the color of an object or image. Fireworks lets you see the details of a color in the Info panel.

To use the Info panel:

1. Make sure the Info panel is open. If not, choose **Windows** > **Info**.

2. Pass the pointer over any objects. The Info panel displays the values for the color the pointer is over ㉒.

3. Click the triangle to open the Info panel menu ㉓.

4. Use the Color Model list to change the way the Info panel displays the color values.

TIP Changing the way the Info panel displays colors does not actually change the colors. Colors in Fireworks are not set until they are exported as a finished file *(see Chapter 15, "Basic Exporting")*.

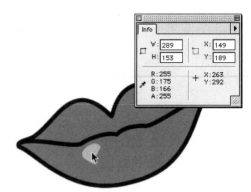

㉒ *The color readings of the* **Info panel.**

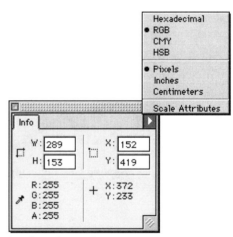

㉓ *The* **Info** *panel menu.*

Info Panel

PATH TOOLS 4

Unlike bitmapped programs, Fireworks does not create images by coloring pixels. It creates images with paths. The path tools create shapes that are then used as the basis of Fireworks images. If you are familiar with programs such as Macromedia FreeHand or Adobe Illustrator, you will find it is easy to understand the path tools in Fireworks. If you have never used a vector program, pay attention to this chapter, because creating paths is the primary source of images in Fireworks.

In this chapter you will learn how to

Create a rectangle.

Create a rounded-corner rectangle.

Create an ellipse.

Create a polygon.

Create a star.

Create straight path segments.

Create curved path segments.

Create a corner curve.

Retract the handle into a point.

Extend a handle out from a point.

Create an open path with the Pen.

Create a closed path with the Pen.

Create lines.

Create paths with the Brush tool.

Draw straight path segments with the Brush tool.

Modify a brush path.

Draw with the Pencil.

Soften the edges of Pencil lines.

Use the Auto Erase feature.

Add points to a path.

Delete points from a path.

Although it is called the Rectangle tool, this tool lets you create rectangles, squares, and rounded-corner rectangles. With the Rectangle tool you can create buttons and banners for your Web graphics.

To create a rectangle:

1. Click the Rectangle tool in the Toolbox ❶. If the Rectangle tool is not visible open the pop-up group to choose the Rectangle tool.

2. Move the pointer to the document area. The cursor changes to the plus (+) sign indicating that you can draw the rectangle.

3. Drag diagonally from one corner to the other of the rectangle you want to draw.

TIP Hold the Shift key as you drag to constrain the rectangle into a square ❷.

TIP Hold the Option/Alt key as you drag to draw from the center point outward.

4. Release the mouse button to create the rectangle.

❶ *The* **Rectangle tool** *in the Toolbox.*

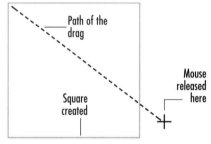

Path of the drag

Mouse released here

Square created

❷ **Holding the Shift key** *constrains the rectangle tool to creating a square even if the path of the drag is not along the correct diagonal of the square.*

Rectangle

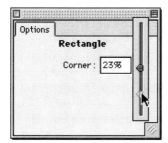

❸ *The* **Corner radius** *slider.*

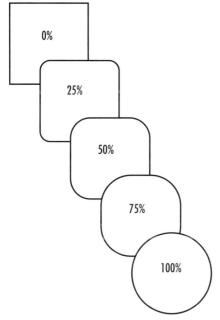

❹ *Rectangles drawn with different percentages for the corner radius.*

❺ *The* **Ellipse tool** *in the Toolbox.*

A rectangle with a rounded corner is a very popular look for buttons and other interactive Web elements.

To create a rounded-corner rectangle:

1. Double-click the Rectangle tool in the Toolbox. This opens the Tool Options for the Rectangle tool.

2. Drag the Corner slider to increase the size of the corner radius ❸.

TIP The size of the corner radius is a percentage of the length of the shorter side of the rectangle.

3. Drag as you would to create a regular rectangle. The corners of the rectangle are rounded by the percentage set for the corner radius ❹.

TIP The percentage size of the corner radius is set once you create the rounded-corner rectangle. If you scale the rectangle up or down *(see page 68)* the corner radius changes accordingly.

You can create ellipses or ovals using the Ellipse tool.

To create an ellipse:

1. Click the Ellipse tool in the Toolbox ❺. If the Ellipse tool is not visible, open the pop-up group to choose the Ellipse tool.

2. Move the pointer to the document area.

3. Drag a line that defines the diameter of the ellipse.

TIP Hold the Shift key as you drag to constrain the ellipse into a circle.

TIP Hold the Option/Alt key as you drag to draw from the center point outward.

4. Release the mouse button to complete the ellipse.

Polygons give your Web graphics a special look. You use the Polygon tool to create both polygons and stars.

To create a polygon:

1. Click the Polygon tool in the Toolbox **❻**. If the Polygon tool is not visible, open the pop-up group to choose the Polygon tool.

2. Double-click the Polygon tool to display the Tool Options panel **❼**.

3. Choose Polygon from the pop-up list.

4. Use the slider or enter a number from 1 to 360 in the field to set the number of sides for the polygon.

5. Move the pointer to the document area and drag. The point where you start the drag is the center of the polygon.

TIP Hold the Shift key as you drag to constrain the orientation of the polygon to 45° increment angles.

6. Release the mouse button to create the polygon.

❻ *The* **Polygon tool** *in the Toolbox.*

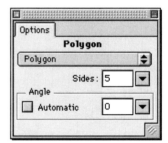

❼ *The* **Polygon tool** *options.*

❽ *The Polygon tool set for the **Star** options.*

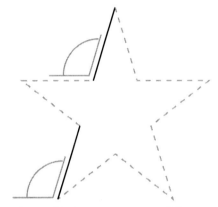

❾ *The two black segments are parallel as a result of setting the star to **Automatic**.*

Fireworks also lets you create stars. When stars have many points they are sometimes called bursts. You can use bursts to call attention to special information.

To create a star:

1. Click the Polygon tool in the Toolbox. If the Polygon tool is not visible, open the pop-up group to choose the Polygon tool.

2. Double-click the Polygon tool to display the Tool Options panel.

3. Choose Star from the pop-up list in the Tool Options. This adds the Angle controls to the panel ❽.

4. Use the slider or enter a number from 1 to 360 in the field to set the number of sides for the star.

5. Check Automatic to create stars with parallel line segments ❾.

   or

   Use the slider to set the angle of the points. Low settings create acute angles. High settings create obtuse angles ❿.

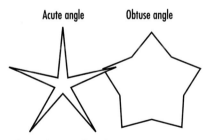

Acute angle   Obtuse angle

❿ *Choose low angle values to create **acute-angled stars** with sharp points. Choose high angle values to create **obtuse-angled stars** with broad points.*

One of the most important tools in any vector program is its Pen tool. The Pen tool allows you to precisely create a wide variety of shapes. The Fireworks Pen tool is very similar to those found in Macromedia FreeHand, Adobe Illustrator, and Adobe Photoshop. If you've never used the Pen tool, you need to learn the elements of paths.

⑪ *The **Pen tool** in the Toolbox.*

Elements of Paths

Anchor points define a path at points where the path changes. *Segments* are the paths that connect anchor points. *Conrol handles* extend out from anchor points; their length and direction controls the shape of curves of the segments.

⑫ *The **start icon** for the Pen tool.*

The best way to learn to use the pen is to start by creating straight segments.

To create a straight path segment:

1. Click the Pen tool in the Toolbox ⑪.

2. Move the pointer to the document area. The cursor changes to the plus (+) sign with a white square dot next to it. This indicates the start of the path ⑫.

3. Click to create an anchor point which defines the beginning of the segment of the path.

4. Move the cursor to where you want the next anchor point of the path. The cursor changes to a plus sign without a dot next to it. This indicates that the next point is connected to the previous one.

5. Click. This connects the two anchor points with a straight line segment ⑬.

6. Continue to create straight segments by repeating steps 4 and 5.

7. To finish the path, move the tool away from the path, hold down the Command/Ctrl key, and double-click.

Path segment ———

Selected anchor point

Anchor point ———

⑬ *Clicking with the Pen tool creates **straight** segments.*

Straight Path Segments

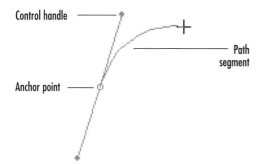

Control handle

Path segment

Anchor point

⑭ *Dragging with the Pen tool creates* **curved segments**.

⑮ *A path with a series of curved segments.*

⑯ *Hold the Option/Alt key to pivot the handles, which creates a* **corner curve**.

You can also create curved segments. Think of a curved segment as the shape that a rollercoaster follows along a track.

To create a curved path segment:

1. Click the Pen tool in the Toolbox.

2. Move the pointer to the document area. The cursor changes to the plus sign with a white square dot next to it.

3. Press and drag to create an anchor point with control handles.

4. Release the mouse button. The length and direction of the handle controls the height and direction of the curve ⑭.

5. Move the cursor to where you want the next anchor point of the path. Drag to create the curved segment between the two anchor points.

6. Continue to create curved segments by repeating steps 3 and 4 ⑮.

7. To finish the path, move the tool away from the path, hold down the Command/Ctrl key, and double-click.

Curves do not have to be smooth. A corner curve has an abrupt change in direction. The path of a bouncing ball is a corner curve.

To create a corner curve:

1. Press and drag to create an anchor point with control handles. Do not release the mouse button.

2. Hold the Option/Alt key and then drag to pivot the second handle ⑯.

TIP The longer the handle, the more steep the curve.

3. Release the mouse button when the second handle is the correct length and direction.

Once you have created a curved segment with two handles, you can retract the second handle back into the anchor point.

To retract the handle into a point:

1. Drag to create an anchor point with two control handles.

2. Move the cursor back over the anchor point. A small arrow appears next to the plus sign.

3. Click. The handle retracts back into the anchor point **⓱**.

4. Continue the path with either a straight segment or a curved segment.

TIP Click to make the next path segment straight. Drag to make the next path segment curved.

⓱ *Move the cursor back over a point and click to* **retract a handle** *along a curve.*

Once you click to create an anchor point with no control handles, you can extend a single handle out from that anchor point.

To extend a handle out from a point:

1. Click to create an anchor point with no control handles.

2. Move the pointer back over the anchor point you just created. A small arrow appears next to the plus sign.

3. Hold the Command+Option keys (Mac) or Ctrl+Alt keys (Win) as you drag out from the anchor point **⓲**. A single control handle extends out from the anchor point.

4. Continue the path with a curved segment.

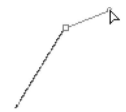

⓲ *Hold the Command+Option keys (Mac) or Ctrl+Alt keys (Win) to* **extend a handle** *out from an anchor point.*

⓳ *An* **Open path.**

⓴ *The* **Closed path** *icon.*

㉑ *The* **Line tool** *in the Toolbox.*

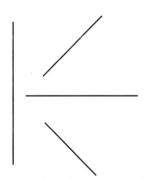

㉒ *The results of* **holding the Shift key** *while drawing with the Line tool.*

There are two ways to finish a path in Fireworks. The first way is to leave the end points of the path open. An open path is like a piece of string.

To create an open path:

1. Move the pen away from the last point of the path.

2. Hold the Command/Crl key and double-click. This leaves the path open **⓳** and allows you to continue using the Pen tool.

   or

   Switch to another tool in the Toolbox. This leaves the path open.

The second way to finish a path is to join the last point of the path to the first. This creates a closed path. A closed path is like a rubber band.

To create a closed path:

1. Move the cursor to the first anchor point of the path. The cursor changes to plus sign with a black square dot next to it **⓴**.

2. Click to close the path.

You can use the Line tool to quickly create straight line segments.

To create a line:

1. Click the Line tool in the Toolbox **㉑**.

2. Move the pointer to the document area. The cursor changes to the plus sign.

3. Drag to set the length and direction of the line.

   TIP Hold the Shift key to constrain the angle of the line to 45° increments **㉒**.

4. Release the mouse button to complete the line.

Fireworks also has a Brush tool that lets you draw more freely, without worrying about how and where you place points.

To draw with the Brush:

1. Click the Brush tool in the Toolbox **㉓**.

2. Move the pointer to the document area. The cursor changes to the brush icon.

3. Drag to create a path that follows the movements of the mouse.

4. Release the mouse button to end the path.

TIP To make a closed path with the Brush tool, move the mouse close to the starting point of the path. A small black dot appears **㉔** indicating that the path will close when you release the mouse button.

As you draw with the Brush tool, you can make straight lines in addition to the curved segments.

To draw straight segments with the Brush tool:

1. Draw the curved portion of the path but do not release the mouse.

2. Hold the Shift key and then release the mouse button. The Brush cursor displays a small plus (+) sign indicating you are adding to the path **㉕**.

3. Still holding the Shift key, position the Brush cursor where you want the straight segment to end.

4. Press the mouse button and release the Shift key.

TIP The straight-line segment is not visible yet.

5. Drag with the mouse to draw the rest of the path. Release the mouse button to complete the path. The straight-line segment appears.

㉓ *The **Brush tool** in the Toolbox.*

㉔ **The small black dot** *next to the Brush tool indicates that the path will be closed.*

㉕ **The plus sign** *next to the Brush tool indicates that part of the path will be a straight line segment.*

㉖ *The* **Redraw Path tool** *in the Toolbox.*

㉗ *The* **Redraw path icon.**

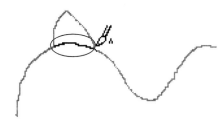

㉘ *A red line (circled) shows the original path as the Redraw Path tool creates the new path.*

Once you have created a path with the Brush tool, you can modify the shape of the path.

To modify a brush path:

1. Select a brush path.

2. Press the pop-up group in the Toolbox to choose the Redraw Path tool **㉖**.

3. Move the tool to the part of the path that you want to redraw. A small triangle sign appears next to the brush icon **㉗**. This indicates that the path will be redrawn.

4. Drag to create the new shape of the path. A red line appears that indicates the part of the path that is modified **㉘**.

5. Release the mouse to redraw the path.

TIP You can use the brush to modify a segment created by the Pen, Line, or Pencil tools. *(See the next set of exercises for working with the Pencil tool.)*

TIP You can also modify the shape of a path by manipulating the the anchor points and control handles of the path. *(See Chapter 5, "Selecting Paths.")*

The Pencil tool lets you draw without worrying about placing anchor points or creating handles. The Pencil tool can also be used in the image-editing mode to color individual pixels. *(For more information on working in the image-editing mode see Chapter 12, "Working With Pixels.")*

㉙ *The **Pencil Tool** in the Toolbox.*

To draw with the Pencil:

1. Click the Pencil tool in the Toolbox **㉙**.

2. Move the pointer to the document area.

3. Drag to create a line that follows the movements of the mouse.

4. Release the mouse button to finish drawing the line.

TIP Release the mouse button where you started to close the path.

㉚ *The **Pencil Tool** options.*

You can soften the look of Pencil lines by turning on the anti-aliasing option. This adds lighter colors that blend to white, softening the edge of the line.

To anti-alias pencil lines:

1. Double-click the Pencil tool in the Toolbox to display the Tool Options for the Pencil **㉚**.

2. Click the Anti-Aliased option to soften the lines created by the pencil **㉛**.

TIP Anti-aliasing creates additional colors in the line create by the Pencil. This can add to the size of the final Web graphic.

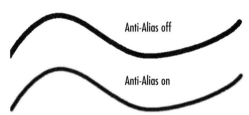

㉛ *The difference between drawing with the **Anti-Aliasing** option on and off.*

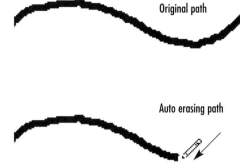

Original path

Auto erasing path

32 *Dragging with the Pencil tool along a path with the **Auto Erase option** lets you erase the path by coloring it with the Fill color.*

The Auto Erase option lets you erase Pencil lines by drawing over them with the Fill color. *(For more information on Fill and Stroke colors, see Chapter 7, "Fills" and Chapter 8, "Strokes.")*

To use the Auto Erase:

1. Double-click the Pencil tool in the Toolbox. This opens the Options panel for the Pencil tool.

2. Click Auto Erase in the Options panel.

3. Place the Pencil over a path colored with the current Brush color.

4. Drag the Pencil. The path changes from the Brush to the Fill color **32**.

TIP When working in the path mode, the Auto Erase option of the Pencil does not actually change the colors of the previously drawn path; rather, it creates a new path on top of the first one.

TIP The Auto Erase option works best when the path is not anti-aliased. This makes it easier to position the Pencil over a pixel colored exactly with the Brush color and not a shade created by anti-aliasing.

Auto Erase

As you work with paths, you may find that you need to add points to a path. This makes it much easier to reshape an existing path. Adding and deleting points on a path requires selecting the path with the Subselection tool. *(See Chapter 5, "Selecting Paths" for more information on working with the Subselection tool.)*

㉝ *The* **Subselection tool** *in the Toolbox.*

To add points to a path:

1. Use the Subselection tool **㉝** to select the path with its points visible.

2. Choose the Pen tool and position the cursor on the segment where you want to add the point. A small caret (^) appears next to the cursor **㉞**.

3. Click. A new point appears.

㉞ *Click with the Pen tool to* **add a point** *to a path.*

Just as you can add points, you can delete points from a path.

To delete points from a path:

1. Select the path.

2. Use the Subselection tool to select the point or points.

3. Press the Delete/Backspace key on the keyboard. The point disappears from the path **㉟**.

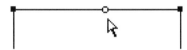

㉟ *A selected* **point on a path can be deleted** *by pressing the delete/backspace key.*

SELECTING PATHS 5

O nce you have created objects using
the path tools, you have many more
options available. You can select and
manipulate the individual points of the
paths. Again, if you are familiar with a
vector drawing program, you will find
many of the steps in this chapter familiar.
However, there are a few new tricks that
Fireworks provides for selecting objects.

In this chapter you will learn how to

Use the Pointer tool.

Marquee selected objects.

Add or subtract objects from a
selection.

Use the Subselection tool.

Use the Select Behind tool.

Use the Select menu commands.

Set the Mouse Highlight option.

Set the Preview Drag option.

Group selected objects.

Select objects within groups.

Create nested groups.

Use the Subselect and Superselect
commands.

Hide the highlight of selected objects.

Change the highlight color.

Several different tools help you select objects. The main selection aid is the Pointer tool. The Pointer tool selects objects as complete paths.

To use the Pointer tool:

1. Click the Pointer tool in the Toolbox ❶.

TIP Hold the Command/Ctrl key to temporarily access the Pointer tool. Release the key to return to the original tool.

2. Position the Pointer arrow over an object and click. A highlight color appears along the path indicating that the object is selected ❷.

TIP If the object has no fill color, you must click the path or stroke color to select the object.

TIP If you are working in the Draft Display mode *(see page 29)*, you must click the path directly to select the object.

3. Hold the Shift key and click to select any additional objects.

4. Hold the Shift key and click to deselect any objects.

You can also select many objects at once by dragging a marquee with the Pointer tool.

To marquee selected objects:

1. Place the Pointer tool outside the area of the objects you want to select.

2. Drag diagonally with the Pointer tool to create a rectangle that encloses your selection.

3. Release the mouse button. All objects inside the rectangle are selected ❸.

❶ *The* **Pointer tool** *in the Toolbox.*

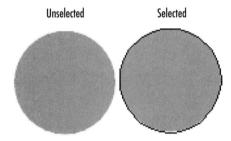

❷ *A highlight color appears on the path of a* **selected object.**

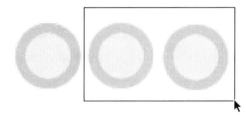

❸ *Drag with the Pointer tool to select objects within the* **rectangular marquee.**

❹ *The* **Subselection tool** *in the Toolbox.*

Object selected but points unselected | Object and points selected

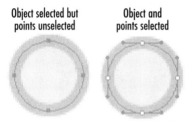

❺ *The* **Subselection tool** *allows you to see the individual anchor points of a selected object. Click to select the specific points.*

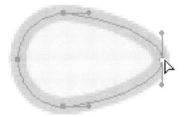

❻ **Drag with the Subselection tool** *to change the position of anchor points.*

Once you have a selection of objects, you can add objects to, or subtract from, the selection.

To add or subtract objects from a selection:

1. Hold the Shift key and click to select any additional objects.

2. Hold the Shift key and click to deselect any objects.

TIP Sometimes it is easier to marquee-select a group of objects and then use the Shift key to deselect the one or two you do not want as part of the selection.

Fireworks creates paths with anchor points defining the shape of the path. You can use the Subselection tool to select those individual points and manipulate them to change the shape of the objects.

To use the Subselection tool:

1. Click the Subselection tool in the Toolbox ❹.

2. Click the object to select the object. The anchor points will be displayed but not selected.

TIP Anchor points filled with the highlight color are unselected ❺.

3. Click a specific point or marquee drag to select multiple points. The anchor points of the object are selected.

4. Shift-click to select additional points.

TIP Anchor points that are white are selected points ❺.

5. Use the Subselection tool to move the selected points ❻.

TIP If you switch from the Pointer tool to the Subselection tool while an object is already selected, you see the unselected anchor points for that object.

Because transparency is so important in creating Fireworks graphics, you may find that your artwork consists of many objects stacked on top of each other. This can make it difficult to select an object behind the rest. The Select Behind tool makes it easy to select through other objects to one at the back.

❼ *The **Select Behind tool** in the Toolbox.*

To use the Select Behind tool:

1. Press the pop-up group for the Pointer tool to choose the Select Behind tool ❼.

2. Click with the Select Behind tool over the objects you want to select. The first click selects the object on top of the others.

3. Click as many times as necessary to select the object you want ❽.

TIP Hold the Shift key as you click to add each object to the selection.

❽ *The Select Behind tool was used to select the star behind the other two objects. The first click selected the square. The second click selected the circle. The third click selected the star.*

In addition to the selection tools, the commands in the Select menu allow you to select and deselect objects.

To use the Select menu commands:

1. Choose **Select > Select All** to select all the objects in a file.

2. Choose **Select > Deselect** to deselect any selected objects. These commands can also be used when working in the Image Editing mode *(see Chapter 12, "Working With Pixels")*.

TIP You can also deselect any objects in a file by clicking the empty space in a document with the Pointer tool.

❾ *The* **Pointer tool options** *for the selection tools.*

If you are working with many overlapping objects, it may be difficult to determine which object you are about to select. The Mouse Highlight feature allows you to know which object is about to be selected with the next click.

To set the Mouse Highlight:

1. Double-click the Pointer, Subselection, or Select Behind tool to open the Options panel.

2. Select Mouse Highlight in the panel **❾**.

3. Move the selection tool over an object. A red line appears around the object indicating that the object can be selected with the next mouse click.

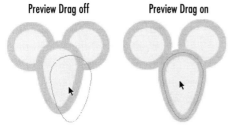

Preview Drag off   Preview Drag on

❿ *The* **Preview Drag** *controls what you see as an object is moved.*

The Preview Drag option controls what the object looks like as you move it.

To set the Preview Drag:

1. Double-click the Pointer, Subselection, or Select Behind tool to open the Options panel.

2. Select Preview Drag in the panel.

3. Move an object. With Preview Drag turned on you see the fill, stroke, and effects of an object as you move it. With Preview Drag turned off, you see only the path shape of the object **❿**.

You may find it easier to select several objects together as a single unit, or group.

To group selected objects:

1. Select two or more objects.

2. Choose **Modify > Group**. Small anchor points appear around the objects indicating they are a group ⓫.

TIP Fireworks lets you group a single object. This lets you select the object without the highlighting its path.

3. You can add objects to the group by selecting the group and additional objects and then choosing the Group command again.

⓫ *A* **Grouped object** *displays four points when selected.*

To ungroup objects:

1. Select the grouped objects.

2. Choose **Modify > Ungroup** to release the objects from the group.

TIP (Win) You can also use the Group/ Ungroup icons on the Modify toolbar.

Grouped objects are considered a single object. However, you do not have to ungroup to select a specific object within the group.

To select objects within groups:

1. Choose either the Pointer, Subselection, or Select Behind tool.

2. Hold the Option/Alt key and click the individual object of the group.

TIP Hold the Shift and Option/Alt keys to add other items to the selection.

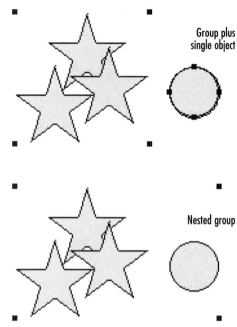

Group plus
single object

Nested group

12 *A nested group is a group that contains a subgroup.*

Groups can be nested within other groups so that one group contains subgroups.

To create a nested group:

1. Select two or more groups or one group and some other objects.

2. Choose **Modify > Group**. The original selections are now subgroups of the nested group **12**.

3. Continue to select additional objects and choose the Group command to create more nested groups.

The Subselect and Superselect commands make it easy to work with nested groups. The Subselect command lets you select the entire group and then select the individual members of the group.

The Superselect command lets you select an individual object in a group and then can select up to select the entire group.

To use the Subselect command:

1. Select a nested group.

2. Choose **Edit > Subselect**. This lets you see and work with the original objects of the nested group.

To use the Superselect command:

1. Select a single item in a nested group.

2. Choose **Edit > Superselect**. This selects the group that contained the selection.

TIP You can reapply both the Subselect and Superselect commands to further select groups within nested groups.

Nested Groups; Subselect; Superselect

If you find the highlight effect interferes with your work, you can hide the highlight while keeping the object selected.

To control the highlight of selected objects:

1. Choose **View>Hide Edges**. This hides the highlight along the path of an object.

2. To reveal the highlight, choose **View> Hide Edges** when there is a checkmark in front of the command.

TIP Anchor points and control handles are still visible when the Hide Edges command is applied **⑬**.

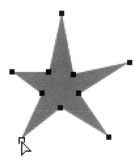

⑬ *The* **Hide Edges** *command hides the highlight along a path but keeps the anchor points and control handles visible when you're using the Subselection tool.*

You may not be able to see the path highlight color if it is too similar to the color of the brush stroke around an object. You can use the Preferences to change the path highlight color.

To change the highlight color:

1. Choose **File>Preferences** to open the Preferences dialog box **⑭**.

2. Click the Highlight Color Well. The Color picker dialog box appears.

3. Choose the color for the highlight and then click OK.

TIP The highlight color is an application preference. Changing it changes the highlight color for all Fireworks documents.

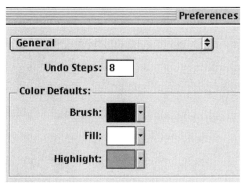

⑭ *Use the* **Highlight Color Well** *in the Preferences dialog box to change the color of the path highlight.*

WORKING WITH OBJECTS 6

O nce you have created objects, there
are many different ways you can work
with those objects. Some of the ways to
work with objects change the shape of the
objects themselves. You can also change
their relationship to other objects. Finally,
you can change the properties of objects so
that they change their appearance.

In this chapter you will learn how to

Move an object by eye.

Move an object numerically.

Copy and paste an object.

Clone an object.

Duplicate an object.

Drag and drop between documents.

Copy an object as you move it.

Scale an object.

Skew an object.

Distort an object.

Rotate an object.

Use the Transform commands.

Set the Transform options.

Use the Freeform tool.

Use the Reshape Area tool.

Use the Eraser tool.

Use the Combine commands.

Use the Alter Path commands.

Align objects.

Use the Arrange commands.

Work with the Layers panel.

Use Single Layer Editing.

Move objects between layers.

Once you have selected an object, you can move it by dragging the mouse.

To move an object by eye:

1. Select the object.

2. Using any of the selection tools, drag the object to the new position.

TIP Drag anywhere on the object except on a point to avoid reshaping the object.

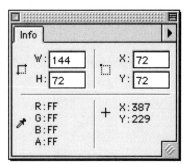

❶ *The* **Info panel** *lets you change the position of an object using the X and Y coordinates.*

You can also move any object by changing its upper-left corner coordinates in the Object Properties dialog box.

To move an object numerically:

1. Select the object.

2. Choose **Window** > **Info**. The Info panel appears **❶**.

3. Change the number in the **X** field to set the position of the left edge.

4. Change the number in the **Y** field to set the position of the top edge.

TIP Use the **W** and **H** fields to change the width and height of an object.

You can copy and paste objects in Fireworks as you can in other programs, but in addition there are a few special features you should know.

To copy and paste an object:

1. Select the object.

2. Choose **Edit** > **Copy**.

3. Choose **Edit** > **Paste** to paste the object into the same position as the original.

TIP Although it may not seem very useful, pasting an object into the same position is helpful when creating rollover buttons *(see Chapter 18, "Behaviors")*.

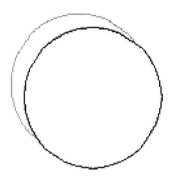

❷ *The* **Duplicate** *command copies the selected object.*

In addition to copy and paste, you can make copies of objects using the Duplicate and Clone commands.

To clone an object:

1. Select the object.
2. Choose **Edit** >**Clone**. A duplicate of the object appears in exactly the same position as the original.

To duplicate an object:

1. Select the object.
2. Choose **Edit** >**Duplicate**. A duplicate of the object appears slightly offset from the original ❷.

❸ Holding the **Option/Alt keys** *as you move an object creates a copy of that object while leaving the original in place.*

Another technique allows you to copy an object as you move it.

To copy an object as you move it:

1. Choose any of the selection tools.
2. Hold the Option/Alt key as you move the object. A small plus sign (+) appears next to the arrow as you move the object ❸.
3. Release the mouse button. A copy of the object appears.

TIP The Clone, Duplicate, Drag and Drop, and Option/Alt-Drag leave the contents of the Clipboard unchanged.

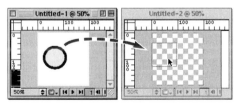

❹ *You can* **drag and drop** *an object from one document to another. (The dashed line indicates direction of the drag and drop.)*

You can also duplicate objects using the drag-and-drop feature.

To drag and drop an object:

1. Position two document windows so that both are visible.
2. Use any of the selection tools to drag an object from one document to the other.
3. Release the mouse button. A copy of the object appears ❹.

(margin tab) Clone; Duplicate; Copy and Move; Drag and Drop

Transformations change the size, shape, or orientation of an object. Fireworks provides many different ways to transform objects. *Scaling* changes an object's size.

To scale an object:

1. Choose the Scale tool in the Toolbox **⑤**.

   or

   Choose **Modify > Transform > Scale**. The transformation handles appear around the object.

2. Place the cursor directly over any of the handles. A small double-headed arrow appears **⑥**.

3. Drag toward the object to reduce it or away to enlarge it.

   TIP Drag one of the corner handles to scale both the horizontal and vertical dimensions of the object.

   TIP Drag the edge handles to change just the horizontal or vertical dimensions.

4. Double-click within the bounding box of the transformation handles to apply the transformation.

   or

   Click the Transform button in the Tool Options panel **⑦**.

   TIP To exit the transformation mode without applying the transformation, switch to any other tool in the Toolbox or press the Esc key on the keyboard.

⑤ *The* **Scale tool** *in the Toolbox.*

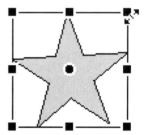

⑥ *Drag a corner handle with the* **Scale tool** *to change the horizontal and vertical dimensions of the object proportionally.*

⑦ *The* **Transform** *Options panel.*

❽ *The* **Skew tool** *in the Toolbox.*

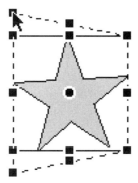

❾ *Drag a corner handle with the* **Skew tool** *to change the dimension of that side of the object.*

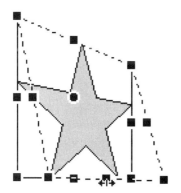

❿ *Drag a side handle with the* **Skew tool** *to change the angles along that side of the object.*

The *skewing* transformation moves two sides of the bounding box together or two control handles in opposite directions. Skewing creates 3-dimensional effects for objects or for text *(see page 127).*

To skew an object:

1. Choose the Skew tool in the Toolbox ❽.

   or

   Choose **Modify > Transform > Skew**. The transformation handles appear around the object.

2. Place the cursor directly over any of the handles.

3. Drag one of the corner handles in or out to move that handle and the one opposite it. This changes the dimension of that side of the object ❾.

4. Drag one of the side handles to change the angle of that side of the object ❿.

5. Double-click within the box created by the transformation handles to apply the transformation.

   or

   Click the Transform button in the Tool Options panel.

TIP To leave the transformation mode without applying the transformation, switch to any other tool in the Toolbox or press the Esc key on the keyboard.

Skew

The *distortion* transformation allows you to distort the shape of object by changing the shape of the box that defines the object.

To distort an object:

1. Choose the Distort tool in the Toolbox **⑪**.

   or

   Choose **Modify** > **Transform** > **Distort**. The transformation handles appear around the object.

2. Place the cursor directly over any of the handles.

3. Drag one of the side handles to change the shape of the object **⑫**.

4. Double-click within the box created by the transformation handles to apply the transformation.

   or

   Click the Transform button in the Tool Options panel.

TIP To exit the transformation mode without applying the transformation, switch to any other tool in the Toolbox or press the Esc key on the keyboard.

⑪ *The* **Distort tool** *in the Toolbox.*

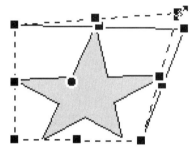

⑫ *Drag a handle with the* **Distort tool** *to change the shape of an object.*

Distort

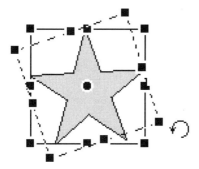

⓭ *Drag with the* **Rotation cursor** *to change the orientation of an object.*

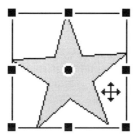

⓮ *The* **four-headed arrow** *appears while moving an object in the transformation mode.*

An additional transformation, *rotation*, is available when you use any of the three transformation tools.

To rotate an object:

1. Choose any of the Transformation tools.

2. Position the cursor outside of the handles. A rounded arrow appears.

3. Drag either clockwise or counter-clockwise to rotate the object ⓭.

TIP Move the small transformation circle to change the point around which the object rotates.

4. Double-click within the box created by the transformation handles to apply the transformation.

or

Click the Transform button in the Tool Options panel.

TIP To leave the transformation mode without applying the transformation, switch to any other tool in the Toolbox or press the Esc key on the keyboard.

You can also move an object while in the transformation mode.

To move an object in the transformation mode:

1. Choose any of the Transformation tools.

2. Position the cursor inside the box created by the transformation handles. A four-headed arrow appears ⓮.

3. Drag to move the object.

4. Continue working with the transformation tools or apply the transformation by double-clicking within the box created by the transformation handles.

Fireworks also gives you a set of transformation menu commands that make it easy to rotate or flip objects 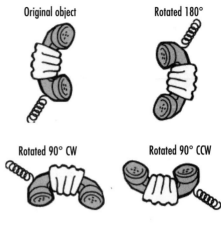.

To use the Transform menu commands:

1. Select an object.

2. Choose one of the commands from the **Modify** > **Transform** menu to rotate or flip the object. For example, to rotate an object so that it is upside down, choose **Modify** > **Transform** > **Rotate 180°**.

TIP (Win) You can also use the rotate buttons on the Modify toolbar to easily apply rotations.

The Numeric Transform dialog box makes it easy to scale, resize, or rotate an object using numeric values, rather than by judging by eye.

To use the Numeric Transform dialog box:

1. Select an object.

2. Rotate or flip the object by choosing a command from the **Modify** > **Transform** > **Numeric Transform**. The Numeric Transform dialog box appears

3. Use the pop-up list to choose Scale, Resize, or Rotate.

4. In the Scale mode, enter the percentage of change in the width or height fields.

   or

   In the Resize mode, enter the pixel amount in the width or height fields.

   or

   In the Rotate mode, use the wheel or enter the angle amount in the field.

5. Click OK to apply the transformation.

TIP Both Scale and Resize change the size of the object. Scale does so using percentages. Resize does so by changing the pixel dimensions.

Original object   Rotated 180°

Rotated 90° CW   Rotated 90° CCW

Flipped Horizontally   Flipped Vertically

 *The effect of* **Transform** *menu commands on the original object (upper left).*

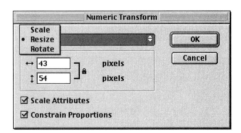

 *The* **Numeric Transform** *dialog box.*

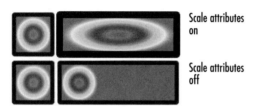

⑰ *The* **Transform** *Options panel.*

Scale attributes on

Scale attributes off

⑱ *The difference between scaling with the* **Scale Attributes** *option on and off. The size of the stroke and the gradient change when the option is turned on. The stroke and gradient do not change when the option is turned off.*

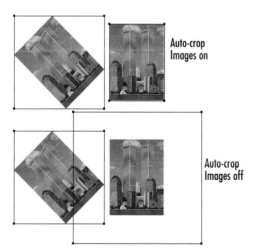

Auto-crop Images on

Auto-crop Images off

⑲ *The difference between rotating with the* **Auto-crop Images** *option on and off. The bounding box around the rotated image shrinks when the option is on. The bounding box expands when the option is off.*

Two options control how the Transformation tools work. The first option, *Scale Attributes,* controls how the scale tool affects the attributes of an object.

To set the Scale Attributes option:

1. Double-click any of the Transformation tools in the Toolbox. The Transformation Options panel appears **⑰**.

2. Choose Scale Attributes to extend any scaling to the size of the stroke, pattern fill, gradient fill, or effect applied to the object **⑱**.

    or

    Deselect Scale Attributes to restrict scaling only to the size of the object, not the stroke, pattern fill, gradient fill, or effect applied to the object.

The second option, *Auto-crop Images,* controls whether or not the bounding box of a pixel-based image shrinks to fit a transformed image. *(For information on pixel-based images, see Chapter 12, "Working With Pixels.)*

To set the Auto-crop Images option:

1. Double-click any of the Transformation tools in the Toolbox. The Transformation Options panel appears.

2. Choose Auto-crop Images to automatically shrink the bounding box of an image to fit the new area of any transformed image **⑲**.

    or

    Deselect Auto-crop Images to leave control of the size of the bounding box to Fireworks.

Transform Options

Once you have created an object, you may find it difficult to work with the control handles to reshape the path. The Freeform tool allows you to change the shape of an object without worrying about adding or modifying points.

To set the Freeform tool options:

1. Double-click the Freeform tool in the Toolbox ⑳ to open the Tool Options panel ㉑.

2. Use the slider or click in the Size field to set the size of tool. This controls how large an area is pushed by the tool.

3. If you have a pressure-sensitive pen and tablet, click Pressure to allow your pressure on the tablet to affect the size of the effect.

TIP If you do not have a pressure-sensitive tablet, press the 1, left bracket ([), or left-arrow key as you drag to decrease the size of the Freeform tool effect.

TIP If you do not have a pressure-sensitive tablet, press the 2, right bracket (]), or right-arrow key as you drag to increase the size of the Freeform tool effect.

⑳ *The* **Freeform tool** *in the Toolbox.*

㉑ *The* **Freeform tool** *options.*

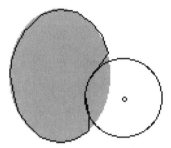

㉒ *The* **Push Freeform tool** *cursor.*

㉓ *The* **Push Freeform tool** *allows you to push on the edges of an object to reshape it.*

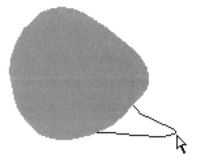

㉔ *The* **Pull Freeform tooll** *cursor.*

㉕ *The* **Pull Freeform tool** *allows you to pull out segments from an object.*

There are two modes to the Freeform tool: the Push mode and the Pull mode. In the Push mode the Freeform tool acts like a rolling pin to modify the shape of the path.

To use the Freeform tool in the Push mode:

1. Set the Freeform tool options, as described on *page 74.*

2. Move the cursor near, but not on, the edge of a selected object. The cursor displays the Push icon, an arrow with a circle next to it **㉒**.

3. Drag around the edge of the object. The shape of the object changes accordingly **㉓**.

TIP The Push Freeform tool can work from either the inside or the outside of an object.

TIP Check Preview to turn off the highlight color on the object as you use the Freeform tool.

In the Pull mode the Freeform tool acts like a magnet that pulls out new segments from the path.

To use the Freeform tool in the Pull mode:

1. Set the Freeform tool options, as described on *page 74.*

2. Move the cursor to the edge of a selected object. The cursor displays the Pull icon **㉔**.

3. Drag in or out from the edge of the object. The shape of the object changes accordingly **㉕**.

The Reshape Area tool also lets you distort paths without manually adding or modifying anchor points or handles.

To set the Reshape Area tool options:

1. Choose the Reshape Area tool in the Toolbox **26**.

2. Double-click the Reshape Area tool in the Toolbox to open the Tool Options panel **27**.

3. Use the slider or click in the Size field to set the size of the Reshape Area tool. The greater the amount, the larger the area that the tool distorts **28**.

4. Use the slider or type in the Strength field to set how long the tool will work during a drag—the higher the setting, the longer the tool distorts the path **29**.

5. Use the slider or click in the Precision field to set the precision amount—the greater the amount, the more sensitive the tool is to movements of the mouse.

6. If you have a pressure-sensitive tablet, check the Size or Strength boxes to set how the pressure on the tablet affects the tool.

TIP If you do not have a pressure-sensitive tablet, press the 1, left bracket ([), or left-arrow key as you drag to decrease the size of the Reshape Area tool effect.

TIP If you do not have a pressure-sensitive tablet, press the 2, right bracket (]), or right-arrow key as you drag to increase the size of the Reshape Area tool effect.

26 *The* **Reshape Area tool** *in the Toolbox.*

27 *The options for the* **Reshape Area tool.**

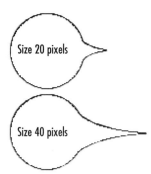

28 *The effect of changing the* size *of the* **Reshape Area tool.**

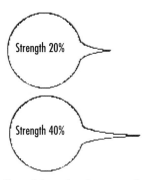

29 *The effect of changing the* strength *of the* **Reshape Area tool.**

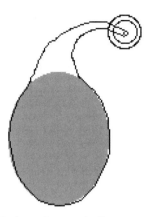

The Reshape Area tool modifies paths as if they were taffy. The size of the tool controls the amount that is pulled. The strength of the tool controls the length of the pull.

To use the Reshape Area tool:

1. Choose the Reshape Area tool.

2. Position the tool either inside or outside the path.

3. Drag to reshape the path ❸⓪.

❸⓪ *The* **Reshape Area tool** *allows you to distort the path of objects.*

You can also modify paths by cutting them with the Eraser tool.

To use the Eraser tool:

1. Choose the Eraser tool in the Toolbox ❸❶.

2. Drag the Eraser tool across a path. This cuts the path ❸❷.

TIP Segments created by the Eraser tool can be moved away from the other objects with any of the selection tools.

❸❶ *The* **Eraser tool** *in the Toolbox.*

TIP The Eraser tool also erases pixels in the Image Editing mode *(see page 156)*.

TIP The Eraser tool cursor resembles an X-acto knife when used to cut paths. It resembles a rubber eraser when erasing pixels.

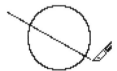

❸❷ *Cutting an object with the Eraser tool.*

One of the secrets to working with vector objects is to use commands that combine simple path shapes into more complex shapes. In FreeHand these commands are called path operations; in Fireworks they are the Combine commands. Each of these commands creates a new object from two or more overlapping objects.

The Union command allows you to create one path that is a combination of two or more objects.

To unite overlapping objects:

1. Select two or more overlapping objects.
2. Choose **Modify** > **Combine** > **Union**. The outside path of the new object follows the original outside path of the overlapping objects **❸❸**.

The Intersect command creates one path from the intersection of two or more paths.

To form the intersection of overlapping objects:

1. Select two or more overlapping objects.
2. Choose **Modify** > **Combine** > **Intersect**. The path of the new object follows the shape of the area where the two paths overlapped **❸❹**.

Original objects   Objects after Union command

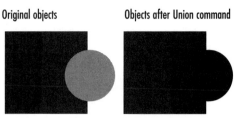

❸❸ The Union command *forms one object from the combination of two or more overlapping objects.*

Original objects   Objects after Intersect command

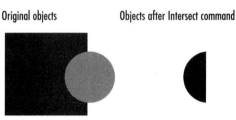

❸❹ The Intersect command *creates an object from the area where two or more objects overlapped.*

Original objects   Objects after Punch command

㉟ **The Punch command** *uses one object to punch a hole in the objects below it.*

The Punch command allows one object to act like a cookie cutter to punch a hole in the objects below it.

To create a hole where objects overlap:

1. Select two or more overlapping objects.

2. Choose **Modify > Combine > Punch**. The top object punches holes in all the objects below it **㉟**.

The Crop command is the reverse of the Punch command. Instead of punching a hole in the objects below, cropping discards the parts that are outside the top object.

To crop overlapping objects:

1. Select three or more overlapping objects.

2. Choose **Modify > Combine > Crop**. This trims away any part of the paths that were outside the original top object **㊱**.

TIP The object created by the combine commands take their appearance from the bottom-most object.

Original objects   Objects after Crop command

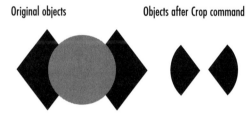

㊱ **The Crop command** *trims away all the area outside the top object.*

Punch; Crop

You can also change the shape of paths using the Alter Path commands. For instance, you can simplify the number of points on a path.

To simplify the shape of a path:

1. Select a path.

2. Choose **Modify** > **Alter Path** > **Simplify**. The Simplify dialog box appears **37**.

3. Enter an amount of simplification in the dialog box and click OK. Fireworks removes as many points as possible to simplify the path **38**.

TIP The higher the number, the greater the distortion that may occur.

You can also an expand the stroke of an open path into a closed path. This lets you apply a fill such a pattern or a gradient. *(For more information on open and closed paths, see page 51. For more information on using patterns and gradient blends as fills, see Chapter 7, "Fills.")*

To expand a path:

1. Select a path.

2. Choose **Modify** > **Alter Path** > **Expand Stroke**. The Expand Stroke dialog box appears **39**.

3. Enter the desired width or thickness of the path (in pixels).

4. Set shape of the corners.

5. Set the miter limit to control the length of the points of any corners.

6. Set the shape of the ends of the path.

7. Click OK. The path is converted into a filled shape **40**.

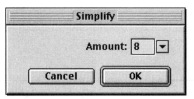

37 The Simplify dialog box.

Original object

After Simplify command

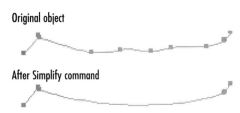

38 The Simplify command *reduces the number of points on a path.*

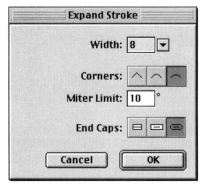

39 *The* Expand Stroke *dialog box.*

Original object   **After Expand Stroke command**

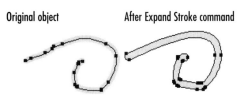

40 The Expand Stroke command *converts an open path into a filled shape.*

Simplify; Expand Stroke

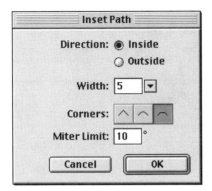

⓵ The Inset Path dialog box.

⓶ The Inset Path command *changes the shape of the path so that it lies inside or outside the original path.*

Fireworks also lets you increase or decrease the size of a path using the Inset Path command. While it might seem like this is the same as the scale command *(see page 68)*, it is actually different and allows you to create a smaller or larger path that exactly follows the contours of the original.

To inset a path:

1. Select a path you want to inset.
2. Choose **Modify** > **Alter Path** > **Inset Path.** The Inset Path dialog box appears **⓵**.
3. Choose the direction of the inset. Inside moves the contours of the path inside the original. Outside moves the contours of the path outside the original **⓶**.
4. Enter the width or amount that the path should be changed.
5. Set shape of the corners.
6. Set the miter limit to control the spikes of any corners.
7. Click OK. The path is converted into a filled shape.

TIP Use the Clone command before applying the Inset Path. This keeps the original image and moves the object created by the Inset Path command inside or outside the original.

Inset Path

You can use the Align menu commands to align the objects or distribute them along the horizontal or vertical axis ❹❸–❹❻.

To use the Align menu commands:

1. Select two or more objects to align.

or

Select three or more objects to distribute.

2. Align or distribute the objects by choosing a command from the **Modify** > **Align** menu, for example, **Modify** > **Align** > **Left**.

TIP Fireworks uses the object on the left as the point to align to on the left. It uses the object on the right to align to the right.

TIP Fireworks uses the object at the top to align to the top. It uses the object on the bottom to align to the bottom.

The Modify toolbar (Win) gives you buttons to apply many object commands. All the Align commands are available in a pop-up list on the Modify toolbar.

To use the Align pop-up list (Win):

1. Select two or more objects to align.

or

Select three or more objects to distribute.

2. Press the Align button on the Modify toolbar ❹❼ and choose an alignment or distribute command.

❹❸ *The* **Align Commands** *for the vertical axis.*

❹❹ *The* **Align Commands** *for the horizontal axis.*

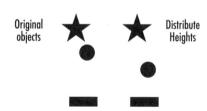

❹❺ *The effect of applying the* **Distribute Heights** *command.*

❹❻ *The effect of applying the* **Distribute Widths** *command.*

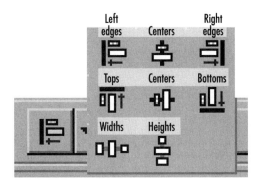

㊼ *The **Align** pop-up list on the Modify toolbar (Win).*

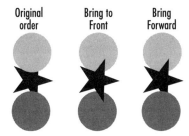

㊽ *The results of applying the **Arrange** menu commands to the star.*

Just as in other vector programs, the order in which overlapping objects appear depends on the order in which they were created. Objects that were created first are at the back of the file. Objects that were created later are in front. You can also change the order of the objects using the Arrange menu commands **㊽**. Objects can be moved to the front or back of a layer.

To send objects to the front or back of a layer:

1. Select the object.

2. Choose **Modify** > **Arrange** > **Bring to Front** to move the object in front of all the other objects on that layer.

   or

   Choose **Modify** > **Arrange** > **Send to Back** to move the object behind all the other objects on that layer.

TIP (Win) You can also use the Front/Back icons on the Modify toolbar to easily move objects within a layer.

Objects can also be moved forward or backward one place at a time in their layer.

To move objects forward or backward in a layer:

1. Select the object.

2. Choose **Modify** > **Arrange** > **Bring Forward** to move the object in front of the next object in the layer.

   or

   Choose **Modify** > **Arrange** > **Send Backward** to move the object behind the next object in the layer.

3. Repeat as necessary to put the object where you want it.

TIP (Win) You can also use the Forward/Backward icons on the Modify toolbar to easily move objects in front or behind each other.

Send to Front or Back; Move Forward or Backward

As you add more objects to your documents, you may want to take advantage of the Fireworks Layers panel. This panel lets you show and hide objects on each of the layers, lock the layers from changes, and change the order in which objects appear.

To work with the Layers panel:

1. Open the Layers panel by choosing **Window>Layers ④⑨**. The two default layers, Layer 1 and Web Layer, appear in the panel.

TIP The Web layer holds objects used to add Web addresses to images and to slice them for exporting. *(For more information on working with Web addresses and HTML information in Fireworks, see Chapter 16, "Hotspots and URLs," and Chapter 17, "Slices.")*

2. To make all the objects on a layer invisible, click the Show/hide icon for that layer.

TIP To make all the layers invisible, hold the Option/Alt key as you click the view icon for any layer.

3. To prevent any objects on a layer from being selected, click the space in the lock area. A padlock icon appears indicating the layer is locked.

TIP Click the layer's padlock icon to unlock the layer.

4. Click the name of a layer to make that layer the active layer. New objects are automatically on that layer.

5. Drag the name of a layer up or down to a new position in the panel to move the that layer to a new position.

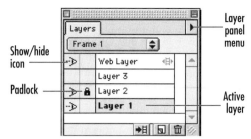

Show/hide icon

Padlock

Layer panel menu

Active layer

④⑨ *The* Layers panel.

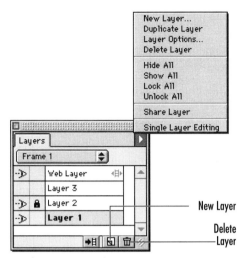

New Layer

Delete Layer

⑤ *The* Layers panel menu.

The Layers panel menu controls additional features of the Layers panel.

To use the Layers panel menu:

1. Press the triangle at the top of the Layers panel to view the panel menu **⑤**.

2. Choose New Layer or click the icon to add a new layer.

3. Choose Duplicate Layer to duplicate the layer currently selected along with its contents.

4. Choose Layer Options to change the name of the currently selected layer.

TIP Double-click the name of a layer to open the Layer Options.

5. Choose Delete Layer or click the icon to delete a layer.

6. Choose Hide All or Show All to change the display status of all the layers in the document.

7. Choose Lock All or Unlock All to change the protection applied to all the layers in the document.

8. Choose Share Layer to display the objects on a layer on all the frames of a document. *(For more information on working with frames, see Chapter 19, "Animations.")*

Layers Panel Menu

The Single Layer Editing mode makes it easy to work only with the objects on one layer.

To use Single Layer Editing:

1. Choose Single Layer Editing from the Layers panel menu. The currently selected layer becomes the only layer you can work on. Objects on other layers cannot be selected.

2. To select objects on other layers, to select the layer in the Layers panel.

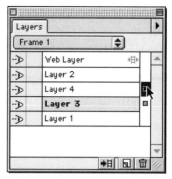

51 Drag the small object square *to move an object from one layer to another.*

You can also move objects from one layer to another.

To move an object between layers:

1. Select the object. A small square appears next to the name of the layer that the object is on.

2. Drag the small square to the layer where you want the object **51**.

TIP Objects can also be copied and pasted from one layer to another.

FILLS 7

Vector objects in Fireworks act like containers that you can fill with colors, patterns, or gradients. Fireworks also lets you manipulate objects so that the objects display their fills in different ways. This means that Fireworks gives you more choices for filling objects than ordinary vector programs.

In this chapter you will learn how to

Apply a solid color fill.

Apply the None fill setting.

Change the edges of a fill.

Apply a Web Dither fill.

Apply a gradient fill.

Edit the colors of a gradient fill.

Save a gradient fill.

Delete a gradient fill.

Change the appearance of a gradient.

Apply a pattern fill.

Add patterns.

Apply a texture to a fill.

Add textures.

Change the object transparency.

Use the Join command.

Use the Split command.

Work with mask groups.

Change the blending modes.

Paste attributes from one object to another.

There are two different ways to style objects in Fireworks: fills and brushes. Fills are the colors, patterns, and gradients that are applied inside paths.

To apply a solid color fill:

1. Choose **Window**>Fill to open the Fill panel.

2. Choose Solid from the Fill category pop-up list. This displays the options for solid fills **❶**.

3. Click the Fill color button to open the Color Well Swatches panel to pick a color

   or.

   Use the Color Mixer to select a color. *(For more information on working with the Color Mixer, see Chapter 3, "Colors.")*

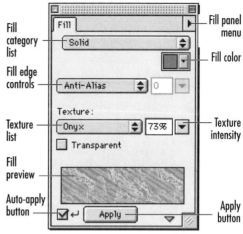

Fill category list

Fill edge controls

Texture list

Fill preview

Auto-apply button

Fill panel menu

Fill color

Texture intensity

Apply button

❶ *The* Fill *panel.*

You can also set an object to have no fill. This makes the inside of the object completely transparent.

To apply the None fill setting:

Choose None from the Fill category pop-up list. This changes the fill of the object to completely transparent **❷**.

TIP You can also apply the None fill by clicking the None button in the Color Well Swatches panel *(see page 11)*.

TIP Click the edge to select an object with a None fill, or use a selection marquee.

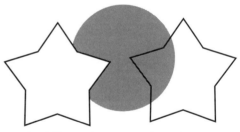

❷ *The difference between a white fill (left star) and a fill of* None *(right star) becomes obvious when the objects appear over another image.*

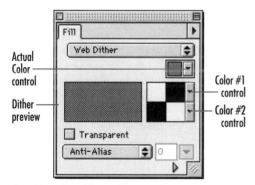

❸ *The three different* **edge** *choices.*

Once you have filled an object, you can control how the edges of the object are filled.

To change the edges of a fill:

1. Select and fill an object.

2. Use the Fill-edge list to change the edge treatment of the fill **❸**.

- Choose Hard Edge to leave the edge of the object as single-colored pixels.

- Choose Anti-Alias to soften the edge of the object.

- Choose Feather and then use the slider to blur the edge of the object.

TIP The feather amount is in pixels and is applied equally to both sides of the edge of the path.

In additon to a solid color fill, Fireworks offers a Web dither fill. This allows you to choose two colors that are combined together in a pattern (also called a *dither*) to simulate a third color. This gives you more control over the number of colors in your document. *(For a color print-out of the Web Dither fill, see the color insert pages.)*

To apply the Web Dither fill setting:

1. Choose Web Dither from the Fill category pop-up list. This displays the options for Web Dither fills **❹**.

2. Use the Color #1 control to set the first of the two dithered colors.

3. Use the Color #2 control to set the second of the two dithered colors. The Dither preview shows how the combination of the two colors looks.

TIP Use the Actual Color control to convert the dithered color into a solid color.

❹ *The* **Web Dither Fill** *controls.*

Actual Color control

Dither preview

Color #1 control

Color #2 control

In addition to solid colors, Fireworks lets you fill objects with gradients, which gradually blend one color into another. You can apply the preset gradients that ship with Fireworks or create your own gradients.

To apply a gradient fill:

1. Select an object.

2. Choose one of the preset gradient fills from the Fill category pop-up list **❺**.

TIP Each of the gradient presets controls how the colors of the gradients are manipulated. These presets control the shape and number of blends of the gradient. They do not control the colors or number of colors of the gradient. *(For a printout of the default settings of the preset gradients, see Appendix A.)*

3. If necessary, change the colors of the gradient by choosing from the gradient colors list **❻**.

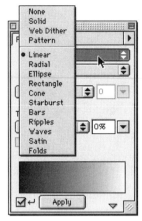

❺ *The* **gradient category** *list.*

❻ *The* **gradient colors** *list.*

Gradient Fill

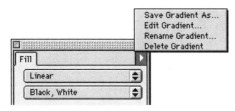

⦿ *The* **Fill panel menu.**

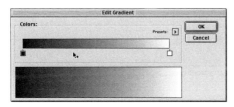

⦿ *The* **Edit Gradient** *dialog box. Click in the area below the gradient ramp to add a new gradient control.*

You can add to or edit the colors in the gradient colors list.

To edit the colors a gradient fill:

1. With a gradient selected, choose Edit gradient from the Fill panel menu **⦿**. This opens the Edit Gradient dialog box **⦿**.

2. Click one of the square gradient controls along the gradient ramp. Drag the control to change the position of the color.

3. Click in the empty area below the gradient ramp to add a new gradient control.

   TIP To delete a gradient control, drag it off of the area below the ramp.

4. Double-click the gradient control to open the Color Mixer. Choose the color you want and then click OK to apply the color to the gradient.

5. Use the preset pop-up list to change the colors in the gradient.

6. Click OK to apply the changes to the gradient.

   TIP For a color printout of the default gradient colors, see the color insert.

If you want to use the gradient in other Fireworks documents, you need to save the gradient preset.

To save a gradient:

1. Choose Save Gradient As from the Fill panel menu. This opens the Save Gradient dialog box ❾.

2. Give the gradient a name and then click OK.

TIP If you give the gradient a new name, you add a new preset to the list.

TIP Gradient colors are saved in the document where they were created. To have a gradient available for all documents, use a style. *(For more information on working with styles, see Chapter 11, "Automation Features.")*

TIP (Mac) When you change the colors of a gradient, a plus sign appears next to its name. This indicates that the gradient has not been saved as a gradient preset.

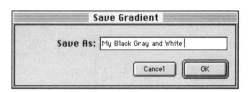

❾ *The* **Save Gradient** *dialog box.*

You can also delete gradients from the Fill panel menu.

To delete a gradient fill:

1. Select the gradient preset you want to delete.

2. Choose Delete Gradient from the Fill panel menu. A dialog box appears asking you to confirm the deletion of the gradient.

3. Click OK. The gradient is deleted from the list.

Save a Gradient; Delete a Gradient

⑩ *The* **Paint Bucket** *in the Toolbox.*

⑪ *The* **vector controls** *over a gradient.*

⑫ *The* **circle control** *defines the start point of a gradient.*

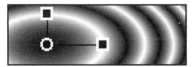

⑬ *The* **square control** *defines the end point of the gradient. A short gradient repeats to fill the object.*

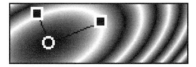

⑭ *The* **angle of the controls** *defines the rotation of the gradient.*

In addition to controlling the colors in a gradient, you can also change the appearance of a gradient by changing its direction, length, and center.

To change the appearance of a gradient:

1. Select an object filled with a gradient.

2. Click the Paint Bucket tool in the Toolbox **⑩**. The vector controls appear in the object **⑪**.

3. Move the circle control to change the start point of the gradient **⑫**.

4. Drag the square control to change the end point of the gradient **⑬**.

TIP Some gradients provide two control handles to control two axes of the gradient.

5. Drag the line of the control to change the rotation of the gradient **⑭**.

TIP Double-click with the Paint Bucket tool to reset the vector controls to the default setting.

Changing a Gradient's Appearance

In addition to gradients, Fireworks has a set of patterns that you can apply as the fill of objects.

To apply a pattern fill:

1. Choose pattern from the Fill category pop-up list. A second Fill name pop-up list appears.

2. Choose one of the preset pattern fills from the pattern list **⑮**. *(For a complete printout of all the default patterns, see Appendix A.)*

TIP A small preview appears next to each name as you move through the list.

TIP The vector controls can also be used to modify the appearance of patterns as well as gradients *(see previous page)*.

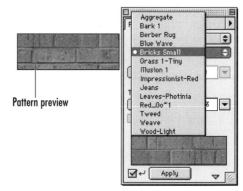

Pattern preview

⑮ *The* **Patterns** *pop-up list.*

Patterns in Fireworks are simply images saved in the PNG format. If you have artwork from a scanner or artwork created in another program, you can use that artwork as a pattern fill in Fireworks.

To add patterns:

1. Scan or create artwork that can be tiled as a pattern.

2. Give the file a name and save it as a PNG file.

3. Put the PNG file in the Patterns folder (Fireworks: Settings: Patterns). The name of the file appears as the name of the texture in the pop-up list.

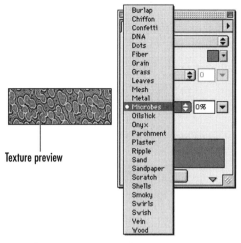

Texture preview

⑯ *The* **Textures** *pop-up list.*

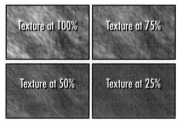

⑰ *Different settings of the Parchment texture on a solid fill.*

Transparency off

Transparency on

⑱ *The effect of the* **Transparent** *settings for a texture.*

Textures change the intensity of fills. You can apply textures to any of the fills— solids, patterns, or gradients. Once a texture is applied to a fill, you can then change the intensity of the texture.

To apply a texture to a fill:

1. Choose one of the textures from the Texture pop-up list **⑯**. *(For a complete printout of all the default textures, see Appendix A.)*

TIP There is always a texture applied to every fill. However, with an intensity of 0% the effect of the texture is not visible.

2. Use the slider or enter a number in the Intensity field to see the effects of the texture on the fill **⑰**.

3. Check Transparent to allow background objects to appear in the light-colored areas of the texture **⑱**.

Like patterns, you can bring in textures from other applications to use within Fireworks.

To add textures:

1. Scan or create artwork that can be tiled as a texture.

2. Save the file as an Indexed Color or Grayscale document.

3. Give the file a name and save it as a PNG file.

4. Put the PNG file in the Textures folder (Fireworks: Settings: Textures). The name of the file appears as the name of the texture in the pop-up list.

Textures

Not only can you change the fill of objects, you can also control the object's transparency or opacity. Transparency—or lack of opacity—allows you to see through an object to the one underneath.

To change the object transparency:

1. Choose **Window** > **Object** to open the Object panel 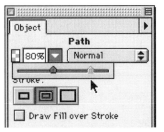.

2. Select the object you want to change.

3. Drag the Opacity slider or type a new percentage in the Opacity field **⑳**.

TIP The Opacity controls in Fireworks are similar to the layer opacity controls in Adobe Photoshop. However, in Fireworks each object on a layer can have its own opacity setting. In Photoshop all the objects on a layer share the same opacity setting.

⑲ *The* **Opacity slider** *of the Object panel.*

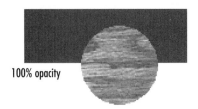

100% opacity

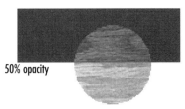

50% opacity

⑳ *The effects of changing the* **opacity** *of an object.*

The Join Objects lets you have one object act as a transparent hole in another.

To use the Join command:

1. Select two or more objects.

2. Choose **Modify** > **Join**. The areas where the objects overlap are transparent **㉑**.

TIP Text characters that have two or more parts, such as the letters *D*, *B*, *o*, or *g* are automatically joined when you convert the text to paths *(see page 130)*.

Objects that have been joined can then be split apart.

To use the Split command:

1. Select the joined objects.

2. Choose **Modify** > **Split**.

TIP (Win) You can also use the Join and Split icons on the Modify toolbar to easily change objects.

㉑ *Applying the* **Join command** *creates a hole where two objects overlap.*

㉒ *Selecting a Mask Group displays the* **Mask Group controls** *in the Object panel.*

Before

After

㉓ *A mask group set to clip to* **Top Object's Image.** *The lightness and darkness as well as the feathering of the mask change the visibility of the photo.*

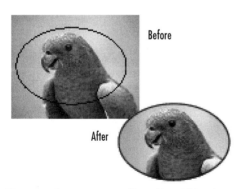

Before

After

㉔ *A Mask Group set to clip to* **Top Object's Path.** *Only the parts of the photo that fit within the mask are visible.*

Masking is the technique of using the shape of one object as a contour to crop— or clip—other objects. Only those parts of the objects that are within the mask are visible. Fireworks masks objects by creating a Mask Group.

To create a Mask Group:

1. Position the objects to be masked below the object that is to act as the mask.

2. Select all the objects and choose **Modify**>**Mask Group**. This opens the Object Inspector **㉒**.

3. Choose the type of Mask Group from the two options in the Object Inspector. Top Object's Image creates an *alpha channel mask* similar to the layer masks found in Adobe Photoshop **㉓**. Top Object's Path creates a mask similar to the Paste Inside command found in FreeHand **㉔**.

TIP The **Edit**>**Paste Inside** command automatically creates a Mask Group set to Top Object's Path.

TIP You can see the fill or brush stroke for an object that has been made into a mask using Top Object's Path.

To release a Mask Group:

1. Use the Selection tool to select the entire Mask Group.

2. Choose **Modify**>**Ungroup** to release the mask.

   or

   In the Object Inspector, change the setting from Mask Group to Group. This releases the Mask Group but the groups the objects together. *(For more information on working with grouped objects, see Chapter 5, "Selecting Paths.")*

Mask Group

You need to use the Subselection tool to select and modify objects within a Mask Group.

To select objects within a Mask Group:

1. Use the Subselection tool to select the objects you want to modify.

2. Make any changes to the object.

    or

    Choose **Edit**>**Clear** delete the object.

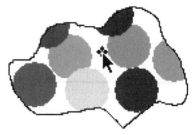

㉕ *The* **Mask handle** *lets you move the contents inside a mask.*

Once you have created a mask, you may want to move the objects inside the mask. This technique works with both types of masks.

To move objects within a Mask Group:

1. Select the mask with the Pointer tool. A small mask handle appears ㉕.

2. Drag the mask handle. This moves the items within the mask.

㉖ *The* **Blending mode** *pop-up list.*

The Object panel lets you change how the colors of one object interact with objects below. This is similar to the layer blending modes in Adobe Photoshop.

To change the object blending mode:

1. Select the top object you want to change.

2. Use the blending mode pop-up list to choose the blending mode for the object ㉖.

❷❼ *The results of the **Multiply** blending mode.*

❷❽ *The results of the **Screen** blending mode.*

❷❾ *The results of the **Darken** blending mode.*

❸⓿ *The results of the **Lighten** blending mode.*

The Normal Blending Mode

Choose **Normal** to have the object not interact with the objects below it. *For a color printout of the blending modes shown in figures ❷❼–❸❽, see the color insert.*

The Multiply Blending Mode

Choose **Multiply** to add the colors of the object to the objects below ❷❼. This is similar to the results of overprinting one object over another.

The Screen Blending Mode

Choose **Screen** to subtract the colors of the object from the objects below ❷❽. This is similar to the results of bleaching out one image from the other.

The Darken Blending Mode

Choose **Darken** to have the colors of the object visible only where they are darker than the objects below ❷❾.

The Lighten Blending Mode

Choose **Lighten** to have the colors of the object visible only where they are lighter than the objects below ❸⓿.

The Difference Blending Mode

Choose **Difference** to have the colors of the object create a difference between them and the objects below. If the colors are the same, the result is black. The greater the difference, the lighter the color ➌➊.

➌➊ *The results of the Difference blending mode.*

The Hue Blending Mode

Choose **Hue** to have the hue of the object applied to the objects below without changing the brightness or saturation of the image ➌➋.

The Saturation Blending Mode

Choose **Saturation** to have the saturation of the object applied to the objects below without changing the hue or brightness ➌➌.

➌➋ *The results of the Hue blending mode.*

The Color Blending Mode

Choose **Color** to have the hue and saturation of the object applied to the objects below without changing the brightness ➌➍.

➌➌ *The results of the Saturation blending mode.*

➌➍ *The results of the Color blending mode.*

35 *The results of the* **Luminosity** *blending mode.*

36 *The results of the* **Invert** *blending mode.*

37 *The results of the* **Tint** *blending mode.*

38 *The results of the* **Erase** *blending mode.*

The Luminosity Blending Mode

Choose **Luminosity** to have the lightness information of an object applied to the objects below without changing the hue, saturation, or brightness **35**.

The Invert Blending Mode

Choose **Invert** to have the shape of the top object reverse the colors of the objects below—for instance, black becomes white, green becomes red, blue becomes yellow. The color of the top object has no effect on the results of the Invert blend **36**.

The Tint Blending Mode

Choose **Tint** to have the color of the top object tint the objects below **37**.

The Erase Blending Mode

Choose **Erase** to have the shape of the top object act like a mask on the objects below. Only objects outside the top object will be visible. The color of the top object has no effect on the results of the Erase blend **38**.

If you have created an object with a certain set of intricate fill settings—for instance a special gradient, feathering, and texture— it might be cumbersome to reapply all those settings to another object created later. Rather, you can copy the settings from one object to another 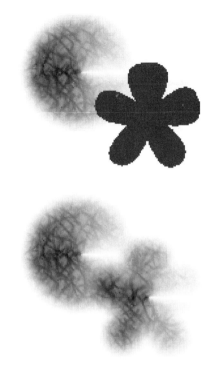.

To paste attributes from one object to another:

1. Select the object with the attributes you want to copy.

2. Choose **Edit > Copy**.

3. Select the object with the attributes you want to change.

4. Choose **Edit > Paste Attributes**. The second object takes on all the settings of the first.

TIP Changes made using the vector controls *(see page 93)* are not saved when copying and pasting attributes.

39 *The results of applying the* **Paste Attributes** *command.*

STROKES 8

art of coloring vector objects in
Fireworks is applying a stroke. A stroke
is the color or effect applied along
the path of an object. If you use other
programs for vector drawing you should
be familiar with the concept of strokes.
Fireworks gives you much more control
over the look of strokes so they can
resemble the brush strokes in programs
such as MetaCreations Painter.

In this chapter you will learn how to

View the Stroke panel.

Apply a basic stroke.

Change the stroke attributes.

Apply textures to a stroke.

Use the Pencil tool.

Save stroke settings.

Create a natural stroke.

Use the Path Scrubber tool.

Create your own strokes.

Change stroke position on a path.

Change how the fill meets a stroke.

A stroke in Fireworks can be a simple colored line resembling a pencil stroke, or it can be a multicolored paint splatter. You control the look of strokes with the Stroke panel.

To view the Stroke panel:

Choose **Window**>**Stroke** to open the Stroke panel ❶.

The best way to understand strokes is to start with a basic stroke and then work your way up to the more sophisticated effects.

To apply a basic stroke:

1. Select the Brush tool in the Toolbox ❷.

TIP Although strokes can be applied to closed paths, such as rectangles, it is easier to understand strokes by creating open paths with the Pen, Pencil, or Brush tools.

2. Open the Stroke panel and select Basic from the stroke category pop-up list.

3. Drag the Brush tool in the document area. A brush stroke appears along the path you just created.

4. Use the Stroke color well to choose a stroke color.

TIP You can also use the Color Well in the Color Mixer or the Toolbox to set the stroke color. *(For more information on working with the Color Mixer, see Chapter 3, "Colors.")*

TIP When you create a path with the Brush or Pencil tools, the fill automatically changes to None. This gives the look of a simple brush stroke, rather than a vector object.

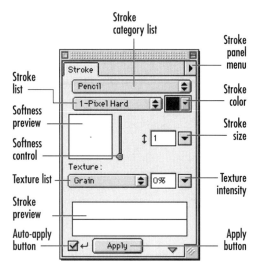

❶ *The* Stroke panel.

❷ *The* **Brush tool** *in the Toolbox.*

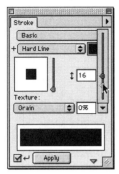

❸ *The* Stroke size *slider.*

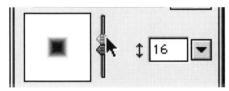

❹ *The* Stroke softness *slider.*

The easiest way to understand the nature of strokes is by experimenting with the attributes of a selected path.

To change the stroke attributes:

1. Start with the basic stroke created in the previous exercise.

2. In the Stroke panel, drag the size slider or enter an amount in the field to change the size of the stroke ❸.

3. Drag the softness slider to blur the edge of the stroke ❹.

TIP You may need to increase the size of the stroke to see the difference in the edge softness.

4. Choose one of the preset strokes from the stroke name pop-up list to change the shape of the stroke.

TIP Each of the 11 stroke categories has its own preset strokes making a total of 48 different strokes to choose from. *(For a printout of all the default stroke categories, see Appendix A.)*

Just as with fills, you can apply a texture to a stroke.

To apply a texture to a stroke:

1. Select a stroke.

2. Open the Stroke panel and choose one of the textures from the Texture pop-up list. *(For a complete printout of all the default textures, see Appendix A.)*

TIP The list of texture for strokes is the same as the list of textures used for fills. However, a stroke can have a different texture than the fill for the object **⑤**.

3. Use the slider or enter a number in the Intensity field to see the effects of the texture on the fill.

TIP As with patterns, you can bring in textures from other applications to use within Fireworks *(see page 95)*.

⑤ *Two different textures applied to the stroke and fill of an object.*

⑥ *The* **Pencil tool** *in the Toolbox.*

The Pencil tool creates paths like the Brush tool. However, the size and shape of the Pencil tool creates the thin lines of a pencil.

To use the Pencil tool:

1. Click the Pencil tool in the Toolbox **⑥**.

2. Drag a path on the page. The Stroke panel settings automatically change to the Pencil tool settings.

3. Choose one of the preset settings for the Pencil tool **⑦**.

4. Drag to create a Pencil path.

TIP When you select the Brush or the Pencil tools, any fill that was set in the Fill panel resets automatically to None.

TIP Paths created by the Pencil tool can be changed by applying any of the stroke categories.

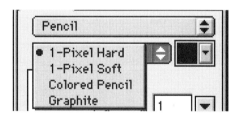

⑦ *The* **Pencil tool** *presets.*

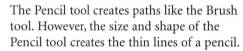

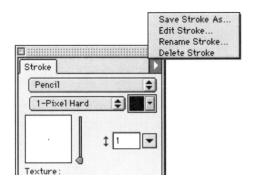

❽ *The* **Stroke panel** *menu.*

Any changes to the Stroke panel, such as the size, edge softness, or texture, are modifications of the stroke preset. You can save those changes as your own stroke preset.

To save Stroke panel settings:

1. Make whatever changes you want to the Stroke panel settings.

TIP (Mac) A plus appears next to the stroke name indicating that the stroke has been modified.

2. Choose Save Stroke As from the Stroke panel menu ❽. The Save Stroke dialog box appears.

3. Type the name of the new stroke and click OK. The new stroke appears as one of the stroke presets.

Brush paused here

❾ *The effect of pausing while creating three brush strokes.*

Pressure means more than just meeting tight deadlines. If you work with a pressure-sensitive tablet, you can easily see how responsive the Fireworks strokes are to changes in how you press with the stylus. Even if you draw with a mouse, you can still make a more natural stroke based on how you drag with the mouse.

To create a natural brush stroke:

1. Select the Brush tool.

2. Choose a brush such as Airbrush set to Basic or Calligraphy set to Quill.

TIP These strokes respond very well to variations in mouse movements.

3. Drag along a path pausing without releasing the mouse button. The width of the stroke increases where you pause in the drag ❾.

You can also alter the look of the stroke after it has been applied to a path by using the Path Scrubber tool. This tool allows you to increase or decrease the pressure on a path. The Path Scrubber has two modes: Path Scrubber Plus and Path Scrubber Minus.

TIP If you have a pressure-sensitive tablet, you can use the Path Scrubber to further refine the look of the path. If you do not have a pressure-sensitive pen and tablet, you can use the Path Scrubber to simulate those effects.

To use the Path Scrubber tool:

1. Select a path with a stroke.
2. Choose the Path Scrubber Plus tool in the Toolbox ❿. (If you do not see the Path Scrubber Plus tool, press the pop-up group to select the tool.)
3. Drag along the path. The width of the stroke increases as you drag ⓫.
4. Choose the Path Scrubber Minus tool in the Toolbox ⓬.
5. Drag across to intersect the path. The width of the stroke decreases as you drag ⓭.

TIP Hold the Option/Alt key to switch between the Path Scrubber Plus and Minus modes.

❿ *The* **Path Scrubber Plus tool** *in the Toolbox.*

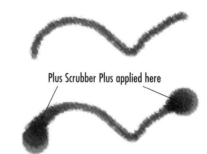

Plus Scrubber Plus applied here

⓫ *The effects of the Path Scrubber Plus tool on a brush stroke.*

⓬ *The* **Path Scrubber Minus tool** *in the Toolbox.*

Path Scrubber Minus applied here

⓭ *The effects of the Path Scrubber Minus tool.*

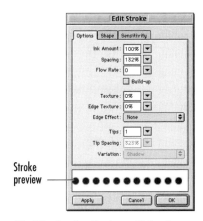

Stroke preview

⓮ *The* **Stroke Options** *dialog box.*

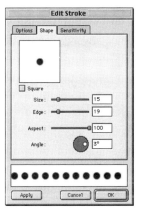

⓯ *The* **Stroke Shape** *dialog box.*

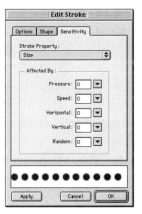

⓰ *The* **Stroke Sensitivity** *dialog box.*

In addition to the settings in the Stroke panel, other controls can affect the appearance of strokes. You do not have to open these settings to use Fireworks. However, as you become more comfortable with the program, you may want to experiment with these controls. For instance, these controls let you create strokes that are dashed or dotted lines.

To create your own strokes:

1. Choose Edit Stroke from the Stroke panel menu. The Edit Stroke dialog box appears.

2. Click the tab for Options to control the appearance of the stroke **⓮**.

3. Click the tab for Shape to control the size, edge softness, shape, roundness, and angle of the stroke **⓯**.

TIP You can override the settings for size by changing the size and edge in the main Stroke panel.

4. Click the tab for Sensitivity to control how the stroke reacts to changes in the mouse or stylus movements **⓰**.

Create Your Own Strokes

Unlike other vector programs, Fireworks gives you a choice as to where a stroke is displayed on a path.

To change the position of a stroke on a path:

1. Select the path.

2. Choose **Modify**>**Object Properties** to open the Object Properties panel **⑰**.

3. Click the Centered, Inside, or Outside buttons to change the position of the stroke along the path **⑱**.

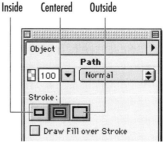

Inside Centered Outside

⑰ *The* **Object Properties** *panel.*

When a path has both a stroke and a fill, you have a choice as to how the fill interacts with the stroke.

To change how the fill meets a stroke:

1. Select the path.

2. Choose **Window**>**Object** to open the Object panel.

3. Check Draw Fill Over Stroke to have the fill of the object extend over the path **⑲**.

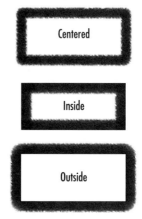

Centered

Inside

Outside

⑱ *The three choices for the* **position of a brush on a path.**

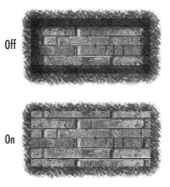

Off

On

⑲ *The effects of changing the* **Draw Fill Over Brush** *setting.*

EFFECTS 9

Beyond fills and brushes, Fireworks lets you add effects to objects. These effects serve two different purposes. First, they let you create special effects such as shadows, glows, and bevels. Second, they give the different looks for rollover buttons. *(For more information on creating rollover buttons, see Chapter 18, "Behaviors.")*

Unlike the effects created in pixel-based programs, the effects in Fireworks can be edited at any time. This means that you can apply an effect and then change it later.

In this chapter you will learn how to
> View the Effect panel.
>
> Apply an Inner or Outer Bevel effect.
>
> Change the color of an Outer Bevel.
>
> Use the bevel presets for buttons.
>
> Apply a drop shadow effect.
>
> Apply an emboss effect.
>
> Apply a glow effect.
>
> Save an effect.
>
> Apply multiple effects.

Any object—path, text, or image—can have an effect applied to it.

To view the Effect panel:

Choose **Window** > **Effect** to open the Effect panel.

or

Click the Effect panel tab to change from the Fill or Brush panel.

TIP If you make changes to the Effect panel, you can save those changes as new preset effects *(see page 117)*.

❶ *Different looks that can be created using the* **Inner and Outer Bevel effects.**

The two most interesting effects are the inner and outer bevel effects ❶.

To apply a bevel effect:

1. Select an object.

2. Choose Inner Bevel or Outer Bevel from the Effect category pop-up list. The Effect panel changes to show the bevel choices ❷.

3. Choose one of the Effect presets from the Effect name pop-up list ❸. *(For a complete printout of all the default effect presets, see Appendix A.)*

4. Press the Size control to open the slider or type in the field to change the size of the bevel.

5. Press the Contrast control to open the slider or type in the field to change the intensity of the light creating the bevel highlights and shadows.

6. Press the Softness control to open the slider or type in the field to change the hardness of the edges of the bevel.

TIP If the bevel around curved objects appears appears bumpy, increase the softness to smooth the bevel.

7. Use the Lighting wheel or type in the field to change the angle of the light.

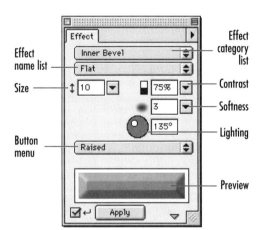

❷ *The* **Bevel effects** *panel.*

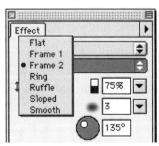

❸ *The* **Bevel preset** *choices.*

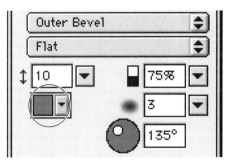

❹ *The* **Color Well** *for the Outer Bevel effect.*

The color of an inner bevel comes from the color of the original object. The color of an outer bevel can be changed using the Effect panel.

To change the color of a bevel:

1. Click the Color Well in the Effect panel **❹**.

2. Choose the color of the Outer Bevel from the Swatches panel.

   or

   Use the Color Mixer to set the color of the Outer Bevel.

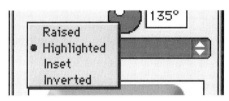

❺ *The* **Button menu.**

Using the Button menu

The Button menu for the bevel effects is used to easily apply variations to the bevels. The four states are Raised, Highlighted, Inset, and Inverted **❺**.

The four states change bevels as follows **❻**:

- **Raised** leaves the object as originally styled.

- **Highlighted** lightens the object as if a 25% white tint were applied over it.

- **Inset** reverses the lighting of the bevel to invert the 3-D effect.

- **Inverted** reverses the lighting and lightens the object with a tint.

TIP The four states of the Button menu are provided as a convenience for quickly changing the appearance of buttons. They do not actually create the code for buttons. *(For more information on creating rollover buttons, see Chapter 18, "Behaviors.")*

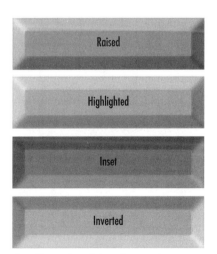

❻ *The effects of applying the* **Bevel Preset** choices.

Drop shadows ❼ are another of the effects you can apply to objects.

To apply a Drop Shadow effect:

1. Choose Drop Shadow from the Effect category list. The Effect panel changes to show the shadow choices ❽.

2. Choose one of the Drop Shadow presets from the Effect names list.

3. Use the Opacity slider or type a number in the field to change the transparency of the shadow. The lower the number the more transparent the object.

4. Use the Softness slider or type a number in the field to change the softness or feather applied to the edge of the shadow.

5. Use the Lighting wheel or type in the field to change the angle of the light casting the shadow.

6. Use the Distance slider or type a number in the field to change how far the shadow falls from the object.

7. Open the Color Well Swatches panel to choose a color for the shadow.

   or

   Click the Color Well and then use the Color Mixer to choose a color for the shadow.

8. Select Knock Out to have only the shadow appear, not the object casting the shadow.

❼ *Different looks that can be created using the* **Drop Shadow** *effect.*

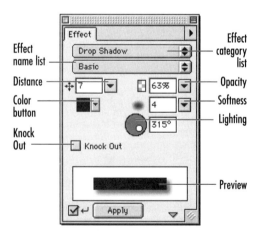

❽ *The* **Drop Shadow effects** *panel.*

Drop Shadows

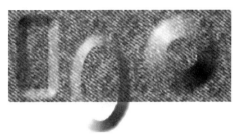

⑨ *Different looks that you can create using the* **Emboss** *effect.*

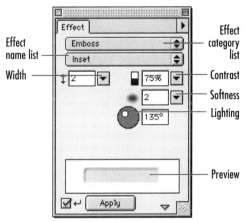

Effect name list — Effect — Effect category list — Width — Contrast — Softness — Lighting — Preview

⑩ *The* **Emboss** *effects* panel.

⑪ *Embossed objects take their color from the objects behind them.*

The emboss effect pushes the shape of one object into the background or into other objects **⑨**.

To apply an Emboss effect:

1. Choose Emboss from the Effect category list. The Effect panel changes to show the emboss effect choices **⑩**.

2. Choose one of the Emboss presets from the Effect names pop-up list.

3. Use the Width slider or type a number in the field to change the width or size of the embossing.

4. Use the Contrast slider or type a number in the field to change the intensity of the light creating the embossing highlights and shadows.

5. Use the Softness slider or type a number in the field to change the sharpness of the edges of the embossing.

6. Use the Lighting wheel or type a number in the field to change the angle of the light on the embossing.

Embossing always takes its appearance from the object it is over, the canvas color of the document, or any placed image **⑪**.

To change the appearance of the embossing:

You control the look of embossing by changing the color of the object, the canvas color *(see page 23)* or the placed image *(see Chapter 12, "Working With Pixels")*.

Embossing: Embossing Color

The glow effect lets you add a color all around the edges of an object .

To apply a Glow effect:

1. Choose Glow from the Effect category pop-up list. The Glow effect choices appear ⓭.

2. Use the Opacity slider or type a number in the field to change the transparency of the glow. The lower the number, the greater the transparency.

3. Use the Softness slider or type a number in the field to change the softness, or feather, applied to the glow.

4. Use the Width slider or type a number in the field to change the size of the glow.

5. Open the Color Well Swatches panel to choose a color for the glow.

   or

   Click the Color Well and then use the Color Mixer to choose a color for the glow.

⓬ *Different looks you can create using the* **Glow** *effect.*

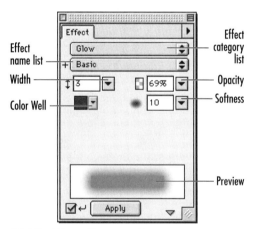

⓭ *The* **Glow** *effects panel.*

Effect name list
Width
Color Well

Effect category list
Opacity
Softness
Preview

Glows

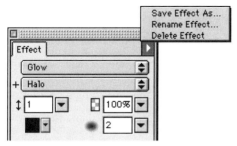

⑭ *The* **Effect panel menu.**

⑮ *The Effect panel set to apply multiple effects.*

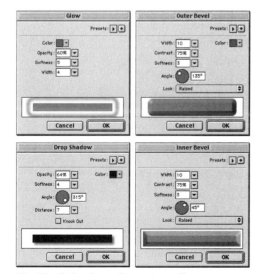

⑯ *The dialog boxes for various effects.*

Every time you change the choices for an effect, you create a new effect. You can save those choices for use on other objects or in other documents.

To save an effect:

1. Make whatever changes you want to the effect.

TIP (Mac) The plus sign next to the name indicates the effect has been modified.

2. Choose Save Effect As from the Effect panel menu ⑭. The Save Effect dialog box appears.

3. Type the name of the new effect and click OK. The new effect appears as one of the effect presets.

TIP The settings created for an effect are specific to that effect category. So the settings for an Inner Bevel do not appear when the Outer Bevel is chosen.

Instead of applying a single effect, you can apply multiple effects to an object.

To apply multiple effects:

1. With the object selected, choose Multiple from the Effect pop-up list. The Effect panel changes to the multiple mode ⑮.

2. Click the check box for the first effect you want to apply. A dialog box appears for that effect ⑯.

3. Set the controls for the effect and then click OK.

4. Click the check box for additional effects.

TIP You can alter the settings for each effect by clicking the ellipsis (…) button in the Effect panel. This reopens the effect dialog box.

TIP Presets for various effects are available only when the Effect panel is set to their respective controls.

Whoever said a picture is worth a thousand words underestimated by several hundred kilobytes. Pictures, or graphics, create much bigger Web files than text. So why convert fast-moving text into slow-moving graphics? It might be to create labels, create a banner design, or just make sure the text looks the same no matter what fonts or system the viewer has. Whatever the reason, Fireworks has many features for working with text.

In this chapter you will learn how to

Use the Text tool.

Open the Text Editor.

Set the font and point size.

Add electronic styling.

Kern text.

Set the range kerning.

Set the leading.

Add a baseline shift.

Set the horizontal scale.

Set the horizontal text alignment.

Set the vertical text alignment.

Reverse the text flow.

Modify text inside a text block.

Transform text in a text block.

Set the object properties for a text block.

Attach text to a path.

Change the position and orientation of text on a path.

Reverse the direction of text on a path.

Apply path attributes to text.

Convert text to paths.

You access text in Fireworks by using the Text tool. You should find working with text similar to the methods you have used in any graphics or page-layout program.

To use the Text tool:

1. Choose the Text tool in the Toolbox **❶**.

2. Click inside the document area or drag to create the area that you want the text to stay inside. This opens the Text Editor **❷**.

TIP If you click with the Text tool, the text box starts at that spot and extends to the edge of the document area.

❶ *The* **Text tool** *in the Toolbox.*

In addition to the formatting controls, there are a few special controls you can use inside the Text Editor.

To use the Text Editor:

1. Type the text inside the Preview area.

2. Use any of the ordinary text techniques to select text, make corrections, or insert new text within the Preview area.

3. Click Font and Size & Color to see the Text as it will appear in the document.

TIP Turn off the Font and Size & Color options if you find it difficult to read the text within the Text Editor.

4. Click Apply to see the formatting changes without leaving the Text Editor.

5. Click OK to close the Text Editor.

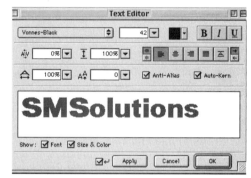

❷ *The* **Text Editor.**

To reopen the Text Editor:

Choose **Text** > **Editor**.

or

Double-click the text block.

Text Tool: Text Editor

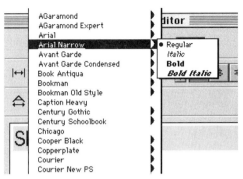

❸ *The* **font list** *in the Text Editor.*

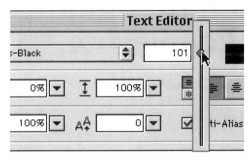

❹ *The* **point size** *control in the Text Editor.*

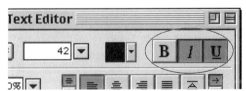

❺ *The* **styling** *controls in the Text Editor include the buttons for applying bold, italic, and underline style to text.*

To set the font:

1. Use the font pop-up list ❸ to choose the typeface.
2. Type text inside the Preview area.
3. Use the font pop-up list to change to a different typeface.

TIP Highlight the text to mix different typefaces within the Preview area.

To set the point size:

Use the point size slider or type in the field ❹ to change the point size.

Fireworks also lets you add bold or italic styling to text.

To add electronic styling:

1. Select the text.
2. Click the bold or italic buttons to change text ❺.

TIP Electronic styling is discarded when text is converted into paths *(see page 130).*

You can apply different text attributes within the Text Editor.

To apply different text attributes:

1. As you are typing the text, make whatever changes you want. The next text you type will reflect those changes.

   or

   Select the text you want to change.
2. Apply the changes to that text.

Kerning is adjusting the space between two letters. Fireworks lets you kern text within the Text Editor.

To kern the text:

1. Click between the two letters you want to kern.

2. Use the Kern slider or type in the field ❻ to kern the text closer together or further apart. Negative values decrease the space; positive values increase the space ❼.

TIP The Preview does not show the effects of kerning. To see those effects, position the Text Editor outside the document area and then use the Apply button to see the changes as you enter the kerning amounts.

Range kerning is kerning applied to a selection of text. (Range kerning is sometimes called *tracking* in other programs.)

To set the range kerning:

1. Drag across a selection of the text.

2. Use the Range Kerning slider or type in the field to change the range kerning for the text ❽. Negative values decrease the space; positive values increase the space ❾.

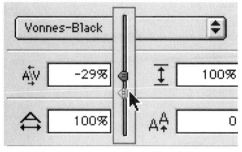

❻ The **kerning** *controls in the Text Editor.*

People Inc.
People Inc.

❼ *The result of kerning to close up the space between the letters* **Pe***,* **pl***, and* **le***.*

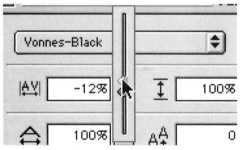

❽ *The* **range kerning** *controls in the Text Editor.*

People Inc.
People Inc.

❾ *The results of applying range kerning to increase the spaces between the characters.*

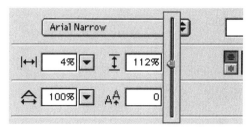

⑩ *The **leading** controls in the Text Editor.*

Leading, or *line spacing*, is the space between multiple lines of text. If your text is only on a single line, you do not have to worry about setting leading.

To set the leading:

Use the Leading slider or type in the field to change the leading for the text **⑩**.

TIP Fireworks measures leading as a percentage of the point size. 100% means the leading is the same as the point size.

TIP Leading is applied to an entire paragraph, not individual characters.

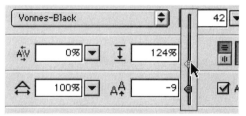

⑪ *The **baseline shift** controls in the Text Editor.*

Baseline shift is the technique of raising or lowering text from its *baseline*, or the line that the text sits on.

To add a baseline shift:

1. Select the text.

2. Use the baseline slider or type in the field **⑪** to raise or lower the text in points from the baseline.

TIP Positive numbers raise the text. Negative numbers lower the text **⑫**.

People Inc.
People Inc.

⑫ *The results of apply a positive baseline shift to the characters **nc**. (The baseline is indicated by the dashed line.)*

Text can also be distorted using a techniques called horizontal scaling. This changes the width of the text without changing the height.

To change the horizontal scale:

1. Select the text.

2. Use the horizontal scale slider or type in the field **⑬** to increase or decrease the horizontal scaling. Amounts lower than 100% make the text width smaller. Amounts higher than 100% make the text wider.

TIP Typography purists (such as this author) disdain the look of electronically scaled type **⑭**. They say it causes ugly distortions to the look of the original typeface.

They also say that if you need to fit text into a specific area you should use the proper condensed or expanded typeface. However, even the purists cannot always tell if small amounts of scaling have been applied.

Text can also be set with a wide variety of alignment options. The text can be set either horizontally or vertically. Horizontal text reads from left to right.

To set the horizontal alignment:

1. Select the text.

2. Click one of the five horizontal alignment settings: left, right, centered, justified, or stretched alignment **⑮**.

TIP Justified alignment increases the range kerning so the line fills the width of the text block **⑯**.

TIP Stretched alignment distorts the shape of the text as it increases the horizontal scale so the line fills the width of the text block **⑰**. This could cause typography purists to cringe (*see tip in previous exercise*).

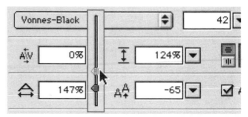

⑬ *The* **horizontal scale** *controls in the Text Editor.*

People Inc.
People Inc.

⑭ *The results of applying horizontal scale to the initial letter* **P**.

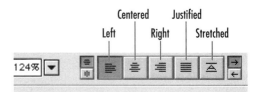

⑮ *The* **alignment** *controls in the Text Editor.*

People Inc.
People Inc.

⑯ *The results of applying the* **justified** *alignment.*

People Inc.
People Inc.

⑰ *The results of applying the* **stretch** *alignment.*

Horizontal Vertical

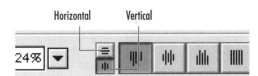

⓲ *The* **vertical alignment** *controls.*

Normal Reversed

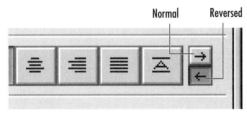

⓳ *The* **text flow** *controls.*

SMSC CSMS

⓴ **Text reversed** *to read from right to left.*

Text can also be set so it reads from top to bottom. This is very useful for creating vertical buttons.

To set the vertical alignment:

1. Select the text.

2. Click the vertical alignment button **⓲** to access the five vertical alignment settings: top, bottom, centered, justified, or stretched alignment.

TIP Vertical alignment does not show in the Text Editor. Use the Apply button to see the actual vertical alignment.

Another special effect you can create with text is to have the text read from right to left. This can also be useful when working with certain foreign typefaces.

To reverse the text flow:

Click the Reversed button **⓳**. All the text in that text block changes so that the letters flow from right to left **⓴**.

Once text is in a text block, you do not have to open the Text Editor to make certain formatting changes.

To modify text inside a text block:

1. Drag any of the text block handles to rewrap the text within the block **21**.

2. With the text block selected, choose Text > Font to change the typeface.

3. With the text block selected, choose Text > Size to change the point size.

4. With the text block selected, choose Text > Style to apply one of the electronic styles.

5. With the text block selected, choose Text > Alignment to apply any of the horizontal or vertical alignment settings.

TIP Changes applied from the Text menu are applied to all the text within the text block. You cannot apply the changes to just some of the text.

TIP You can also select multiple text blocks and apply the changes to them all at once.

21 Drag the text block handles *to change the way the text wraps within the block.*

㉒ *The results of applying a distortion to the text within a text block.*

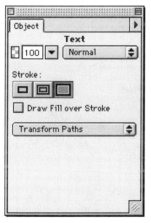

㉓ *The* **Object Properties** *panel when a text block is selected.*

You can use the transformation tools on text with some spectacular results.

To transform text in a text block:

1. Select the text block.

2. Use any of the the Transform tools *(see pages 68–71)* to distort the text within the block **㉒**.

TIP The transformation tools change the size of the text by distorting the text, not by changing the point size.

TIP Choose **Modify** > **Transform** > **Remove Transformations** to restore the text to its original formatting.

When you distort text, you have a choice as to how the text is distorted. This is controlled by the object properties for text.

To set the object properties for a text block:

1. Select the text block.

2. Choose **Window** > **Object** to open the Object Properties panel **㉓**.

3. Choose Transform Paths or Transform Pixels.

TIP Transform Paths results in distortions that preserve crisp text. Transform Pixels results in distortions in which the text may be blurred.

One of the most popular effects in graphics is to attach text so it flows along a path.

To attach text to a path:

1. Select the text block.

2. Select the path.

3. Choose **Text** > **Attach to Path**. The text automatically aligns to the path .

TIP Text attached to a path can still be edited using the Text Editor *(see page 120)*.

㉔ *The results of* attaching text to a path.

Once you have text on a path, you can change the alignment, or the position where the text appears on the path.

To change the alignment of text on a path:

Choose **Text** > **Align** and then choose one of the alignment settings. This changes where the text is positioned **㉕**.

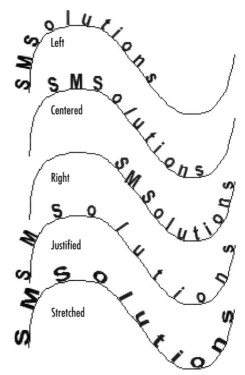

㉕ *The results of* applying the different **alignment settings** *to text on a path.*

Palettes

The illustrations below show three of the most important preset Swatches palettes.

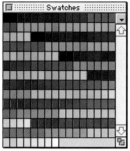

The **216 Web-safe colors** *Swatches panel discussed on page 37.*

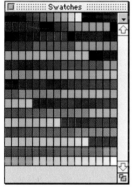

The **Macintosh System Colors** *Swatches panel discussed on page 37.*

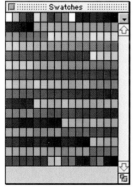

The **Windows System Colors** *Swatches panel discussed on page 38.*

Web Dither Fill

The Web Dither Fill allows you to use two colors in a checkerboard pattern to create the illusion of a third color. The following is a colored example of a Web dithered fill. For a detailed explanation of this type of fill, see page 89.

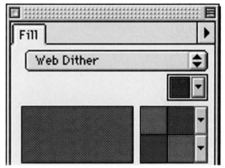

The **Web Dither** *fill allows you to choose two different colors and combine them as a fill. This panel shows how red and blue can be picked to create purple.*

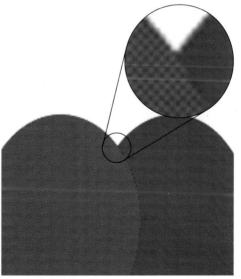

The **Web Dither** *fill of red and blue in the left circle approximates the actual purple in the right circle. However, as the blowup shows, the color is actually a checkerboard pattern.*

Adaptive Color File Sizes

The illustrations below show how exporting as a GIF with an Adaptive palette shrinks the file size significantly: the lower the number of colors, the lower the file size. For more information on exporting as GIF images, see pages 182–187.

All the colors of the original image are maintained when exported with the **Adaptive palette using 256 colors** *(8.01 K).*

*Just a few colors are changed when exported with the **Adaptive palette using 64 colors** (5.35 K).*

*Even more colors are noticeably changed when exported with the **Adaptive palette using 8 colors** (3.58 K).*

Web Palette or Adaptive Palette

The illustrations below show the effects of exporting using the Adaptive palette or using a Web palette with or without dithering. For more information on exporting using the Web Adaptive palette, see pages 184–185.

*The **Adaptive palette** maintains as many of the original colors as possible. Notice the subtle shade for the face and hands.*

*The **Web 216 palette with dithering on** creates a pattern of dots in the shirt, face, and hands to simulate non-Web colors. This is unacceptable for flat color art.*

*The **Web 216 palette with dithering off** shifts the colors in the shirt, face, and hands to the closest Web-safe color.*

JPEG or GIF Comparisons

The illustrations below show how much better JPEG images are than GIF files in maintaining the tones of an image. For more information on exporting as JPEG images, see pages 188–189.

JPEG Comparisons

The illustrations below show the effects of exporting with different JPEG settings. Notice how the quality of the image degrades only slightly while the file size is reduced greatly. Notice also the effects of smoothing. For more information on file quality and smoothing JPEG images, see page 188.

GIF Web 216 Dithered with 88 colors *(37.7 K).*

JPEG at 100% Quality *(16.58 K).*

GIF Adaptive Dithered with 64 colors *(38.67 K).*

JPEG at 80% Quality *(5,00 K).*

JPEG at 90% *(29.4 K).*

JPEG at 40% Quality *(2.80 K).*

JPEG at 70% *(15.98 K).*

JPEG at 40% Quality, Smoothing of 4 *(2.52 K).*

The PhotoOptics Xtras

The following is a sample of the effects that you can create with the eight PhotoOptics Xtras. For more information on these Xtras, see pages 166–168.

*The **original image** with no effect applied.*

*The **GradTone** effect.*

*The **PhotoFilter** effect.*

*The **HueSlider** effect.*

*The **Noise** effect.*

*The **MonoChrome** effect.*

*The **Levels** effect.*

*The **PseudoColor** effect.*

*The **Negative** effect.*

The Default Gradient Colors

For more information on working with gradients, see pages 90–93.

The **Black, White** *gradient.*

The **Pastels** *gradient.*

The **Blue, Red, Yellow** *gradient.*

The **Red, Blue** *gradient.*

The **Blue, Yellow, Blue** *gradient.*

The **Red, Green, Blue** *gradient.*

The **Cobalt Blue** *gradient.*

The **Silver** *gradient.*

The **Copper** *gradient.*

The **Spectrum** *gradient.*

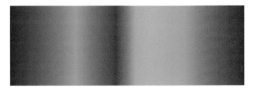

The **Emerald Green** *gradient.*

The **Violet, Orange** *gradient.*

The Blending Modes

*For a detailed explanation of these modes,
see pages 99–101.*

*The **Normal** blending mode.*

*The **Multiply** blending mode.*

*The **Screen** blending mode.*

*The **Darken** blending mode.*

*The **Lighten** blending mode.*

*The **Difference** blending mode.*

*The **Hue** blending mode.*

*The **Saturation** blending mode.*

*The **Invert** blending mode.*

*The **Tint** blending mode.*

*The **Color** blending mode.*

*The **Luminosity** blending mode*

*The **Erase** blending mode.*

The Default Styles

For a detailed explanation of working with styles, see pages 132–135.

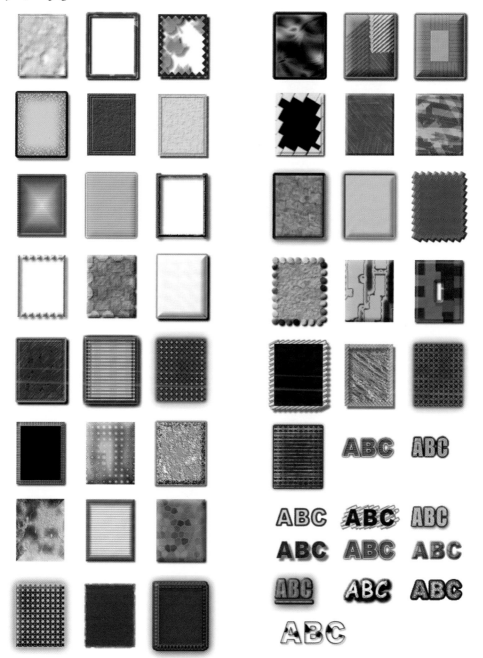

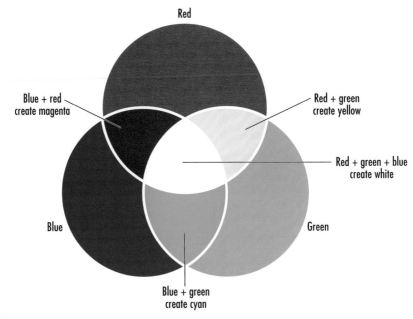

Red

Blue + red
create magenta

Red + green
create yellow

Red + green + blue
create white

Blue

Green

Blue + green
create cyan

*An example of **additive colors**, sometimes called RGB (for more information see page 32).*

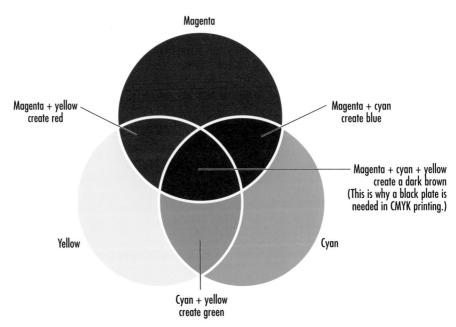

Magenta

Magenta + yellow
create red

Magenta + cyan
create blue

Magenta + cyan + yellow
create a dark brown
(This is why a black plate is
needed in CMYK printing.)

Yellow

Cyan

Cyan + yellow
create green

*An example of **subtractive colors**, sometimes called process colors (for more information see page 34).*

⑳ *The Object Properties dialog box for* **text attached to a path.**

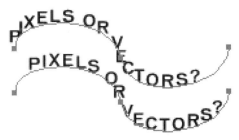

㉗ *The effects of adding a 20 pixel* **text offset** *to shift the text along a path.*

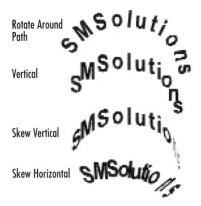

Rotate Around Path

Vertical

Skew Vertical

Skew Horizontal

㉘ *The results of applying the* **different orientation settings** *to text on a path.*

You can also control where the text is positioned along the path. This is called the text offset.

To change the text offset along a path:

1. Select the text that has been attached to the path.

2. Choose **Window**>**Object** to show the Object panel **⑳**.

3. Change the amount in the Offset field and then click Apply or OK. The text moves along the path **㉗**.

You can also change how the individual characters of the text are positioned in relation to the angle of the path. This is called the *orientation* of the text.

To change the orientation of the text:

Choose **Text**>**Orientation** and then choose one of the orientation settings to change how the text is positioned on the path **㉘**.

- **Rotate Around Path** has the text keep a perpendicular orientation as it moves around the path.

- **Vectical** makes each character stand up straight no matter how the path curves.

- **Skew Vertical** maintains a vertical rotation but distorts the characters' shapes as the text follows the path.

- **Skew Horizontal** exaggerates the text's horizontal tilt up to a 90° rotation and distorts the characters' shapes as the text follows the path.

You can also reverse the direction of the path. This causes the text to flip to the other side of the path.

To reverse the direction of text on a path:

Choose **Text** >**Reverse Direction** to flip the text so that it flows on the other side of the path **29**.

29 *The results of applying the* **Reverse Direction** *command settings to text on a path.*

You can apply any of the path attributes—fills, strokes, or effects—to text **30**.

To apply path attributes to text:

1. Select the text block or text on a path.
2. Use any of the Fill settings to change the inside of the text.
3. Use any of the Stroke settings to add a stroke around the edge of the text.
4. Use any of the Effect settings to add effects to the text.

30 *The results of* applying various fill, brush, and effect settings *to text.*

The text in a text block or attached to a path is called editable text. This means that you can work with the text—change the font or the letters—at any time. However, there are some effects you might want to create that require that the text be converted into paths.

To convert text to paths:

1. Select the text block or text on a path.
2. Choose **Text** >**Convert to Paths**. This converts the text into grouped paths.
3. Use any of the path selection tools to manipulate the paths **31**.

TIP Once you convert text to paths, you can no longer edit it in the Text Editor; you can edit it only as path objects then.

People Inc.

People Inc.

31 *The results of* converting text to paths *and then manipulating the converted paths.*

AUTOMATION FEATURES

One of the challenges of creating Web graphics is that a typical Web site has hundreds of different images for graphics, buttons, and special typographic elements. Once you have created those items you may find it necessary to repeatedly change the look of many different elements. Fortunately Fireworks provides you with many ways to automate creating objects and making changes.

In this chapter you will learn how to

Create styles for the look of objects.

Create styles for text formatting.

Apply styles to objects.

Import and export styles in documents.

Work with the Styles panel.

Automate changes using the Find & Replace commands.

Work with the Project Log.

Use the batch processing commands.

Save the batch processing commands as scripts.

Run the scripts for automated commands.

macromedia
FIREWORKS

Styles are simply a way to store all the information about the fill, stroke, effects, or text settings. You can then easily apply the style to other objects without applying all the settings one by one.

The Styles panel contains an assortment of object and text styles that you can use. There are many other styles located on the Fireworks CD. However, most likely you will want to define your own styles.

To define an object style:

1. Open the Styles panel by choosing **Window>Styles ❶**.

2. Select an object and use the Fill, Stroke, and Effect panels to give the object any look you want.

3. With the object selected, click the New Style button at the bottom of the Styles panel. The Edit Style dialog box appears ❷.

4. Name the style.

5. Check the boxes for the properties you want the style to control.

- Check Fill Type to control a pattern, gradient, or Web dither.

- Check Fill Color to control the color of the fill.

- Check Effect to control the effect.

- Check Stroke Type to control the size and tyle of stroke.

- Check Stroke Color to control the color of the stroke.

6. Click OK to store the style in the Styles panel.

TIP The preview in the Styles panel is always a square, regardless of the shape that was used to define the style.

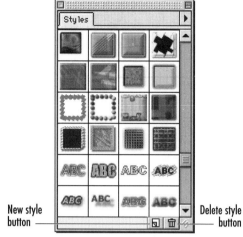

New style button ————— Delete style button

❶ *The* **Styles panel** *stores visual previews of the styles. These styles all come preset with Fireworks.*

❷ *The* **Edit Style dialog box** *lets you name the style and set which properties are included as part of the style.*

❸ *The* **Edit Style** *dialog box lets you name the style and set which properties are included as part of the style.*

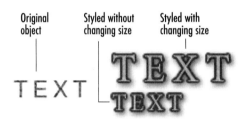

Original object | Styled without changing size | Styled with changing size

❹ *The difference between applying a style that does not change the text size and one that does change the size.*

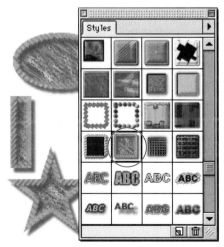

❺ *Click the* **style preview** *(circled) to apply a style to a selected object.*

In addition to styles for objects, you can also define styles that apply text properties.

To define a text style:

1. Select a text block and use the Text Editor as well as the Fill, Stroke, and Effect panels to format the text in the way you want.

2. With the formatted text block selected, click the New Style icon at the bottom of the Styles panel. The Edit Style dialog box appears ❸.

3. Use the Name field to name the style.

4. In addition to the object properties described on the previous page, check the boxes for which text properties you want the style to control.

- Check Text Font to control the font.

- Check Text Size to control the point size ❹.

- Check Text Style to control styling such as Bold or Italic.

5. Click OK to store the style in the Styles panel.

TIP The preview in the Styles panel is always *ABC*, regardless of the text that was used to define the style.

Once you have defined a style, it is easy to apply that style to objects.

To apply a style to objects:

1. Select the object or objects to which you want to apply the style.

2. Click the preview of the style ❺. The object changes according to the definition of the style.

TIP Unlike the styles in FreeHand or other programs, styles can't be used to update objects.

Define Text Styles; Apply Styles

Once you define a style, it continues to appear in the Styles panel where you can access it for other documents. You can also save styles and share them with other people working on the same project. That is called exporting styles.

To export styles:

1. In the Styles panel, select the style you want to export.

2. Select additional styles by holding the Command/Ctrl key and clicking the styles.

TIP To select adjoining styles, select the style at one end of the group, hold down the Shift key, and click the style at the other end of the group. All styles between the first and last style are selected.

3. Choose Export Styles from the Styles panel menu ❻. A dialog box appears.

4. Use the dialog box to name the document that contains the styles and click Save.

❻ *The* Style menu panel.

To import styles:

1. Choose Import Styles from the Styles panel menu ❻.

2. Navigate to find the document that contains the styles you want to import.

3. Choose Open. The styles appear in the Styles panel.

TIP Exporting and then importing styles lets you clear the Styles panel so that it contains only the styles applicable to the project you are working on.

Export Styles; Import Styles

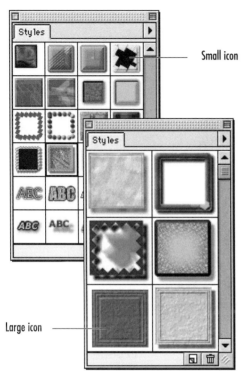

Small icon

Large icon

❼ *The difference between the* **Small icons** *and the* **Large Icons** *in the Styles panel.*

Once you have defined a style you can edit which properties of the style are applied to objects.

To edit styles:

1. Choose Edit from the styles menu. This opens the Edit Styles dialog box.

2. Make whatever changes you want and click OK.

TIP You must create a new style and then apply it to objects to change the fill, stroke, effects, or text settings.

There are several commands that help you work with styles in the Styles panel.

To change the Style views:

1. Choose Large Icons from the Styles panel menu. This increases the size of the preview in the Styles panel.

2. If Large Icons is already chosen, choose it again to change the previews to the small icons ❼.

To reset the styles:

1. Choose Reset Styles from the Styles panel menu.

2. Click OK when the dialog box asks for confirmation.

To delete styles:

1. Select the styles you want to delete.

2. Click the Delete Style button at the bottom of the Styles panel.

   or

   Open the Styles panel menu and choose Delete Styles.

Edit Styles; Style Views; Reset Styles; Delete Styles

Once you have applied formatting, you may want a way to quickly change the attributes of many different objects. The Find & Replace panel gives you that control.

Fireworks lets you choose the locations where the Find & Replace commands should search.

To set the Find & Replace search location:

1. Choose **Window** > **Find & Replace** to open the Find & Replace panel **❽**.

2. Open the Search In pop-up menu **❾** and choose a place for the Find & Replace to occur.

- Choose Selection to search among the currently selected items.

- Choose Frame to search in the current Frame of the document. *(For more information on working with Frames, see Chapter 19, "Animations.")*

- Choose Document to search throughout the current document.

- Choose Project Log to search within all the files listed in the Project Log. *(For information on adding files to the Project Log, see page 141.)*

- Choose Files to search within a specific list of files.

3. If you choose Files, use the dialog box that appears **❿** to navigate to add files from different locations.

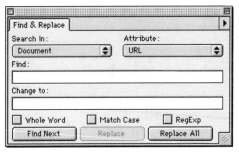

❽ *The* **Find & Replace** *panel.*

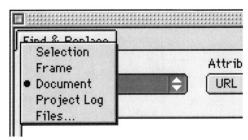

❾ *The* **Search In** *choices.*

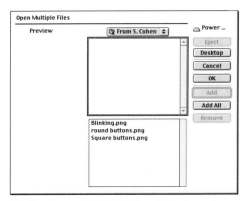

❿ *The* **Open Multiple Files** *dialog box where you can add a list of files to change using the Find & Replace panel.*

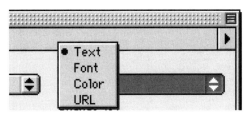

⓫ *The* **Attribute list** *in the Find & Replace panel.*

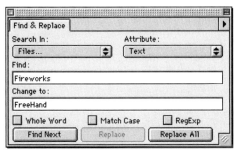

⓬ *The* **text attributes** *in the Find & Replace panel.*

⓭ *The* **Find Next, Replace,** *and* **Replace All** *controls in the Find & Replace panel.*

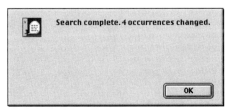

⓮ *The* **Search complete** *dialog box tells you the results of the Find & Replace command.*

The Find & Replace Text attributes allows you to search for specific words and change them to others. For instance, you can find one product and replace it with another.

To find and replace text attributes:

1. Choose **Window > Find & Replace.**

2. If necessary, change the search location as explained on page 136.

3. Choose Text from the Attribute pop-up list ⓫. The text attributes appear ⓬.

4. In the Find field type the text you want to locate.

5. In the Change To field type the replacement text.

6. Check Whole Word to make sure the text only appears as a whole word, and not part of another word.

7. Check Match Case to make sure the upper and lowercase letters match the text exactly as typed.

8. Check RegExp to allow the use of Regular Expressions in your search and replace text strings. For instance entering *s$* will search for the letter *s* that appears only at the end of a word or line. *(See Appendix C for a list of some Regular Expression controls.)*

9. Choose Replace All to change all the occurrences of the attribute without reviewing each one ⓭.

   or

   Click the Find Next button to find each occurrence and then choose Replace to change that one instance of the attribute ⓭.

TIP If you choose Replace All, a dialog box appears telling you when the search is complete and how many changes were made ⓮.

You can use the Font attribute to find and change the typeface, point size, or the style applied to text. For instance, if you previously changed *Help* to *Assistance*, you may need to change the typeface and point size so the new text fits better in the layout.

To find and replace Font attributes:

1. Choose **Window** > **Find & Replace** and then narrow the search, if necessary, as explained on page 136.

2. Choose Font from the Attribute pop-up list. The font attributes appear ⓯.

3. Choose the typeface to search for from the Find typeface pop-up menu.

4. Set the replacement typeface from the Change typeface pop-up menu.

5. Set the type style to locate from the Find style pop-up menu.

6. Set the replacement type style from the Change style pop-up menu.

7. Set a range of point sizes to be changed by entering minimum and maximum amounts in the Min and Max fields.

TIP To set a single point size to change, delete any amount in the Min field and enter an amount in the Max field.

8. Set the point size to be changed to by entering the amount in the size field.

9. Choose Replace All to change all the occurrences of the attribute without reviewing each one.

   or

   Click the Find Next button to find each occurrence and then choose Replace to change that one instance of the attribute.

TIP If you choose Replace All, a dialog box tells you when the search is complete and how many changes were made.

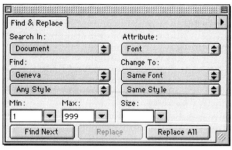

⓯ *The* **Font Attributes** *in the Find & Replace panel. The search options take up the left side; the replace options fill the right side.*

Find and Replace Font Attributes

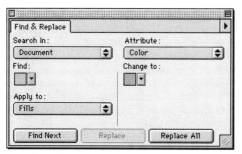

⑯ *The* **Color Attributes** *in the Find & Replace panel. The search options are on the left; the change options on the right.*

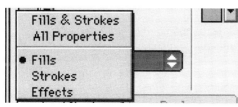

⑰ *The* **Apply to** *list for the color attributes changes.*

The color attribute allows you to search for a specific color. For instance, you can search for all instances of red and change them to a different color such as blue.

To set the Color attributes:

1. Choose **Window** > **Find & Replace** and then narrow the search, if necessary, as explained on page 136.

2. Choose Color from the Attribute pop-up list. The color attributes appear ⑯.

3. Use the Find color well to select the color to change.

4. Use the Change color well to set the replacement color.

5. Use the Apply pop-up list ⑰ to set which properties should change.

- Choose All Properties to change the fills, strokes, and effects.

- Choose Fills & Strokes to change the fills and strokes but not effects.

- Choose Fills, Strokes, or Effects to change just one of those attributes.

6. Choose Replace All to change all the occurrences of the attribute without reviewing each one.

   or

   Click the Find Next button to find each occurrence and then choose Replace to change that one instance of the attribute.

TIP If you choose Replace All, a dialog box appears telling you when the search is complete and how many changes were made.

The URL attribute allows you to search for the text in URL links and change it. This makes it easy to update a Web site when a URL link changes from one address to another. Changing URL links changes the Web-address information stored in rollovers, slices, or image maps. This information is not the same as the visible text. *(For more information on working with URL links, see Chapter 16, "Hotspots and URLs.")*

To Find and Replace URL attributes:

1. Choose **Window**>**Find & Replace** and then narrow the search, if necessary, as explained on page 136.

2. Choose URL from the Attribute pop-up list. The URL attributes appear ⓲.

3. In the Find field, type the URL to search for.

4. Type the replacement URL in the Change To field.

5. Choose Replace All to change all the occurrences of the attribute without reviewing each one.

   or

   Click the Find Next button to find each occurrence and then choose Replace to change that one instance of the attribute.

TIP If you choose Replace All, a dialog box appears telling you when the search is complete and how many changes were made.

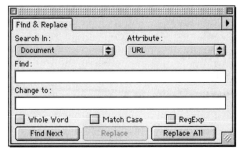

⓲ *The* URL *attributes.*

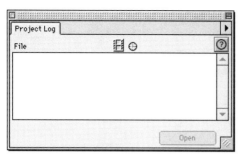

⑲ *The* **Project Log** *panel.*

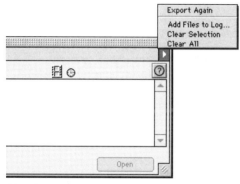

⑳ *The* **Project Log menu.**

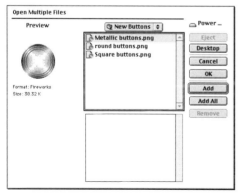

㉑ *The* **Open Multiple Files dialog box** *allows you to add multiple files to the Project Log.*

It may become difficult to remember all the files associated with a specific Web site or project. The Project Log gives you an easy way to organize these files into groups. A group might be all the files that pertain to a specific project, or the files for a specific client. Once you have added files to the Project Log, you can use the Project Log as part of a Find & Replace routine *(see pages 136–140).*

To add or delete Project Log files:

1. Choose **Window** > **Project Log** to open the Project Log panel **⑲**.

2. Choose Add Files to Log from the Project Log menu **⑳**. The Open Multiple Files dialog box appears **㉑**.

3. Use the Open Multiple Files dialog box to select the files to be added to the Project Log.

4. Select an item or items in the Project Log and then choose Clear Selection to delete the selected files from the Project Log.

   or

   Choose Clear All to delete all the files from the Project Log.

The files in the Project Log can also be exported using the current export settings.

To export files from the Project Log:

1. Set the Export defaults as desired. *(See Chapter 15, "Basic Exporting," for setting the Export defaults.)*

2. Select the files in the Project Log that you want to export.

3. Choose Export Again from the Project Log menu. This lets you save each of the exported files.

The most powerful automation feature in Fireworks is its batch processing. This allows you to combine the Find & Replace feature together with exporting files into one automated command that can be applied to many files at once. So not only can you make changes to many Fireworks files, you can also efficiently export them as GIF or JPEG files for use in Web pages. This makes it easy to do the maintenance for a large Web site.

㉒ *The* Batch Processing *dialog box.*

The first stage is to determine what files will be part of the batch processing.

To set the files for batch processing:

1. Choose File>Batch Process. The Batch Processing dialog box appears ㉒.

2. Use the Files to Process pop-up menu ㉓ to choose which files should be included in the batch processing.

㉓ *The* Files to Process *options for Batch Processing.*

- Choose Current Open Files to include all files currently open.

- Choose Project Log (All Files) to include all the files listed in the Project Log. *(See page 141 for information on working with the Project Log.)*

- Choose Project Log (Selected Files) to include only the selected files in the Project Log.

- Choose Custom to open the Open Multiple Files dialog box *(see page 136)* which allows you to pick a specific set of files to batch process.

3. Set the replacement and export options, as described on the next page.

4. Set the backup and script options, as described on page 144.

5. Click OK to batch process the files.

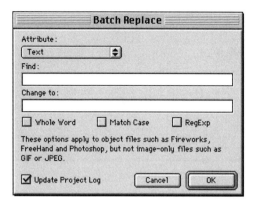

ⓩ *The* **Batch Replace** *dialog box.*

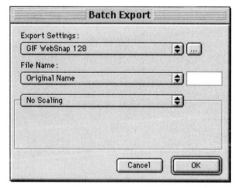

㉕ *The* **Batch Export** *dialog box.*

Once you have set the files for batch processing, you need to set the actions to perform on all the files. You can include two types of actions: Batch Replace and/or Batch Export.

To set Batch Replace options:

1. Check the box for Find and Replace under the Actions label in the Batch Processing dialog box **㉒**. This opens the Batch Replace dialog box **㉔**.

TIP If the box is already checked, click the Find and Replace ellipsis (…) to open the dialog box.

2. Set the options like the Find & Replace settings covered on pages 136–140.

3. Check Update Project Log to have Fireworks note the new status of the files in the Project Log.

To set Batch Export options:

1. Check the box for Find and Replace under the Actions label in the Batch Processing dialog box **㉒**. This opens the Batch Export dialog box **㉕**. *(For more information on exporting files, see Chapter 15, "Basic Exporting.")*

TIP If the box is already checked, click the Export ellipsis (…) to open the dialog box.

2. Set the Export Settings to use the setting from the file, a custom setting or a specific export preset.

3. Use the File Name pop-up list to keep the original name of the file or add a suffix or prefix.

4. Use the Scaling pop-up list to control the size of the final exported file.

The batch processing options also let you keep backups of the original versions of the file after they are modified.

To set batch Backup Original Files options:

1. Open the Batch Processing dialog box and change any necessary processing and export settings.

2. Click the Backup Original Files ellipsis (…) in the Batch Processing dialog box to open the Save Backups dialog box **㉖**.

2. Choose Overwrite Existing Backups to keep only the previous version of the file and not any versions created before.

3. Choose Incremental Backups to keep all previous versions of the file, renaming any older versions if necessary.

㉖ The **Save Backups** dialog box.

Fireworks lets you save batch processing settings as a script that can be applied later.

To save the batch process settings as a script:

1. Open the Batch Processing dialog box and change any necessary processing and export settings.

2. Click the Script button in the Batch Process dialog box. This opens a dialog box where you can save the script as a .jsf file.

TIP Fireworks scripts are written in the JavaScript language and can be edited using a word processing program **㉗**.

To run a script:

1. Choose **File > Script**.

2. In the dialog box choose a previously saved script.

3. Click OK.

```
                    if (batch.doBackupFiles) {
                        var backupPath = GetBackupFile(sourceDocumentPath
    batch.doIncrementalBackup);
                        if (backupPath == null) {
                            alert(Errors.EFileNotFound);
                            break;
                        }
                        var errorString =
    SafeCopyFileTo(sourceDocumentPath, backupPath);
                        if (errorString != null) {
                            alert(errorString);
                            break;
                        }
                    }
                    if (batch.findAndReplaceParms != null) {
                        var theFinder =
    theDoc.makeFind(batch.findAndReplaceParms);
                        var replaceAnything = theFinder.replaceAll();
                        if (theDoc.filePathForSave == null) {
                            theDoc.filePathForSave =
    Document.makeGoodNativeFilePath(sourceDocumentPath);
                            if (theDoc.filePathForSave == null) {
                                // this should never happen.
                                alert(Errors.EInternalError);
                                break;
                            }
                        }
                        theDoc.save();
                        if (theDoc.filePathForSave == null) {
                            // this should never happen.
                            alert(Errors.EInternalError);
                            break;
                        }
                    }
                    if (batch.exportOptions != null) {

                        var curExportFormatOptions;
                        if (batch.useFormatOptionsFromEachFile) {
                            curExportFormatOptions =
    theDoc.exportFormatOptions;
                        } else {
                            curExportFormatOptions =
    Document.findExportFormatOptionsByName(batch.exportOptions.exportFormatOptions.
    name);
                            if (curExportFormatOptions == null)
                                curExportFormatOptions =
    batch.exportOptions.exportFormatOptions;

                            // copy scaling/cropping info back over since we
    may have
                            // gotten that info from the doc or the named
    settings
```

㉗ A portion of a **Fireworks JavaScript** as displayed in a word processing program.

WORKING WITH PIXELS 12

It is the vector objects in Fireworks that make it so easy to use. But what if you want to use images such as photographs or scanned art that cannot be created by vector objects? Fortunately there is an alter ego to the vector side of Fireworks—a complete set of features for creating, importing, and working with pixel-based artwork. Technically the correct term for these graphics is pixel-based images. However, it is easier to call them *image objects* to differentiate them from the vector objects covered previously.

In this chapter you will learn how to

Access the image-editing features.

Open and import pixel-based images.

Combine or convert objects.

Create an empty image.

Use the Marquee and Lasso tools.

Use the Magic Wand.

Change the shape of selections.

Use the Selection commands.

Use the Similar command.

Use the Feather command.

Use the Rubber Stamp tool.

Use the Eraser.

Use the Eyedropper.

Use the Paint Bucket.

If you want to work with photographs, scans, or other pixel images, you must switch to the image-editing features of Fireworks. You can do that by opening or selecting a pixel-based image. You can also insert an empty image if you want to start with a blank pixel-based canvas.

To switch to the image-editing features:

Choose **File > Open** and choose a scanned or pixel-based image.

TIP The thick striped line around the image indicates that the image-editing tools are available **❶**.

or

With either the Pointer or Subselection tools chosen, double-click a pixel-based image.

or

Use the Marquee, Lasso, or Magic Wand tools to make a selection in the image. *(See pages 149-152 for working with the selection tools.)*

or

Choose **Insert > Empty Image**.

Striped line   Exit image-edit button

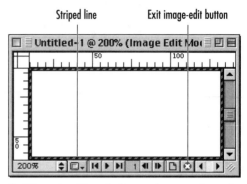

❶ *The* **striped line** *indicates the artwork can be edited using the image editing tools.*

To switch back to vector drawing:

Choose **Modify > Exit Image Edit**. This brings you back to the normal vector-drawing mode.

or

Click the Exit image-editing button.

❷ *The* **corner symbol** *for imported artwork.*

❸ *Dragging the corner symbol places the imported artwork at a specific size.*

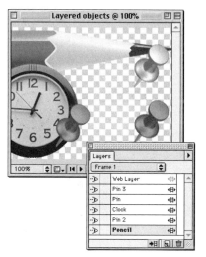

❹ **Layers from Photoshop** *are imported with the objects on their own Fireworks layers.*

❺ *The* **Crop handles** *let you discard portions of imported images.*

You can import or place pixel-based images into Fireworks files.

To import pixel-based images:

1. Choose **File** >**Import** and then find the file you want to import. Click OK. A small corner symbol ❷ indicates the file is ready for placing on the currently selected Fireworks layer.

2. Drag the corner symbol to draw a rectangle that scales the image to fit ❸.

    or

    Click to simply place the image at its original size.

To import pixel-based images:

1. Choose **File** >**Open**.

2. Find the Photoshop file and click OK.

   TIP If the Photoshop file contains layers, each of the layers appears as its own pixel-based image ❹.

If you have image objects in your Fireworks files, you may want to crop those images so they take up less space in the file.

To crop image objects:

1. Select a pixel-based image.

2. Choose **Edit** >**Crop Selected Image**. A set of handles appears around the image ❺.

3. Drag the handles so that they surround the area you want to keep.

4. When you have defined the area you want, double-click inside the handles. The excess image is deleted.

You can also combine imported images, turn vector objects into image objects or add vector objects to image objects.

To combine or convert objects:

1. Select the objects you want to combine or convert ❻.

TIP Select a single vector object to convert it to a pixel-based image object.

2. Choose **Modify > Merge Images.** Vector objects are converted to pixels and imported images are combined into one image object ❼.

TIP If you convert vector objects into image objects, you lose the ability to edit the paths that defined the vector objects.

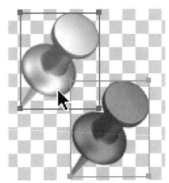

❻ *Two imported images can be moved or manipulated as separate images.*

You can also create an empty image, which acts like a transparent image area. You can paint or fill the transparent area using any of the image object tools.

To create an image from scratch:

1. Choose **Insert > Empty Image.** The striped line appears around the edge of the image, indicating you are working in the Image Edit Mode.

2. Use any of the image-editing tools to paint or modify the area inside the empty image ❽.

3. Choose **Modify > Exit Image Edit.** The area of the empty image shrinks to the size of the area that was painted or modified.

❼ *The* **Merge Images** *command combines the two imported images into one image object.*

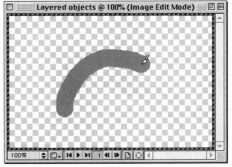

❽ *An* **Empty Image** *allows you to use any of the image-editing tools to paint inside the area.*

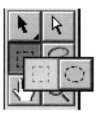

❾ *The* **Marquee tools** *in the Toolbox.*

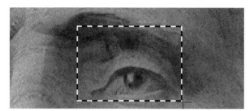

❿ *The* **marching ants** *of the marquee surround the selected area.*

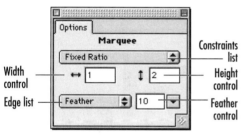

Width control
Edge list

Constraints list
Height control
Feather control

⓫ *The* Marquee Options *panel.*

Unlike vector objects, pixels are selected as areas of the image. The basic selection tools are the two Marquee tools and the two Lasso tools.

To use the Marquee tools:

1. Press the Marquee tool in the Toolbox and choose either the rectangular or elliptical shape **❾**.

2. Move the cursor over the image area and drag diagonally to create a selection. A series of moving dashed lines (sometimes called *marching ants*) indicates the selected area **❿**.

TIP Press the mouse and then hold the Option/Alt key to draw the selection from the center outward.

TIP Press the mouse and the hold the Shift key to constrain the selection to a square or circle.

3. Position the cursor inside the selection and drag to move that portion of the image to a new area.

The marquee tool *constraints* allow you to change the tool so that the area selected is a certain size or proportion.

To change the Marquee tool constraints:

1. Double-click either of the marquee tools in the Toolbox to open the Marquee Tool Options panel **⓫**.

2. Press the Constraints pop-up list to choose Normal, Fixed Ratio, or Fixed Size.

3. In the Fixed Ratio mode, enter the ratio for the width and the height of the selection. This constrains the marquee to those proportions.

4. In the Fixed Size mode, enter the pixel amounts for the width and height of the selection. This constrains the marquee area to that size.

Marquee Tools

You can also change the appearance of the edges of a marquee selection.

To change the Marquee tool edges:

1. In the Marquee Options panel, press the edge list to choose Hard Edge, Anti-Alias, or Feather ⓬.

- Choose Hard Edge to give the selection a jagged edge ⓭.

- Choose Anti-Alias to give the selection a smoother edge ⓭.

- Choose Feather to blur the edges of the selection ⓭.

2. If you choose the Feather, set the amount of the blur with the feather control slider or type the amount of the feather (in pixels) in the field.

⓬ *The* **Edge list** *choices.*

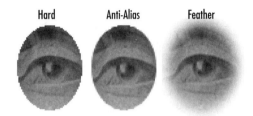

⓭ *The effects of* **changing the edge choices** *of a selection.*

You might want to select shapes besides rectangles and ellipses. To do so, you can use either of the Lasso tools.

To use the Lasso tools:

1. Press the Lasso tool in the Toolbox and choose either the regular or the polygon lasso ⓮.

2. In the regular lasso mode, drag around the area you want to select. The marching ants indicate the selected area ⓯.

3. In the polygon lasso mode, click the cursor around the area you want to select. Each click creates a point of the polygon ⓯.

4. Use the edge list in the Options panel to choose among Hard Edge, Anti-Alias, or Feather.

TIP The regular lasso is useful for following the curved contours of images. The polygon lasso is best for creating selections with straight sides.

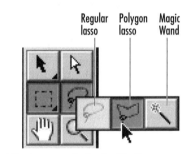

⓮ *The* **Lasso tools** *in the Toolbox.*

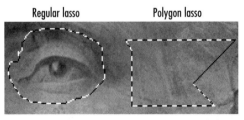

⓯ *A comparison of the Regular lasso and the Polygon lasso.*

Marquee Tool Edges; Lasso Tools

⑯ *The* **Magic Wand** *in the Toolbox.*

Edge list

Tolerance control

Feather control

⑰ *The* **Magic Wand Tool Options.**

You can also select areas by their color. For instance, you might want to select the background behind an image and then delete it or change its color. To do this, you use the Magic Wand.

To use the Magic Wand:

1. Press the Lasso tool to choose the Magic Wand in the Toolbox ⑯.

2. In the Magic Wand Tool Options panel ⑰, use the Tolerance slider or type a number in the field.

3. Use the edge list in the Tool Options panel to choose among Hard Edge, Anti-Alias, or Feather (*see page 150*).

4. Click the area you want to select. The marching ants indicate the selected area ⑱.

TIP Tolerance controls how many colors the Magic Wand selects adjacent to the pixel you click. The lowest tolerance, 0, selects only one color, the exact color of the pixel you select with the tip of the Magic Wand. Increasing the tolerance up to a higher setting, to a maximum of 255, selects a greater range of colors.

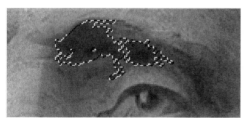

⑱ *The* **area selected with the Magic Wand.**

After you finish working within a selection, you can deselect the selected area.

To deselect a selected area:

Click outside the selection with one of the Marquee or Lasso tools.

TIP You cannot deselect with the Magic Wand tool by clicking outside the selection. This only selects a different area.

or

Choose **Edit > Deselect.**

You may find that the Magic Wand tool has selected too little area, or you may find you need a different shape. You can change a selected area by using modifier keys with the selection tools.

To change the shape of selections:

With an area selected, use any of the selection tools.

- Hold the Shift key to add to the selected area. A plus (+) sign indicates you are adding to the selection **⑲**.

- Hold the Option/Alt key to delete from the selected area. A minus (−) sign indicates you are subtracting from the selection **⑳**.

TIP You can switch tools at any time. For instance, if the original selection was created by the Magic Wand, you can use the Lasso to modify it.

TIP The additional selection does not have to touch the original. For instance, you can select the top and bottom of an image, leaving the middle untouched.

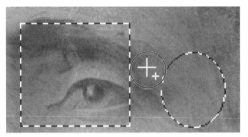

⑲ *Hold the Shift key to* **add to a selection.**

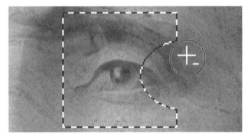

⑳ *Hold the Option/Alt key to* **delete from a selection.**

Rather than use marquee or lasso selection tools, you can also use the Edit menu commands for images.

To use the Selection commands:

- Choose **Edit > Select All** to select all the pixels in the image.

- Choose **Edit > Deselect** to deselect the pixels enclosed by the marching ants.

- Choose **Edit > Select Inverse** to swap the status of the selected pixels, that is, deselect the selected pixels and select everything else.

㉑ *The* Feather Selection *dialog box.*

Once you have selected a certain area with the Magic Wand, you might not want to keep clicking to select similar colors.

To use the Similar command:

With an area selected, choose **Edit**>**Select Similar**. This selects all the areas of the entire image that have the same color.

TIP The Select Similar command uses the tolerance set for the Magic Wand.

TIP You can also use the Select Similar command on selections created by the Marquee or Lasso tools.

Glow indicates feathering

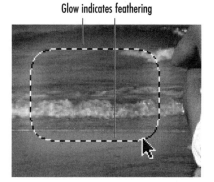

㉒ *The* Feather Selection *dialog box.*

Sometimes it may be easier to select an area with the feather option turned off and then feather the edge afterwards.

To feather an existing selection:

1. With the area selected, choose **Edit** > **Feather** to open the Feather Selection dialog box **㉑**.

2. Enter the number of pixels that you want to blur along the edge of the selection and then click OK.

TIP The marching ants may not change their appearance when you feather a selection. To see the feathering, position the cursor directly over the marching ants and then press the mouse button. The feathering is displayed as a glow in the image **㉒**.

Similar Command; Feather Selections

Most tools, such as the Paint Brush and Pencil have both vector and pixel-based modes. The Rubber Stamp tool, however, works only on pixel images, not vector objects. This tool lets you copy an image and paint with it.

To set the Rubber Stamp options:

1. Choose the Rubber Stamp tool in the Toolbox **㉓**.

2. In the Rubber Stamp Tool Options **㉔**, use the source list to choose Aligned Source or Fixed Source.

   TIP Use Aligned Source when you want to be able to release the mouse button but not lose the position of the area you are copying. This is useful when working on large images.

   TIP Use Fixed Source when you want to make multiple copies of one image. Each time you release the mouse, the source is restored to the original position.

3. Use the Sample list to choose Image or Document.

   TIP Image allows the Rubber Stamp to sample only the area inside the image. Document allows the Rubber Stamp to sample anywhere inside the document. This means you can sample the look of vector objects to paint them as pixels.

4. Use the edge size control to specify the size of the Rubber Stamp brush.

5. Use the edge softness control to change the softness of the Rubber Stamp edge.

㉓ *The **Rubber Stamp** in the Toolbox.*

㉔ *The **Rubber Stamp** Options.*

Area being sampled   Image being painted

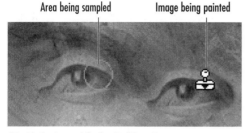

㉕ *Painting with the Rubber Stamp.*

To use the Rubber Stamp tool:

1. Position the Rubber Stamp tool over the image and click to define the source: the area that you want to copy. A circle indicates the source area.

2. Move the Rubber Stamp tool to the area where you want to copy the source.

3. Drag with the Rubber Stamp. The source circle follows your movements. The Rubber Stamp acts like a brush that paints with the image that appears under the source **㉕**.

4. To change the source, hold the Option/Alt key and click a new area. Then paint with the Rubber Stamp tool with the new source area.

TIP The Rubber Stamp tool does not act like a real rubber stamp. Digital rubber stamps (such as the ones found in Fireworks or Photoshop) simply copy the image from one area and paint it onto another. They do not recognize specific shapes or items. If you drag with the Rubber Stamp in a large enough area, you copy the image from one area to another.

Rubber Stamp

The image-editing Eraser works very differently from its vector counterpart. Rather than cutting paths, the image-editing Eraser paints with a color or deletes pixels from an area.

To set the Eraser options:

1. Choose the Eraser in the Toolbox **26**.

2. In the Eraser Tool Options **27**, choose between the round or square shape.

3. Use the edge size control slider or type in the field to set the size of the Eraser.

4. Use the softness control to change the appearance of the Eraser edge.

5. Use the Erase-to list to choose Transparent, Fill Color, Stroke Color, or Canvas Color.

TIP The Erase-to-Transparent option removes the pixels from the image allowing the underlying image to show through **28**.

26 *The* **Eraser** *in the Toolbox.*

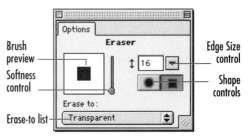

Brush preview

Softness control

Erase-to list

Edge Size control

Shape controls

27 *The* **Eraser Tool Options.**

28 *The effects of* **erasing to transparent.**

㉙ *The* **Eyedropper** *in the Toolbox.*

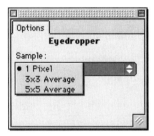

㉚ *The* **Eyedropper Options** *let you control the size of the area sampled by the Eyedropper.*

The Eyedropper allows you to choose colors by sampling them from images.

To use the Eyedropper:

1. Choose the Eyedropper tool in the Toolbox **㉙**.

2. Use the Eyedropper Options **㉚** to set the size of the area the Eyedropper uses to judge the color.

- The 1 Pixel setting picks up the color from the single pixel directly underneath the Eyedropper.

- The 3×3 Average setting picks up the color averaged from nine pixels within the 3×3 pixel area.

- The 5×5 Average setting picks up the color averaged from the twenty-five pixels within the 5×5 pixel area.

Eyedropper

With image objects, the Paint Bucket acts as a speedy way to fill an area with a color.

To set the Paint Bucket options:

1. Choose the Paint Bucket tool in the Toolbox ③.

2. In the Paint Bucket Options ②, use the Tolerance slider or type a number in the field to set how wide an area the Paint Bucket fills ③.

3. Use the Edge list to set the edge of the area filled by the Paint Bucket to Hard Edge, Anti-Aliased, or Feather.

4. If the edge is set to Feather, use the Feather amount to set the width of the feathered border.

TIP The Fill Selection Only option causes the Paint Bucket to fill the selected area or image object regardless of the tolerance setting.

③ *The* **Paint Bucket** *in the Toolbox.*

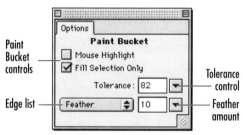

② *The* **Paint Bucket Options.**

To use the Paint Bucket:

1. Choose the Paint Bucket tool in the Toolbox.

2. Click the Paint Bucket over the image. This fills the image with the currently selected Fill color.

TIP If the image has a selected area and you click the Paint Bucket within the selected area, the Paint Bucket fills only within the selected portion of the image ③.

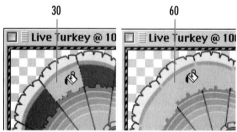

③ *At a setting of 30 (left), the Paint Bucket fills a small area of color. At a setting of 60 (right) the Paint Bucket fills a larger area of color.*

Paint Bucket

X tras are features that are added to Fireworks. There are nine Xtras included as part of Fireworks. (Although they ship with Fireworks, they are called "extras" because they are not part of the core program.) These nine Xtras change the appearance of pixel images in Fireworks in different ways. You can also use the plug-ins for programs such as Adobe Photoshop within Fireworks.

In this chapter you will learn how to

Apply Xtras to vector objects.

Blur images.

Apply the Gaussian blur.

Sharpen images.

Apply the Unsharp Mask.

Invert images.

Find Edges.

Mask using the Convert to Alpha Xtra.

Use the CSI PhotoOptics filters.

Reapply Xtras quickly.

Add Xtras from other companies.

Change the image area to make Xtras work better.

Xtras work only on pixel objects. However, you can convert vector objects to image objects and then use the Xtras. In fact, you can do that all in one step; just make sure you really are ready to lose the paths before you make the conversion.

To apply Xtras to vector objects:

1. Select one or more vector objects.

2. Choose an Xtra from the Xtras menu. A dialog box appears indicating that the image will be converted into a pixel image ❶.

3. Click OK. The object is converted and the Xtra is applied.

Three Xtras create different types of blur effects. The first two, Blur and Blur More, you apply via a simple menu command. These two blur commands are useful for concealing small imperfections in a scan. They can also help erase the lines between images that have been composited together.

To apply the Blur and Blur More Xtras:

1. Select an object or image.

2. Choose Xtras > Blur > Blur to give the image a slight blur effect ❷.

   or

2. Choose Xtras > Blur > Blur More to give the image a greater blur effect ❸.

TIP The blur Xtras work by changing some of the blacks and whites in an image to shades of gray. This means that some of the detail of an image is lost.

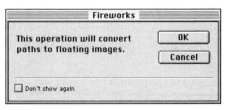

❶ *The dialog box that appears when you want to apply an Xtra to a vector object.*

❷ *The effect of applying the* **Blur Xtra** *to an image.*

❸ *The effect of applying the* **Blur More Xtra** *to an image.*

Preview
area

Zoom in | Zoom out | Radius slider

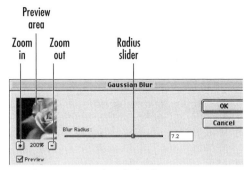

❹ *The* **Gaussian Blur** *dialog box.*

Original   Gaussian Blur

❺ *The effect of applying the* **Gaussian Blur Xtra** *to an image.*

The third blur effect, Gaussian Blur, is applied through a dialog box. The Gaussian Blur Xtra gives you more control over the amount of the blur. This blur is useful for making objects appear as if they are positioned behind others.

To apply the Gaussian Blur Xtra:

1. Select an object or image.

2. Choose **Xtras** > **Blur** > **Gaussian Blur**. The Gaussian Blur dialog box appears ❹.

3. Use the slider to increase or decrease the amount of the blur.

4. Use the Preview area to see the effects of the blur.

5. Press and drag inside the Preview area to see a different portion of the image.

6. Click the plus sign (+) to zoom in on the Preview area.

7. Click the minus sign (−) to zoom out from the Preview area.

8. When you are satisifed with the look of the Gaussian Blur, click OK to apply the Xtra ❺.

Gaussian Blur

Just as you can blur images, so can you sharpen them. This is especially useful when working with scanned images that tend to look a little soft, or out of focus. Three different sharpen Xtras come with Fireworks. The first two Xtras sharpen the image very simply, with little control over how the sharpening is added.

To apply the Sharpen and Sharpen More Xtras:

1. Select an object or image.

2. Choose **Xtras** > **Sharpen** > **Sharpen** to slightly sharpen the image ❻.

   or

   Choose **Xtras** > **Sharpen** > **Sharpen More** to sharpen the image slightly more ❼.

TIP The sharpen Xtras work by changing some gray pixels in the image to black or white. Although it may seem that more detail is revealed, strictly speaking some of the detail is lost.

❻ *The effect of applying the* **Sharpen Xtra** *to an image.*

❼ *The effect of applying the* **Sharpen More Xtra** *to an image.*

Preview Threshold Radius
area slider slider

Zoom Zoom Amount
in out slider

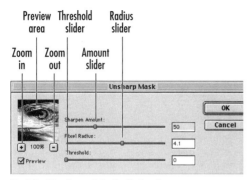

❽ *The **Unsharp Mask** dialog box.*

Original   Unsharp Mask Xtra

❾ *The effect of applying the **Unsharp Mask Xtra** to an image.*

Original   Unsharp Mask Xtra at high settings

❿ *The **Unsharp Mask Xtra** at a high sharpen and low threshold can create a glow around objects.*

The third sharpen Xtra is the Unsharp Mask Xtra. Despite its name, this filter does sharpen images, and in a very sophisticated fashion. This is the most widely used command to compensate for the blurring that occurs when scanning images.

To apply the Unsharp Mask Xtra:

1. Select an object or image.

2. Choose **Xtras > Sharpen > Unsharp Mask**. The Unsharp Mask dialog box appears ❽.

3. Drag the Amount slider or type in the field to change the amount of contrast that is applied—the greater the amount, the greater the sharpening.

4. Drag the Threshold slider or type in the field to set how different the pixels must be before they are sharpened.

TIP A Threshold of 0 means that all the pixels in the image are sharpened.

TIP A low threshold means that pixels that are only slightly different in brightness are sharpened. A high threshold means that only those pixels that are very different in brightness are sharpened. For instance, in illustration ❾, a high threshold means that only the sharp line in the beak would be sharpened. A low threshold means that the gray feathers in the lower-right corner would be sharpened.

5. Drag the Radius slider or type in the field to set the number of pixels around the edge that have the sharpening effect applied.

6. Click OK to see the effects of the Unsharp Mask Xtra ❾.

TIP High Unsharp Mask settings with a high sharpen and low threshold settings can cause an unwanted glow around objects ❿.

The Invert Xtra reverses selected images into negatives. Black becomes white; red becomes green; yellow becomes blue; and so on.

To apply the Invert Xtra:

1. Select an object or image.

2. Choose Xtras > Invert > Invert. The colors of the image are reversed **⓫**.

Original   Invert Xtra

⓫ *The effect of applying the* **Invert Xtra** *to an image.*

The Find Edges Xtra looks for pixels in the image with different shades or colors. Boundaries between the colors are considered edges. The Find Edges Xtra changes the colors of the pixels so that a line appears where there was an edge. This gives the effect of converting photographs into line art.

To apply the Find Edges Xtra:

1. Select an object or image.

2. Choose Xtras > Other > Find Edges. The image is converted **⓬**.

TIP Photographs tend to appear white on black after applying the Find Edges Xtra. Use the Invert Xtra after the Find Edges command to convert the image to black on white.

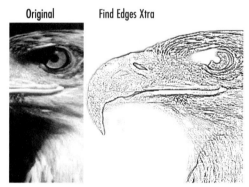
Original   Find Edges Xtra

⓬ *The effect of applying the* **Find Edges Xtra** *and then the Invert Xtra to an image.*

Invert; Find Edges

⓭ *To* **create an Alpha mask** *draw a rectangle over an image and then apply a gradient.*

⓮ *The result of* applying the Convert to Alpha Xtra *to a gradient.*

⓯ *The result of applying* the Mask Group.

The next Xtra, Convert to Alpha, lets you create the same effect as a Mask Group *(see page 97)*. Because the Convert to Alpha Xtra turns vector objects into pixels, it is not as useful as the Mask Group.

To mask using the Convert to Alpha Xtra:

1. Find an object or image to mask. For instance, you might want a scanned image to fade in intensity from top to bottom.

2. Draw a rectangle that covers the image you want to mask and position it over the original object or image **⓭**.

3. Manipulate the rectangle to create the effect you want in the masked area. In the example shown, the rectangle contains a gradient that fades the image below it.

TIP When working with Alpha masks, remember that Alpha areas that are black allow the images underneath to be seen. Alpha areas that are white make the images underneath transparent. Alpha values between black and white show the images with amounts of transparency in between.

4. With the rectangle selected, choose **Xtras > Other > Convert to Alpha**. This converts the vector object to a grayscale image that can be used as an Alpha mask **⓮**.

5. Select both the original image and the Alpha mask and choose **Modify > Mask Group**. The original image is seen through the Alpha mask **⓯**.

TIP The Alpha masks in Fireworks are similar to the Alpha channels in Adobe Photoshop. However, the Fireworks Alpha masks can be applied on an object-by-object basis, rather than to an entire layer as in Photoshop.

Fireworks also provides you with a powerful set of color-correction and effects filters from Cytopia Software. These are the CSI PhotoOptics filters found under the Xtras menu. These filters make it easy to do all your color correction and enhancement within Fireworks.

To work with the PhotoOptics filters:

1. In the Image Edit mode, choose **Xtras**> **PhotoOptics**>**Filter Name.** This opens the dialog box for the filter.

2. Choose settings for the filter in the dialog box.

3. Use the Before and After previews to judge the effects of the filter.

4. When you are satisfied with the results, click OK to apply the filter to the image.

TIP Each of the filters has various presets, or you can create your own to easily apply consistent settings.

(For a color printout of the effects of the CSI PhotoOptics filters, see the color insert.)

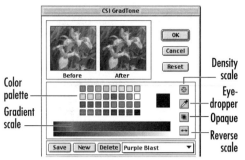

⓰ *The* **CSI GradTone** *dialog box.*

CSI GradTone

The CSI GradTone filter ⓰ is analogous to using a split field or graduated chromatic filter on a camera lens. These traditional filters have color spread over only half of their field, or in differing densities over the entire surface. Clicking any point along the gradient scale changes the colors in the image that correspond to that position.

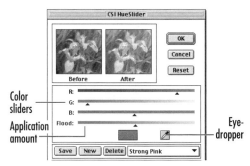

Color sliders

Application amount

Eye-dropper

⑰ *The* **CSI HueSlider** *dialog box.*

Hue slider

Eye-dropper

⑱ *The* **CSI MonoChrome** *dialog box.*

Hue slider

Eye-dropper

⑲ *The* **CSI PhotoFilter** *dialog box.*

CSI HueSlider

The CSI HueSlider **⑰** is used to slide an image toward a specified target color. Each of the primary colors has a separate slider: red, green, and blue. The fourth slider, Flood, controls the amount of color mixing and the saturation of the color.

CSI MonoChrome

The CSI MonoChrome filter **⑱** converts a color image into a monochromatic image. It also includes Hue, Saturation and Exposure controls. This combination allows you to customize effects and eliminates the need to process the image multiple times. Keep in mind that multiple passes of color correction eventually degrade an image.

CSI PhotoFilter

The CSI PhotoFilter **⑲** modifies the color cast of the entire image, matching the effects of gels and optical filters used by photographers. In addition to adding or subtracting specific colors, you can also manipulate the exposure of the image.

CSI HueSlider; CSI MonoChrome; CSI PhotoFilter

CSI Negative

The CSI Negative filter ❷ converts a scanned negative to a positive image with additional control over highlight, shadow and overall exposure to counter the effect of tonal compression found in negative film. It can be used to create pop-art effects or to mimic the look of infrared film.

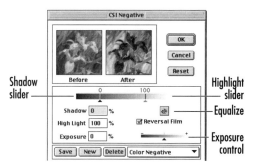

❷ *The* CSI Negative *dialog box.*

CSI Noise

The CSI Noise filter ❷ creates photo-realistic random noise throughout the image. Apply noise in varying size and density of grain. A Luminance control switches the Noise filter from color noise to brightness noise. Use this filter to simulate grain in film and also to make mono-chromatic backgrounds blend seamlessly into composites.

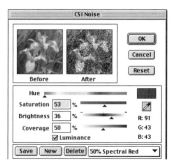

❷ *The* CSI Noise *dialog box.*

CSI PseudoColor

CSI PseudoColor ❷ creates startling false color images. You can use this filter to create extremely stylized pop-art effects. The PseudoColor effect simulates the look of infrared color film that has had different colored filters applied to it.

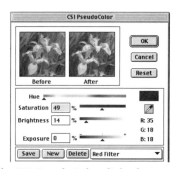

❷ *The* CSI PseudoColor *dialog box.*

CSI Levels

CSI Levels ❷ allows you to manipulate the tonal range and exposure settings for an image to allow for a maximum range for highlights and shadow detail. This lets you to assign deep blacks to parts of shadow areas without compressing the rest of the tonal range.

❷ *The* CSI Levels *dialog box.*

24 *The* **Mac Folders Preferences** *dialog box.*

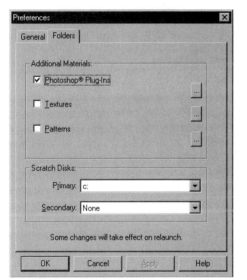

25 *The* **Windows Additional Materials Preferences** *dialog box.*

Once you have applied an Xtra, it appears as the Repeat [Xtra] command. The Repeat [Xtra] command also has a keystroke to make it even easier to reapply an Xtra.

To reapply Xtras quickly:

With an object selected, choose **Xtras** > **Repeat [Name of Xtra]**.

TIP The Mac keystroke for the Repeat [Xtra] command is Command-Option-Shift-X.

TIP The Win keystroke for the Repeat [Xtra] command is Ctrl-Alt-Shift-X.

In addition to the Xtras that are installed as part of Fireworks, you can also use any Photoshop-compatible plug-ins. You can install these plug-ins in their own folder for Fireworks, or you can just use the ones currently installed for Photoshop or other applications.

To add Xtras from other companies:

1. Choose **File** > **Preferences**. This open the Preferences dialog box.

2. On the Mac press the pop-up list to choose Folders. This open the settings for choosing other folders for Fireworks features **24**.

   or

   On Windows click the Folders tab **25**.

3. Click the box next to Photoshop Plug-ins and then click the ellipsis button.

4. Navigate to find the plug-ins folder and then click the select button.

TIP The Xtras do not appear in the Fireworks Xtras menu until after you restart Fireworks.

TIP Once you have added Xtras from other companies, you can apply them just as you do the built-in Fireworks Xtras.

If you are working with Xtras, you may find that you need more space around the image so that the Xtra gives you the proper effect 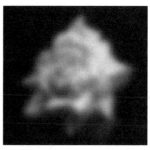. For instance, the Gaussian Blur does not blur the edges of an image; it only blurs the area within the image. Fortunately, you can blur the edges by increasing the area around the image.

To increase the area around an image:

1. Draw a rectangle larger than the image.

2. Fill the rectangle with the canvas color.

3. Choose **Modify** > **Arrange** > **Send to Back**.

4. Select both the rectangle and the image and choose **Modify** > **Merge Images**. This adds area around the image which makes it easier to create certain effects with Xtras .

㉖ *Xtras such as the Gaussian Blur cannot work on the edges of objects unless you add space around the image.*

㉗ Adding extra space around the image *allows the Xtra to work on the outside of the image.*

IMPORTING 14

Although Fireworks boasts a wealth of tools, fills, and effects, it cannot do everything. So it is very likely that you have artwork created in other programs that you want to import into Fireworks. For instance, you probably have images from pixel-based programs such as Adobe Photoshop. You might also have logos and other artwork created in vector-drawing programs such as FreeHand or Illustrator. The decisions you make about importing artwork into Fireworks depend on the software that created the original artwork, as well as the type of Web graphic you want to create.

In this chapter you will learn how to

Open scans as a background layer.

Import scans as image objects.

Import Photoshop artwork with layer masks.

Open vector artwork.

Set the size of vector artwork.

Set the pages of vector artwork.

Set the layers of vector artwork.

Render vector art into pixel images.

Set the edge of vector artwork.

Set additional folders for textures or patterns.

macromedia
FIREWORKS

You can bring scans into Fireworks two different ways. The first is to open the scanned image.

To open a scanned image:

1. Choose **File** > **Open** and then choose the scan you want to open.

2. Click OK. The scan automatically opens ready for image editing.

TIP The scanned image appears on a layer called *background* which is set to be shared across frames ❶. *(For more information on sharing layers across frames, see Chapter 19, "Animations.")*

TIP The Fireworks document opens with the same resolution and size as the original scan.

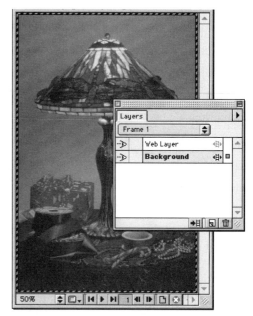

❶ *A scan opened in image-editing mode on the background layer of a Fireworks document.*

You can also import scans into Fireworks.

To import scans as image objects:

1. Choose **File** > **Import** and then find the scan you want to import. Click OK. A small corner symbol indicates the file is ready for placing on the currently selected Fireworks layer.

2. Drag the corner symbol to draw a rectangle that scales the image to fit.

   or

   Click to place the scanned image at the original size.

3. The scan appears as an image object on the currently selected object layer ❷. *(For more information on working with image objects, see Chapter 11, "Working With Pixels.")*

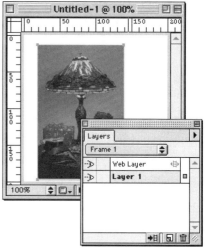

❷ *A scan imported as an image object on a layer of a Fireworks document.*

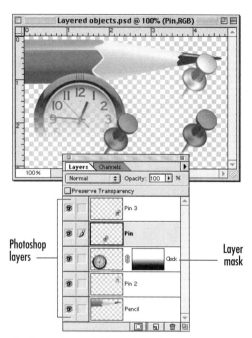

❸ *How a* **layered Photoshop document** *appears in Photoshop.*

Adobe Photoshop uses a feature called layer masks to mask the image in a layer using a grayscale channel. When you use Fireworks to open a Photoshop file that contains layer masks, Fireworks applies the mask to the image objects created from the layer. *(For more information on opening Photoshop files in Fireworks see Chapter 12, "Working with Pixels.")*

To open Photoshop files with layer masks:

1. Choose **File** > **Open** and then find the Photoshop file you want to open.

2. Click OK. The file opens as a Fireworks document. Each layer in Photoshop creates its own layer in Fireworks **❸**. The layer masks that were applied in Photoshop create transparency in the Fireworks image object **❹**.

TIP Use the Photoshop Conversion setting in the Preferences to retain the layers or flatten the image.

TIP If you do not want the layer mask applied to the Photoshop layer, remove the layer mask before you open the file in Fireworks.

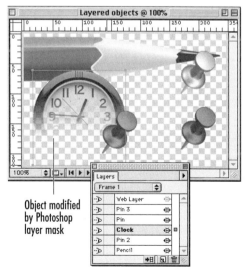

❹ *How a* **layered Photoshop document** *opens in Fireworks.*

Open Layered Artwork; Import Layered Artwork

Fireworks can also open artwork created in vector-drawing programs such as Macromedia FreeHand, Adobe Illustrator or CorelDraw. Artwork created in those programs opens in Fireworks as vector objects. This means you can use the more sophisticated tools in the vector-drawing programs and then add the artwork to your Fireworks document as editable objects.

To open vector artwork:

1. Choose **File**>**Open** and then find the vector file you want to open. Click OK. The Vector File Options dialog box appears ❺.

2. Set the options for opening the vector artwork. *(See the instructions that follow here and on pages 176 for specific details.)*

To set the size of imported vector artwork:

1. Open the artwork in Fireworks and use the top third of the Vector File Options dialog box.

2. Use the Scale control to import the art at a specific size compared to its original size.

    or

    Change the width or height field to change the size of the art to fit a space.

    or

    Set the resolution to something other than 72 pixels per inch to change the size of the art.

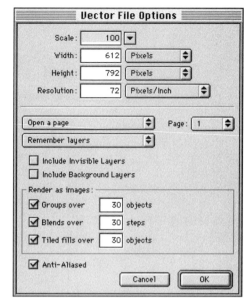

❺ *The* Vector File Options *dialog box.*

❻ *The* **Page options** *for importing vector artwork from a program that lets you specify multiple pages.*

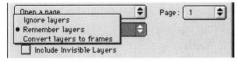

❼ *The* **Layer options** *for importing vector artwork.*

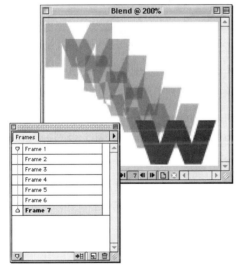

❽ *The composite shows how a* **vector blend imports into Fireworks** *onto individual frames.*

If your artwork has pages or layers, you can set how those pages or layers are opened.

To set which pages of vector artwork to open:

1. Choose **File**>**Open** and then find the vector file you want to open. Click OK. The Vector File Options dialog box appears.

2. Use the page-number list to choose which page is imported **❻**.

   or

   Choose Open Pages As Frames from the Open As list to open each of the pages as a Fireworks frame **❻**.

TIP Opening multiple pages as frame makes it easy to convert vector artwork into animations.

To set the layers of opened vector artwork:

1. With the vector artwork open in Fireworks, in the Vector File Options dialog box choose Remember Layers to import the layers as Fireworks layers **❼**.

   or

   Choose Ignore layers to import the artwork onto one Fireworks layer.

   or

   Choose Convert Layers to Frames to open each of the layers as a Fireworks frame.

TIP If you use FreeHand, you can set its blends to appear on individual layers. Opening that document with Convert Layers to Frames in Fireworks allows you to animate the blend **❽**.

2. Check Include Invisible Layers to bring in artwork on the layers that are not visible in the vector program.

3. Check Include Background Layers to bring in artwork on the background layers in FreeHand.

Because vector artwork can easily contain hundreds of objects, you may not want all those objects opened as individual vector objects. Fireworks lets you convert some of the vector objects into pixel images.

To render imported vector art into pixel images:

1. In the Vector File Options dialog box, check Groups Over and fill in the field to set what type of groups should be converted into pixel images ❾.

2. Check Blends Over and fill in the field to set what types of blends should be converted into pixel images ❾.

3. Check Tiled Fills Over and fill in the field to set what types of tiled fills, or patterns, should be converted into pixel images ❾.

TIP Rendering vectors as pixels helps when importing photorealistic or very intricate images ❿.

When you open vector artwork in Fireworks, you have a choice as to how the artwork appears: either with a hard edge or a softer, anti-aliased edge.

To set the edge of opened vector artwork:

In the Vector File Options dialog box, check Anti-Aliased to import the artwork with the Fill edge setting as Anti-Aliased.

or

Deselect Anti-Aliased to import the artwork with the Fill edge setting as Hard Edge *(see page 89).*

❾ *The* **Render as Images** options *controls whether objects are imported as vectors or images.*

❿ *The difference between importing as vectors and rendering the vector objects as pixel images.*

Vector Art into Pixel Images; Set the Edge of Vector Artwork

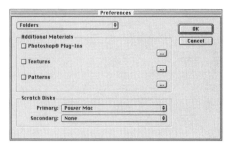

⓫ *The Mac* **Preferences** *dialog box.*

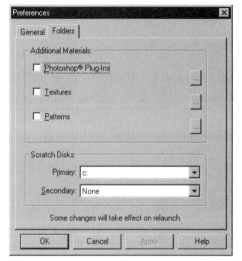

⓬ *The Windows* **Preferences** *dialog box, showing its Folders panel.*

Importing does not just mean bringing in artwork. Fireworks also lets you set a specific folder that holds the artwork that is used for textures or patterns. This allows you to specify a folder in addition to the ones in the Fireworks application that holds textures and patterns such as a project folder.

To set additional folders for textures or patterns:

1. Choose **File** > **Preferences**. This opens the Preferences dialog box.

2. On the Mac use the pop-up list to choose Folders. This open the settings for choosing other folders for Fireworks features ⓫.

   or

   On Windows click the Folders tab ⓬.

3. Click the box next to Textures, click the ellipsis button, and then navigate to find the folder that holds the textures.

4. Click the box next to Patterns, click the ellipsis button, and then navigate to find the folder that holds the patterns.

⫸ Textures and patterns can be saved as PNG formats

⫸ The textures and patterns do not appear in the pop-up lists until after you restart Fireworks.

Set Folders for Textures and Patterns

BASIC EXPORTING

15

Converting graphics and exporting them embodies the very heart and soul of the Fireworks application. In fact, you may have started learning Fireworks by skipping directly to this chapter. Fireworks gives you exceptionally simple yet powerful ways to convert images one at a time or in batches for the Web or for other graphics programs. This chapter covers the basics of converting and exporting images.

In this chapter you will learn how to

Convert and export images.

Open and work within the Export Preview window.

Decide between GIF or JPEG.

Set the GIF palette options.

Save and load palettes.

Set the JPEG options.

Create images that appear gradually.

Compare export settings.

Create a Transparent GIF.

Choose the matte color.

Save export settings.

Export in other file formats.

Set the export defaults.

Batch process images.

Scale an exported image.

Export a portion of an image.

Use the Export Special command.

Use the Export Size Wizard.

Use the Export Wizard.

Use the Export Special command.

This first exercise gives a real quick start in exporting using Fireworks to anyone who already knows enough about Web graphics to be able to choose the export settings without assistance. If you are new to Web graphics, the exercises through the rest of this chapter give details on which settings are right for different situations.

To export an image:

1. With a file open choose **File> Export** to open the Export Preview ❶ and adjust the image in the preview area or zoom in or out, if necessary. (*See page 181.*)

2. Choose a file format. (*See pages 182 and pages 193 for more about file formats.*)

3. Choose a color palette and how many colors should be used in the palette. (*See pages 183–186 for details on color palette and number of colors.*)

4. Make the image background transparent, if necessary. (*See the techniques on page 191.*)

5. Choose compression settings, if necessary, to make the image smaller. (*See page 188 for more details.*)

6. Compare the look, file size, and loading speed of the different settings you are considering to determine which one is best. (*See page 190 for details on making those comparisons.*)

7. If desired, set the graphic to load as interlaced or progressive. (*See page 189 for explanations of those settings.*)

8. If you expect to export other images the same way, save the export settings to use again. (*See page 192.*)

9. Click Next and use the dialog box to give the file a name and save it in the proper location.

Export an Image

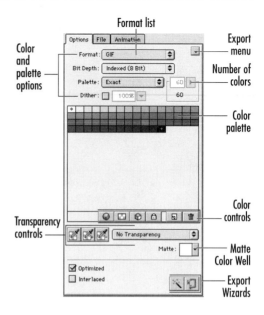

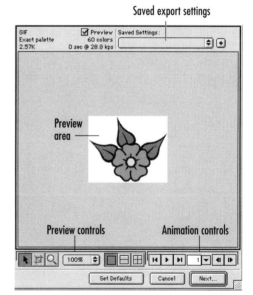

❶ *The* **Export Preview** *window.*

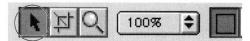

❷ *The* **Pointer Tool** *in the Export Preview window.*

In order to set any of the export or conversion features, you must first open the Export Preview window.

To open the Export Preview window:

Choose **File > Export** to open the Export Preview window **❶**.

❸ *The* **Hand cursor** *lets you move the image within the Preview area.*

As soon as you open the Export Preview window, you see a preview of the image in the file. There are several different ways to control the magnification and area shown within the Preview area.

To change the Preview area views:

1. To move the image within the Preview area, select the Pointer tool **❷** and drag the image. The Hand cursor moves the image within the Preview area **❸**.

2. Use the magnification list **❹** to choose one of the preset magnifications.

   or

   To zoom in on a specific area of the image, select the Zoom tool and click the image.

   TIP Hold the Option/Alt key to zoom out from the image.

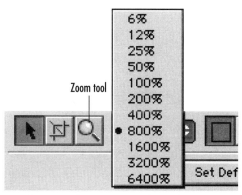

❹ *The* **Magnification controls** *in the Export Preview window.*

The first choice you need to make in exporting a graphic is which format you need. For basic exporting to the Web, choose either GIF or JPEG. *(Fireworks does export in formats for uses besides the Web; for a brief explanation of those formats see page 193.)*

As a general rule, use the **GIF format** for images with flat or solid areas of color . Plain type, solid fills, cartoons, and flat-color logos usually look best when saved as GIF images. GIF images are 8-bit files, which mean they are limited to 256 colors.

⑤ The type of graphic that converts well as a GIF.

Use the **JPEG format** for photographic images or images with subtle blends ⑥. JPEG images are 24-bit images with up to 16.7 millions of colors. When people with 8-bit monitors view a JPEG image, they do not see millions of colors. Only those with high-quality monitors will see all the colors in your image. *(For a color comparison of GIF and JPEG images, see the color insert.)*

TIP If an image has both flat art and a photograph, dithering a GIF image may help maintain the photograph as well as the flat art.

TIP Slicing images can also help work with images that combine photos and flat art *(For more information on slices, see Chapter 17, "Slices.").*

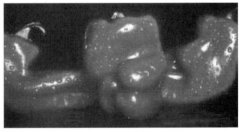

⑥ The type of image that converts well as a JPEG.

To choose a file format:

Use the Format list ⑦ to choose a format. For Web graphics choose GIF or JPEG. These are the main formats for exporting static images on the Web. *(For exporting in the Animated GIF format, see Chapter 19, "Animations.")*

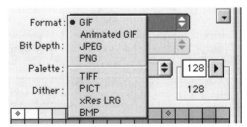

*⑦ The **Format list**. (The PICT format is available only on the Macintosh platform.)*

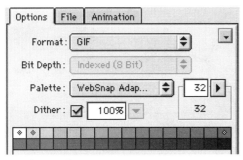

❽ *The* GIF format *options.*

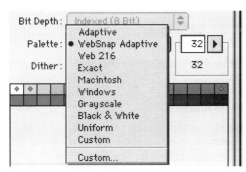

❾ *The* GIF Palette *list.*

When working with a GIF file, you have many other choices for exporting the file. The primary choice is the type of color palette used to create the image. The three choices for GIF graphics are Web 216, Adaptive, and WebSnap Adaptive. Web 216 palette lets you limit your GIF image to only Web-safe colors. These are the 216 colors that will always look the same no matter what browser or platform people use to view your site.

To set the GIF Web 216 palette options:

1. Choose GIF from the Export Preview window Format list. This gives you the GIF options ❽.

2. Choose Web 216 from the Palette list ❾.

   TIP This limits the colors in the file to the Web-safe colors. However, most GIF images do not need 216 colors to display properly.

3. Use the Number of Colors list to reduce the number of colors in the document.

   TIP As you reduce the number of colors, Fireworks automatically changes the artwork in the Preview area.

4. If necessary, check the Dither option to create a mixture between two colors to create the illusion of a third.

   TIP It is rarely necessary to dither in Fireworks; dither only if all other options are unsatisfactory.

5. If you choose the Dither option, use the slider to change the dither amount.

6. Check Optimized to automatically lower the number of colors in the document to the minimum amount.

GIF Web 216 Palette

Using the Web-safe palette can cause problems with artwork that has blends ❿–⓫. A better alternative for artwork with blends is the *Adaptive* palette. Adaptive means that Fireworks first chooses those colors in the image that match the Web-safe palette. It then adds the non–Web-safe colors ⓬. This means that you have a combination of colors that are Web-safe and not Web-safe. *(For a comparison of the results converting images using Web 216 or Adaptive palettes, see the color insert.)*

To set the GIF Adaptive palette options:

1. Choose GIF from the Export Preview window Format list.

2. Choose Adaptive from the Palette list.

3. Use the rest of the GIF palette options described in the previous exercise to lower the number of colors in the document.

TIP If you choose an Adaptive palette, it means that when your artwork is viewed on an 8-bit monitor, the colors will be dithered.

Other Palette Options

- Use Macintosh or Windows palettes when creating artwork for presentations or software to be shown on a specific platform.

- Choose Grayscale or Black and White for certain print applications.

- Choose Custom to open a swatches palette saved from Fireworks *(see page 187)* or from Photoshop.

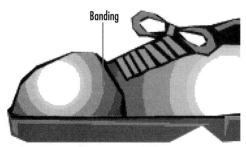

Banding

❿ *The Web-safe palette limits the number and selection of colors. This can cause* **banding** *in the transition of blends.*

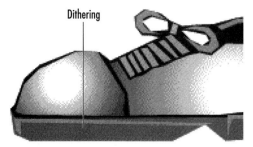

Dithering

⓫ *Applying* **dithering** *for the Web-safe palette reduces the banding, but the dithering in the areas of solid color may not be desirable.*

⓬ *Using the* **Adaptive palette** *allows a mixture of Web-safe and other colors. This gives a smooth, nondithered look for blends and flat art.*

⓭ *The type of image that converts well using the* **WebSnap Adaptive palette.** *This allows the flat color of the heart and paper to stay within Web-safe colors while the photograph of the pen uses an adaptive palette of many other colors.*

Many Web sites try to limit all their graphics to Web-safe colors. Many times, especially with photos, it is not possible to use the Web-safe palette. However, Fireworks has another palette that allows you to combine both the Web-safe and Adaptive palettes. This is the WebSnap Adaptive palette.

When the WebSnap Adaptive palette is chosen, if a color is within 7 units of a Web-safe color, that color is converted into a Web-safe color. The benefit is that areas filled with flat color can be shifted so they do not get dithered when viewed on 256-color monitors **⓭**.

To set the WebSnap Adaptive palette options:

1. Choose GIF from the Export Preview window Format list.

2. Choose WebSnap Adaptive from the Palette list.

3. Use the rest of the GIF palette options described in the exercise on page 183 to lower the number of colors in the document.

TIP The WebSnap Adaptive palette is excellent for images that have large areas of flat colors in photographic images.

In addition to lowering the number of colors for a GIF image, you can control the individual color swatches in the palette. For instance, you can lock a color so it cannot be removed as you lower the number of colors. You can shift a color to the Web-safe palette. You can replace the values of a color. You can also add or delete colors.

To control the colors in a GIF palette:

1. Click a color in the palette that you want to control.

   TIP Shift-click to select contiguous colors. Command/Ctrl-click to select non-contiguous colors.

2. Click the Replace Color button **⑭** to open the system color picker where you can modify the values for the selected color.

3. Click the Web Color button **⑭** to shift the selected color to the nearest Web-safe color.

4. Click the Lock Color button **⑭** to lock the color so that it cannot be shifted nor deleted.

5. Click the Add Color button **⑭** to add a new swatch to the color palette.

6. Click the Delete Color button **⑭** to delete the selected color.

   TIP Colors that have been locked or modified can be identified by the swatch feedback symbols **⑮** in the color palette.

   TIP Deselect Show Swatch Feedback in the Export Color menu *(see page 187)* to hide the swatch feedback symbols.

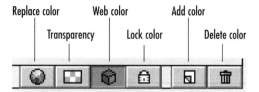

⑭ *The* **color palette controls** *let you change the GIF palette colors.*

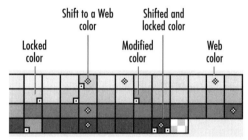

⑮ *The* **swatch feedback symbols** *in the GIF palette tell you if the color has been locked or modfied.*

Control GIF Palette

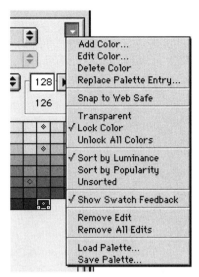

⓰ *The* Export color menu.

In addition to the color controls under the color swatches, the Color Export menu **⓰** gives you additonal controls for organizing an export palette.

To use the Color Export menu:

1. Choose Unlock All Colors to unlock all the colors in the color palette.

   TIP A locked color may be deleted when Unlock All Colors is chosen, depending on the number of colors in the palette.

2. Choose Sort by Luminance or Sort by Popularity to rearrange the colors.

3. Choose Remove Edit or Remove All Edits to restore the selected swatch or all swatches to their original state.

You can also save and load palettes to use in other images. This can help give your site a unified appearance.

To save a palette:

1. Open the Color Export menu and choose Save Palette **⓰**.

2. Name the palette and specify where you want to save it.

3. Click Save.

To load a palette:

1. Choose Load Palette from the Color Export menu in the Export Preview window.

2. Find the palette you want to load and then click OK.

   TIP Fireworks can load palettes saved using Adobe Photoshop.

The JPEG file format allows you to keep more colors in your document. The size of the file is lowered by *compressing* the image. Unlike some compression methods that save all the information in an image, JPEG compressions are *lossy*. This means that information in the image is thrown away, or lost, as the image is made smaller. *(For a color illustration of saving with various compression settings, see the color insert.)*

TIP Do not use JPEG compression on your only copy of a file because you lose information in the image. Save the file as a Fireworks PNG file to preserve all the information.

To set the JPEG options:

1. Choose JPEG from the Format list.

2. Drag the quality slider to change the file size—the lower the quality, the smaller the file **⑰**.

TIP Lowering the file size can make the image look coarse or splotchy **⑱**.

3. Set the Smoothing amount to slightly blur the image. This softens the effects of lowering the file quality **⑲**. *(See the color insert for examples of the various JPEG settings.)*

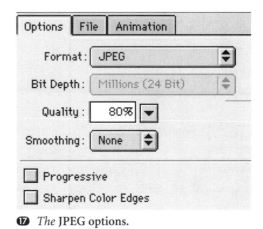

⑰ *The* JPEG options.

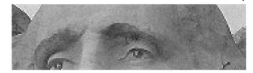
80% Quality

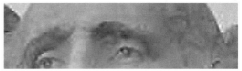
20% Quality

⑱ Lowering the quality of a JPEG image *degrades the image by deleting details and creating square blocks in the image*

With smoothing   Without smoothing

⑲ Adding Smoothing *to a JPEG can reduce the coarseness of the image, but it blurs the image.*

Sharpen
Edges off

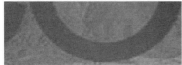

Sharpen
Edges on

⓴ *The* **Sharpen Edges** setting *helps keep the flat areas of color, such as type, crisp against the background of an image.*

If you have added type to an image, it may become blurred or splotchy when it is exported as a JPEG image. The Sharpen Color Edges setting helps avoid that situation **⓴**.

To sharpen the edges of a JPEG image:

1. Choose JPEG from the Format list.

2. Choose Sharpen Color Edges from the JPEG controls.

TIP Sharpen Color Edges does not sharpen the entire image, just where there is a flat area of color against a different colored background.

TIP Sharpen Edges adds a small amount to the size of the file.

You have a choice as to how your graphics are revealed as they download. You can set the image to be revealed gradually **⓴**. This lets visitors decide faster whether or not the image is important to see completely.

To create images that appear gradually:

For GIF images choose Interlaced.

or

For JPEG images choose Progressive.

⓴ *How* **interlaced or progressive images** appear as they are downloaded into a file.

Creating Web graphics is a balancing act between lowering the file size and maintaining the image quality. With all the choices available, you might find it hard to remember which settings give you the best image. Fireworks lets you compare different settings so you can see for yourself which setting produces the best image while lowering the file size. This is one of the most important aspects of working within the Export Preview window.

To compare export settings:

1. In the Export Preview window, change from the 1-Preview icon to either the 2- or 4-Preview icons ㉒. This divides the Preview area into smaller sections ㉓.

2. Click each of the sections to set export options.

TIP The active section is surrounded by a black line which indicates that the settings are being applied to that part of the preview area.

3. Use the image details to compare the image quality as well as the file size and estimated download time.

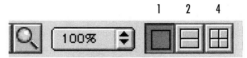

㉒ *The* 1-, 2-, *and* 4-Preview Window *icons.*

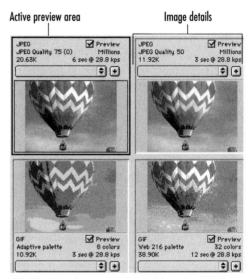

㉓ *The* **Preview area** *divided into four sections.*

Compare Export Settings

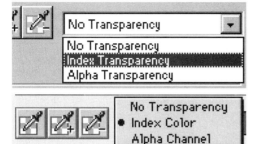

㉔ *The* **Transparent GIF** *controls for Windows (top) and Macintosh (bottom).*

One of the main advantages of the GIF format is that certain areas of an image can be made transparent. This allows you to have a Web graphic that blends into the background of the page. There are two ways to create a transparent GIF. The first method lets you pick the colors within the color table and set them to be transparent. The second method lets you pick the colors directly in the image.

To create a transparent GIF (by color table):

1. Set the image that you want to make transparent over the background color of the Web page. This makes it easier to have the transparency blend smoothly.
2. Choose Index Color from the Transparency list **㉔**.
3. Use the Eyedropper to click the color in the color table that you want to make transparent. The transparent area is indicated with a checkerboard grid **㉕**.
4. Use the Eyedropper with the plus (+) sign **㉔** to select additional colors to make transparent.
5. Use the Eyedropper with the minus (–) sign **㉔** to deselect colors.

㉕ *The* **Eyedropper** *allows you to select those colors in the image that should be transparent.*

To create a transparent GIF (directly in image):

1. Place the image over the background color of the Web page.
2. Choose Index Color from the Transparency list.
3. Use the Eyedropper to click the portion of the image that should be transparent **㉕**.
4. Use the plus Eyedropper to add more colors to the transparency.
5. Use the minus Eyedropper to delete colors from the transparency.

Once you give an image a transparent background, you then need to control the matte setting. This makes the image blend better with other images it passes over . Strictly speaking, JPEG images don't have transparency. However, setting the matte color lets you change the background of the JPEG and make sure the image blends into the background seamlessly.

To choose the matte color:

1. Set the GIF transparency.

2. Use the matte color well to open the pop-up swatches panel.

3. Choose the color closest to the backgrounds or images that you expect the file to be placed over.

TIP If you do not know the color of the background, use the none button in the swatches panel to set no matte color.

Gray matte

Black matte

26 *Changing the* **matte color** *changes the color of the edges of a transparent image.*

Once you have selected export settings, you can save them for use later.

To save export settings:

1. Choose File > **Export** and set the Export settings to the way you want.

2. Click the Save Current Settings button at the top of the Preview windows to open the Preset Name dialog box.

3. Give the settings a name and then click OK. This adds the settings to the Saved Settings list.

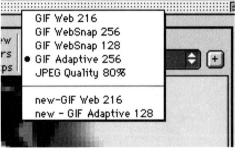

27 *The* **Export settings** *list.*

To use saved export settings:

1. Choose File > Export.

2. Choose the previously saved export setting from the the Saved Settings list **27**.

3. Export the file as usual.

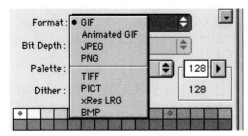

❷❽ *The* **Export format** *list.*

❷❾ *The* **Set Defaults** *button sets the export defaults for the file.*

Although Fireworks was designed for Web graphics, Fireworks does convert images for other purposes.

Exporting Other File Formats

Choose among the other file formats shown in the Export Preview window's format list **❷❽**.

- Choose **Animated GIF** to create animations. *(See Chapter 19, "Animations.")*

- Choose **PNG** for on-screen presentations such as Microsoft PowerPoint, Macromedia Director, or Authorware.

- Choose **PNG** for Web graphics that can be seen with specialized plug-ins.

- Choose **TIFF** for graphics to be inserted into page-layout programs such as QuarkXPress or PageMaker.

- Choose **PICT** (Mac) or **BMP** (Win) for applications that cannot read any of the other formats.

- Choose **xRes LRG** to convert your graphics to Macromedia's imaging program xRes.

You can also set the default export settings for a document. This saves the export settings so they are always available in the Export Preview.

To set the export defaults:

1. Choose File > Export and set the export options as desired.

2. Click the Set Defaults button **❷❾**. This saves the settings with the file.

TIP The export defaults are the options listed in the Export list for Slice objects *(see page 211).*

As discussed in Chapter 11, Fireworks has a powerful batch-processing command to process and export multiple files.

To set the export options for batch processing:

1. Choose File>**Batch Process**. This opens the Batch Processing dialog box ㉚.

TIP (Win) The dialog box is called Batch Process.

2. Click Export and then click the Export ellipsis (...) button. This opens the Batch Export dialog box ㉛.

3. Choose an export preset from the Export settings list *(See page 192 for how to add to the export settings list.)*

    or

    Choose the Use Settings from Each File to use the Export Defaults for each file.

    or

    Click the ellipsis (...) button to open the Export Preview dialog box where you can set specific export options.

4. Click OK to start the batch processing.

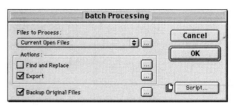

㉚ *The* **Batch Processing** *dialog box.*

Export settings   Custom button

㉛ *The* **Batch Export** *dialog box.*

You can scale the document as part of the export process.

To scale an exported image:

1. Click the File tab of the Export Preview dialog box. This opens the File Scale and Export Area options ㉜.

2. Use the Percentage (%) slider or type in the field to scale the image to a percentage of its original size.

    or

    Enter an amount in the *W* (width) or *H* (height) fields to scale the image to an absolute measurement.

TIP With Constrain selected, the width and height of the image keep the proportions of the original image.

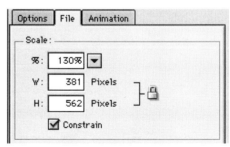

㉜ *The* **Scale controls** *of the File tab of the Export Preview dialog box.*

➂➂ *The* **Export Area** *tool in the Toolbox.*

➂➃ *Use the* **Export Area** *tool to* **drag a rectangle** around the area you want to export.

➂➄ *The* **Export Area tool** *in the Export Preview dialog box.*

➂➅ *Move the* **Export Area handles** *to set the area to be exported.*

As you are working on a document, you may want to export just a certain portion of the image. You can use the Export Area tool to select and export a portion of the image.

To export a portion of an image:

1. Choose the Export Area tool from the Toolbox **➂➂**.
2. Drag a rectangle around the area you want to export **➂➃**.
3. Adjust the handles so they are around the area you want to export.
4. Double-click inside the rectangle or click the Export button in the Tool Options panel. Only the selected area appears in the Export Preview window.

TIP Press the Esc key on the keyboard or choose another tool to leave the Export Area tool.

5. Export the file as usual.

You can also crop an image while you are working inside the Export Preview area.

To use the Export Area tool in the Export Preview:

1. Choose File > **Export** to open the Export Preview dialog box.
2. Click the Export Area tool **➂➄** at the bottom the the preview area.
3. Adjust the handles **➂➅** so the rectangle surrounds the area you want to export.
4. Export the file as usual.

TIP Choose another tool at the bottom of the preview area for the handles to disappear.

You can also control the size of the export area numerically using the Export Area controls of the File tab in the Export Preview dialog box.

To export a portion of an image numerically:

1. Select Export Area within the File tab ③⑦.

2. Use the *X* and *Y* fields to set the upper left corner of the area to be exported.

3. Use the *W* and *H* fields to set the width and height of the exported area.

TIP When you set the export area numerically, you see the same handles as when you use the Export Area tool. You can drag the handles in the box that surrounds the selected portion to adjust the selection.

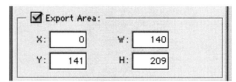

③⑦ *The* **Export Area controls** *of the File tab of the Export Preview dialog box.*

Once you have exported an image using certain settings, you can easily export the document again using those same settings.

To use the Export Again command:

1. Use Export command on a document.

2. Make whatever changes you want and then choose **File > Export Again.** This bypasses the Export Preview dialog box and lets you name and save the file.

TIP The Export Again command is available when you reopen a saved file.

Export Wizard   Export To Size Wizard

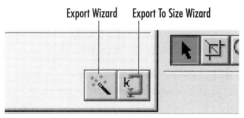

38 *The* **Export Wizard and Export Size Wizard** *can guide you through exporting files.*

39 *Use* **Export Wizard dialog screens** *to select the proper export format for your image or to analyze the current format.*

40 *The* **Export To Size Wizard dialog box.**

You can use the Export Wizard to guide you through the various export settings.

To use the Export Wizard:

1. Choose **File > Export** and then click the Export Wizard button **38** in the Export Preview window. This opens the Export Wizard screen **39**.

   or

   Choose **File > Export Wizard**. This opens the Export Wizard screen **39**.

2. Click Select an Export Format to have the Export Wizard choose the format that is most appropriate for your image.

   or

   Click Analyze Current Settings to have Fireworks analyze whether or not the current format is appropriate.

3. Check Target Export File Size to limit the size of the final exported file.

4. Click Continue for each of the Export Wizard screens to complete the Export Wizard process.

Many web site managers set a maximum size (K count) for images on the site. Rather than trying to calculate the settings to reduce each file, you can use the Export To Size Wizard.

To use the Export Size Wizard:

1. In the Export Preview dialog box, click the Export To Size Wizard button **38**. This opens the Export To Size Wizard dialog box **39**.

2. Set the Target export file size and then click OK. Fireworks automatically computes the settings to export the file at this size.

3. Check to make sure the final size is at the correct level and save the file.

Export Size Wizard; Export Wizard

In addition to exporting Web graphics, Fireworks lets you export files in special formats for use in other applications.

To use the Export Special command:

1. Choose File >Export Special and then choose from one of the submenu options.

2. Choose Export as Files. This opens the Save As dialog box where you can choose to save as Layers, Slice Objects or Frames **❹**.

   or

   Choose Export as CSS Layers. This opens the Save As dialog box where you can save the document as cascading style sheets that can be used in web page layout programs such as Dreamweaver.

   or

   Choose Export as Image Well. This saves the file in the format used with Lotus Domino Designer R5.

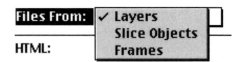

❹ *The Export Files command lets you choose exporting* layers, slice objects, or frames.

HOTSPOTS AND URLS 16

One of the popular uses of Web graphics is as hotspots that act like buttons users can click to move to another Web page. So, for example, a graphic of the United States, could have hotspots over the different parts of the country. If viewers click over the hotspot for the Northeast, it brings them to a Web page for that region. Similar hotspots could be created over the Southeast, the Midwest, and so on. Fireworks offers powerful tools for working with links and applying them to hotspots in an image.

In this chapter you will learn how to

Draw hotspot objects.

Show and hide hotspot objects.

Convert objects into hotspots.

Move and modify hotspots.

Change the shape of hotspots.

Apply a single URL link.

Work with the History list.

Set the hotspot options.

Import links.

Organize links into Libraries.

Delete links.

Edit existing links.

Set the Document Properties.

You can draw hotspots directly on your image using one of the three hotspot tools. Hotspots are automatically drawn on the Web layer even if that layer is not the selected layer.

To draw a rectangular or circular hotspot object:

1. Choose the Rectangle or Circle hotspot tool in the Toolbox ❶.

2. Drag to create a rectangle or circle that defines the hotspot area ❷.

TIP Hold the Shift key to constrain the Rectangle to a square. (The Circle tool creates only circles, not ellipses.)

TIP Hold the Option/Alt key to drag from the center outward.

To draw a polygon hotspot object:

1. Choose the Polygon hotspot tool in the Toolbox ❶.

2. Click to set the first point of the polygon.

3. Click the next corner of the polygon to make the first line segment.

4. Click again to set the remaining segments.

5. Close the the hotspot object by clicking again on the first point.

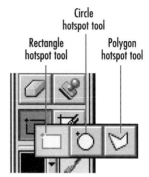

❶ *The hotspot tools.*

Circle hotspot tool
Rectangle hotspot tool
Polygon hotspot tool

❷ **Hotspots** *can be rectangular, circular, or irregularly shaped polygons.*

You use the Web layer to control the visibility of hotspots.

To show and hide hotspot objects:

1. To hide the hotspot objects, click the Eye icon for the Web layer ❸.

2. To show the hotspot objects, click the empty area in the Eye icon column for the Web layer.

    or

    Use any of the hotpsot tools on the image. This automatically shows the Web layer.

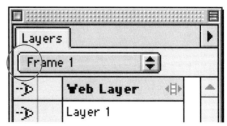

❸ *The Show/Hide icon for the Web layer.*

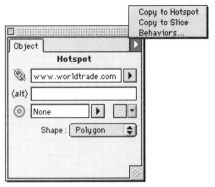

④ *The* Hotspot Object panel menu.

⑤ *Use the Selection or Subselection tools to* modify hotspot objects.

⑥ *The* **Shape menu** *of the Hotspot Object panel.*

You can also convert any Fireworks paths into hotspot objects.

To convert objects into hotspots:

1. Choose the path or paths you wish to convert.

2. Choose **Insert > Hotspot**.

   or

   Choose Copy to Hotspot from the Object panel menu **④**.

   or

   Drag the object square in the Layers panel from the object layer to the Web layer *(for more information, see page 86)*. This copies the shape of the selected object into a hotspot object.

   TIP When curved objects are converted to hotspots, they are converted to polygons with a series of small straight-line segments.

Once you have created a hotspot object, you can still move or modify it.

To move and modify hotspot objects:

1. Choose either the Selection or the Subselection tools in the Toolbox.

2. Drag inside a hotspot object to move it to a new positon.

3. Drag one of the anchor points of the hotspot object to change its shape **⑤**.

You can also convert hotspot objects from one shape to another.

To convert hotspot shapes:

1. Choose the hotspot object you want to convert.

2. Choose a shape from the hotspot panel shape list **⑥**.

Hotspot Objects

URL stands for Uniform Resource Locator, which is an address of a specific page or file on the Internet. Once you have created hotspot objects, you can then apply URL links to them. This lets visitors to your site click an area of the image and switch to a different Web page.

❼ *The* **Links field** *in the Hotspot Object panel.*

If you need to apply only one or two URL links, you can easily type them directly into the Hotspot Object panel.

To apply a single URL link:

1. Select the hotspot object that needs a URL link.

2. Type the URL in the Links field in the Hotpsot Object panel **❼**.

❽ *The* **history list** *in the Hotspot Object panel.*

As you apply or create URL links, a record of each link is retained as the history list. This list makes it easy to reapply a URL link without having to type it.

To work with the history list:

1. Select the hotspot object you want to apply a URL link to.

2. Press the pop-up history list next to the Links field in the Hotspot Object panel **❽**.

3. Choose the link you want to apply to the hotspot.

TIP When you open a Fireworks file that has URL links, those links are automatically added to the history.

TIP The history list is only a temporary list and is deleted when you quite Freworks. If you want a permanent record of all the URL links, you can add the list to a library *(see page 205)*.

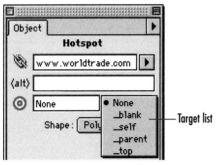

⑨ *The* **Hotspot panel commands.**

Hotspots do not have to have URL links assigned to them. You can also leave the hotspot unlinked.

To appy no link to a hotspot:

1. Select the hotspot.

2. Choose No URL (no HREF) from the History listing.

TIP This can be useful when working with behaviors. *(See Chapter 18, "Behaviors" for more information.)*

Alternate text field   Target menu

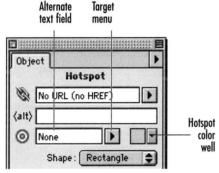

⑩ *The* **Hotspot options.**

In addition to the URL links, there are several other settings for hotspot objects. These are optional and do not affect the URL link.

To set the Hotspot options:

1. In the (alt) field ⑨, type the Alternate text to be displayed in a browser while the image is loading or if it is unavailable.

2. Use the Target list or type in the field ⑨ the window or frame you want the link to open to.

3. Use the hotspot color well ⑩ to set the color for different hotpsots.

Typing URL links is fine if you only have a couple of links to add; however, complicated Web sites can have hundreds of links. Fortunately, Fireworks offers you many features for working with large numbers of links. For instance, rather than type in links one by one, you can import import URLs from any HTML file, Netscape Navigator bookmarks, or Internet Explorer favorites.

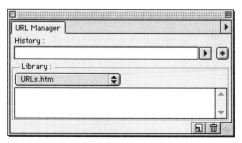

⓫ *The* **URL Manager** *panel.*

To import links:

1. If the URL Manager **⓫** is not visible, choose **Window**>**URL Manager.**

2. Choose Import URLs from the panel options list **⓬**.

3. Navigate to find an HTML files, Navigator bookmarks file, or Internet Navigator favorites file.

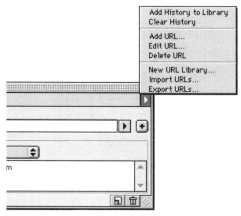

⓬ *The* **URL Manager** *options list.*

Finally, you can also create *libraries,* or groups of URLs. The default library is called URLs.html. However, you can create your own libraries. This allows you to group all the URLs for a certain Web site or client.

To create a URL library:

1. Choose New URL Library from the URL Manager options list. This opens the New URL Library dialog box **⓭**.

2. Type the name of the library and click OK. This adds the library to the library list.

TIP Libraries are available between documents.

TIP To delete a library from the list, remove the library file located in the folder Fireworks: Settings: URL Libraries.

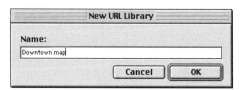

⓭ *The* **New URL Library** *dialog box.*

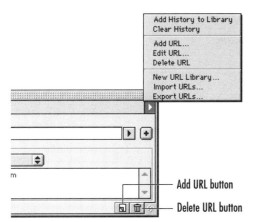

Add URL button

Delete URL button

⑭ *Click the* **Add URL icon** *or choose Add URL from the menu to add URL links to a library.*

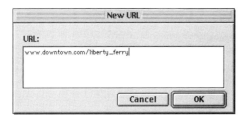

⑮ *The* **New URL dialog box** *lets you type in new links for the selected library.*

As mentioned, the history is a temporary list. However, if you want to keep a permanent record of the links you are working with, you can add them to a Library.

To add the history list to a Library:

1. Create a new library or choose a library from the library list.

2. Choose Add History to Library from the URL Manager menu.

TIP Choose Clear History to delete the URLs in the History list.

To add a new URL link to a Library:

1. Select the library where you want to add the URL link to.

2. Choose Add URL from the URL Manager menu or click the Add URL button ⑭. This opens the New URL dialog box ⑮.

3. Type the URL in the field and then click OK. This adds the URL to the library.

To delete URL links:

1. Choose a library from the URL Manager library list.

2. Choose a link in the library.

3. Choose Delete Link from the URL Manager menu or click the Delete URL button ⑭.

Add History List; Add New URL Link; Delete URL Links

One of the facts of life of working with URL links is they change continually. Fortunately Fireworks provides a simple way to edit URL links in a document.

To edit URL links:

1. Click the URL you want to edit.

2. Choose Edit URL from the URL Manager menu. This opens the Edit URL dialog box 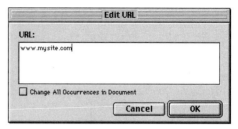.

3. Make whatever changes you want to the URL.

4. Check Change all Occurrences in Document to change all the objects that use that URL.

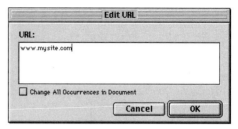

⑯ *The* **Edit URL** *dialog box lets you edit URLs and apply the changes to all occurrences of the URL in the document.*

Before you export a document that contains hotspots, you need to set its Document Properties.

To set the Document Properties:

1. Choose File>Document Properties to open the Document Properties dialog box 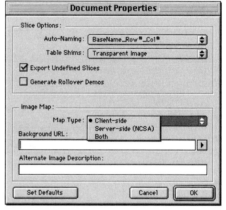.

2. Use the Map Type pop-up list to choose Client-side, Server-side, or Both.

TIP Client-side maps respond more quickly and can be run from any type of server; however, some old browsers cannot read them. Server-side maps require the cooperation of the Internet service provider that hosts your Web site.

3. Use the Background URL list to set a URL link for those areas not controlled by a hotspot.

4. In the Alternative Image Description field type the text you would like to have shown if, for any reason, the browser does not display the image.

⑰ *The* **Document Properties** *dialog box.*

SLICES 17

Why would anyone, after spending hours creating a Web graphic, want to cut it up into pieces? Well, that technique, called *slicing*, creates regions in an image that you can set to behave differently. Slicing images lets you accomplish various effects. Because slicing is actually part of exporting, you should understand how to export files *(see Chapter 15, "Basic Exporting")* before you start this chapter.

In this chapter you will learn how to

Understand the reasons for slices.

Slice using ruler guides.

Create slice objects.

Show and hide slice objects and slice guides.

Set the Slice options.

Set the Export options.

Create a Text slice.

Set the slice options in the Document Properties.

Change the naming conventions.

Custom name slices.

Control table shims.

Work with both hotspots and slice objects.

Export the HTML code for slices.

View graphics in a Web browser.

Copy the HTML code into a Web page layout program.

Why Slices? (Part One)

Slices make it easier to update the images on your Web site ❶. For instance, you might have a portion of the Web-page graphic that changes periodically. Slicing that part of the image makes it easier to update.

Sliced images also are likely to appear faster. Some Web servers can send out multiple images. So the individual slices of an image are downloaded together.

Also the first time visitors view images on the site, those images are *cached*, or stored, on their computers, so the next time visitors come to that image, even on another page, it appears faster because it is already downloaded.

Needs to be cached for many pages   Needs to be updated easily

❶ *Disparate areas of an an image, such as standing elements and elements that must be updated frequently, such as the framed areas shown here, should be sliced.*

The easiest way to slice an image is to use ruler guides to define the slice area.

To slice using ruler guides:

1. Drag a guide from a ruler around the side of the area you want to slice.

2. Drag additional guides until you have defined all the slices for the image ❷.

3. When you save the exported file, set the Slicing to Slice Along Guides ❸.

TIP Fireworks opens Photoshop files with the Photoshop guides intact. They can then be used as slices in Fireworks.

TIP Use hotspot objects *(see Chapter 16)* to add links to slices created by guides.

❷ *Ruler guides can be used to define slices.*

❸ *Use the Slice Along Guides option to use the ruler guides to slice images.*

❹ *The* Slice tool *in the Toolbox.*

Ruler guides may not provide enough control to slice all the areas of the image accurately. For instance, a guide around one area may cut through another area that you don't want sliced. Slice objects let you select the areas that are sliced.

To create Slice Objects:

1. Choose the Slice tool from the Toolbox **❹**. (Be careful, it is sharp.)

2. Drag a rectangle around the area that you want to slice **❺**. This creates a slice object.

3. Use the Selection tools to move or modify slice objects.

❺ *Drag the* Slice tool *to create a* Slice object.

Slice objects create a grid of slice guides that divide the image. There are several controls for showing and hiding slice objects and slice guides.

To show and hide slice objects and slice guides:

1. To show or hide the slice guides **❻**, choose View > **Slice Guides.**

2. To show or hide slice objects **❼**, click the Show/Hide icon for the Web Layer in the Layers panel.

TIP Slice guides are still visible when you hide the slice objects.

TIP The Web Layer is automatically revealed when you create a new slice object.

❻ *The* slice guides *that divide the image are created by the slice objects.*

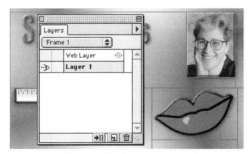

❼ *Use the* Show/Hide icon in the Web Layer *to hide slice objects.*

Create Slice Objects; Show/Hide Slice Objects and Guides

You set the options for slice objects using the Slice object panel.

To set the slice options:

1. If the Object panel is not visible, choose Window>Object.

2. Select a slice object to display the slice object options ❽.

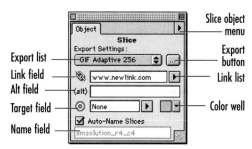

❽ *The* Slice object panel.

Slice objects can also contain URL Links.

To set the link for a slice object:

1. Use the link list ❾ to choose a link from either the current history or the current Library selected in the URL Manager. *(For more information working with the history, libraries, and the URL Manager, see Chapter 16, "Hotspots and URLs.")*

2. To enter a link not in the list, type the link directly into the Link field.

TIP The no URL (noHREF) setting lets you slice an image without a URL link.

❾ *Use the* link list *to display the current history list or the current library in the URL Manager.*

Like hotspot objects, slice objects let you enter the (alt) text and target information. *(For a description of the (alt) text and target fields, see page 203.)* You can also control the color of the slice object.

To set the alt text, target, or slice display:

1. Type the text for the Alt field.

2. Use the Target field or list to set a specific frame or window for the link.

3. Use the Color Well to set the display color for the Slice object.

Flat art for GIF export   Photograph for JPEG export

ⓘ *Slice objects are used for files that mix different types of images such as flat art and photographs.*

Why Slices? (Part Two)

Slicing also comes in handy when you need to use more than one export format for an image **ⓘ**. For instance, artwork that contains primarily flat colors should be exported as GIF files, but artwork with photographic images needs to be saved in the JPEG format. If one file contains both types of artwork, you can use the slice tool to set different export options for each of the different areas.

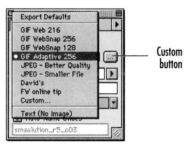

                                    Custom
                                    button

ⓘ *The* **Export list** *controls the export settings for the area defined by the slice object.*

You control how the image under the slice object is exported by choosing the option in the Export list.

To set the slice object Export options:

1. Open the Export list in the Slice object panel **ⓘ**.

2. Choose Export Defaults to apply whatever settings are the current default export settings for the document.

3. Choose one of the saved export settings that are listed in the Export list *(see page 192)*.

4. Click the Custom button to open the Export Preview dialog box where you can set the export settings. *(See Chapter 15, "Basic Exporting," for working with the Export Preview dialog box.)*

What if you want to add some ordinary HTML text to an area of the graphic? This makes it easy to update the information without creating new graphics. Fireworks lets you create a text slice that adds HTML text to that area of the image.

To create a text slice:

1. Select the slice object and set the Export Settings to Text (No Image). The text settings appear **⑫**.

2. Type whatever text you want in the image.

TIP Use whatever HTML codes you want to set the style, color, size, and other attributes of the text. (For more information on the various HTML codes, see *HTML for the World Wide Web: Visual QuickStart Guide* by Elizabeth Castro.)

3. Export as usual.

TIP The area inside a text cell is transparent and uses the canvas color as its background.

TIP You cannot see the text in a text slice in the Fireworks file. You need to export the image and view it in a Web browser before you can see the text **⑬**.

⑫ *The* slice object text settings.

⑬ *The information in a* text slice *as seen through a browser.*

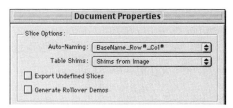

⑭ *The* **Slice Options** *in the Document Properties dialog box.*

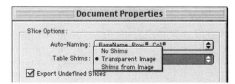

⑮ *The* **Table Shims choices** *in the Document Properties dialog box.*

You also need to set the the Documents Properties dialog box to control how slice objects export.

To set the Document Properties slice options:

1. Choose **File** > **Document Properties** to open the dialog box **⑭**.

2. Check Export Undefined Slices to export all the areas in the document, not just the ones under the slice objects.

   or

   Uncheck Export Undefined Slices to export only areas under slice objects.

TIP When Export Undefined Slices is unchecked, parts of the image create blank cells with the cell color set to the document's canvas color.

When you slice a graphic, Fireworks creates special HTML code that arranges the sliced images into a table. To make sure that the table assembles correctly, Fireworks creates additional 1-pixel images, called *shims*. (In carpentry, shims are thin pieces of wood that you use to make things fit snugly.)

To control table shims:

1. Open the Table Shims list in the Document Properties dialog box **⑮**.

2. Select the shim appearance you prefer.

   - Choose Transparent Image to make the shims transparent. This lets the color of the page show through the shim.

   - Choose Shims from Image to make the shim color the same as the edge of the image. This gives you a more uniform look, especially when one table is nested inside another.

   - Choose No Shims to not create any shims. This is not recommended as your table may not assemble correctly.

Fireworks automatically names the files created by slicing; however, you can choose one of six options as to how those names are created.

To set the auto-naming conventions:

Open the Document Properties dialog box and choose from the Auto-Naming list ⓰. The six choices for naming the file are as follows:

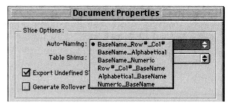

⓰ *The* **Auto-Naming options** *Document Properties dialog box.*

- **BaseName_Row#_Col#** adds suffixes indicating row and column position of the slice.

- **BaseName_Alphabetical** adds an alphabetical suffix.

- **BaseName_Numeric** adds a numbered suffix.

- **Row#_Col#_BaseName** adds a prefix indicating the row and column position of the slice.

- **Alphabetical_BaseName** adds an alphabetical prefix.

- **Numeric_BaseName** adds a numbered prefix.

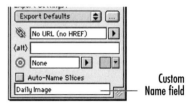

Custom Name field

⓱ *The* **Custom Name field** *in the Slice objects panel.*

You can also override the auto-naming conventions and set your own custom name for a slice. This makes it easy to designate a specific slice for later updating.

To set a custom name for slices:

1. Select the slice object

2. Deselect Auto-Name slices in the Slice object panel. This activates the Custom Name field ⓱.

3. Enter a name in the field.

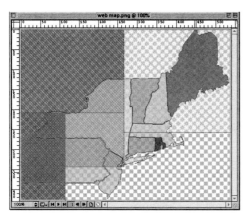

⓲ **Mixing hotspot and slice objects** *creates an image map that is sliced into sections.*

You may think of slice and hotspot objects an "either/or" situation; you either use hotspot objects or you use slice objects. However, there are many instances where you might want to use both. For instance, you can use hotspot objects to set the links for an image map; at the same time you can use slice objects to divide the graphic so it downloads faster **⓲**.

To work with both slice and hotspot objects:

1. If a hotspot overlaps a slice, use the Select Behind tool *(see page 60)*.

2. Use the Arrange commands to send the objects to the front or back of the Web Layer *(see page 83)*.

3. Assign unique colors to the hotspot and slice objects *(see pages 203 and 210)*.

⓳ **The Export dialog box** *lets you control the type of HTML code and its location.*

Sliced graphics require HTML code to reassemble the table correctly.

Exporting HTML code for Slices:

1. In the Export dialog box, open the HTML Style list **⓳**.

2. Set the style of HTML code to Generic. This allows you to paste the code directly into your page-layout program.

3. If you are working with Dreamweaver 2 or FrontPage, set the code for those programs.

4. Use the Location list to control where the HTML file will be created.

5. Use the Setup button to review the Document Properties dialog box.

6. Set the name and other export settings as desired and click the Export button.

It is possible that the HTML code may be assembled differently by different applications. Fireworks lets you set two browsers to preview your files to see how the file will actually appear on the Web. This is especially important when working with behaviors or animations. *(See Chapter 18, "Behaviors" and Chapter 19, "Animations.")*

To set the Web browser and preview a file:

1. Choose File > Preview in Browser > Set Primary Browser and navigate to pick the first Web browser application you want to use to preview files.

2. Choose File > Preview in Browser > Set Secondary Browser and choose the second Web browser application.

3. Choose File > Preview in Browser and choose either of the browsers listed.

TIP Be patient as it takes time for Fireworks to create the code to preview the file.

Once you have created the images and HTML file for a sliced graphic, you can add that HTML code to a Web page-layout program such as Dreamweaver.

To copy HTML code into a Web page:

1. Open the HTML code of the Web page.

2. Use a word processor or text editor to open the HTML code exported by Fireworks ❷⓿.

3. Follow the instructions written in the HTML code for what to copy and where to paste it.

Why Slices? (Part Three)

Another reason for working with slices is to create special behavior effects such as rollovers or image swaps. Behavior effects are covered in the next chapter.

❷⓿ *Fireworks HTML contains the instructions for copying and pasting the code into page-layout programs.*

BEHAVIORS 18

People expect Web pages to do something. With Fireworks you can easily create interactive elements using behavior commands. For instance, a simple rollover behavior allows users to click an object to move to a new Web page. Behaviors also let visitors move over one area to display pictures or animations in another. Adding Behaviors to your Web pages is a way to give visual feedback and enjoyment to people visiting a Web site.

In this chapter you will learn how to

Understand what the rollover states do.

Create the frames for a simple rollover.

Duplicate frames.

Modify the frames of a rollover.

Share an element across frames.

Assign a simple rollover behavior.

Create multiple rollovers.

Edit a behavior.

Delete a behavior.

Assign a Display Status Message behavior.

Create the elements of a swap-image behavior.

Define the areas of a swap-image behavior.

Assign a swap-image behavior.

Create a toggle group.

Export files with behaviors.

When you create image maps *(see Chapter 16, "Hotspots and URLs")*, you give visitors to your Web page only a very subtle hint that they can click there: the cursor changes as it passes over links in the image ❶. Rollovers create a clickable region with visual cues depending on the position or action of the mouse ❷. Some rollovers are simple and only change the appearance of the area under the mouse cursor. Others are more sophisticated and can trigger actions anywhere on the page. There are four states that can be used in rollovers ❸:

- **Plain image** is the look of the image when there is no mouse inside the image. This is the regular state of the rollover image area.

- **Over** is the look of the image when the mouse cursor is moved over the rollover area.

- **Down** is the look of the image when the mouse is released after clicking the rollover. This state is seen on the destination Web page, that is, the page to which the button links.

- **onClick** is the look of the image when the mouse button is pressed. This state is seen as the browser switches to the linked page. Because this state is seen so briefly, Web designers rarely use it.

❶ *When the mouse* **passes over an image map,** *it shows a simple hand cursor.*

❷ *When the mouse* **passes over a rollover.** *it shows the hand cursor and the image variation that was created for the Over state. In this case a glow was added to the silhouette.*

❸ *The* **four rollover states** *can be set for whatever looks you want. Each state gives a different response to the action of the mouse.*

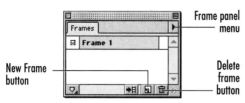

New Frame button

Frame panel menu

Delete frame button

❹ *You create the different rollover states in the* **Frames** *panel.*

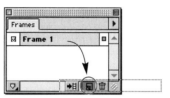

❺ *Drag a frame onto the* **New Frame button** *to duplicate that frame.*

❻ *The* **Duplicate Frame** *command in the* **Frames** *panel menu.*

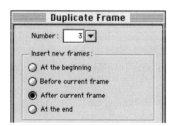

❼ *The* **Duplicate Frame** *dialog box.*

❽ *The first four frames are used for the different rollover states.*

Before you can create a simple rollover, you need to prepare the image by creating the artwork for each of the frames.

To create the frames for a simple rollover:

1. Open the Frames panel by choosing **Window>Frames** ❹.

2. Create the image (with text if necessary) for the basic rollover state.

3. Drag the listing for Frame 1 onto the New Frame button three times to duplicate the frame ❺.

   or

   Choose Duplicate Frame from the Frames panel pop-up list ❻ to open the Duplicate Frame dialog box ❼.

To use the Duplicate Frame dialog box:

1. Adjust the slider control or use the field to enter the number of additional frames. For a four-frame rollover, enter the number 3.

2. Choose After Current Frame to insert the new frames after Frame 1.

3. Click OK. Three additional frames appear in the Frames panel ❽.

   TIP The four frames you have just created are all identical. They now need to be modified to show different looks in the rollover.

Each rollover state comes from the first four frames of the image.

- The Regular state comes from Frame 1.
- The Over state comes from Frame 2.
- The Down state comes from Frame 3.
- The onClick state comes from Frame 4.

Once you have artwork on all four frames for a rollover, you need to modify the individual frames to create the image variations for the rollover states.

To modify the frames of a rollover:

1. Click Frame 2 in the Frames panel to make it the active frame **❾**.

2. Make changes to the appearance of the object.

3. Do the same for frames 3 and 4 of the document.

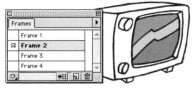

❾ *Change the artwork in each frame to create the different rollover states.*

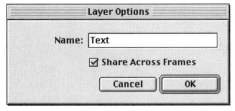

❿ *The* **Layer Options** *lets you set a layer to be shared across frames.*

You may have an element that you want to appear in all the rollover states. Rather than copy and paste this element onto all the frames, it is simpler to put the element on a layer that is shared across frames.

To share an element across frames:

1. Open the Layers panel and create a new layer *(see Chapter 6, "Working With Objects," for more information on working with layers)*.

2. Add the element to be shared onto this layer.

3. Choose Share Layer from the Layers panel menu or choose Layer Options to open the Layer Options dialog box and check Share Across Frames **❿**. The Shared Layer icon appears next to the layer name **⓫**.

TIP Any changes you make to an object on a shared layer are seen across all the frames of the document **⓬**.

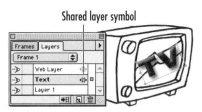

⓫ *A* **shared layer** *lets you see the elements of that layer on all frames.*

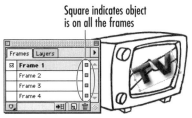

⓬ *When an object on a shared layer is modified, the changes appear on all the frames of the Frames panel.*

⓫ *A* **Slice object** *drawn over an image for a simple rollover.*

Add Behavior   Delete Behavior   Behavior panel menu

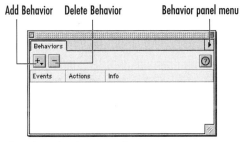

⓮ *The* **Behaviors panel.**

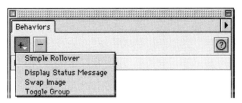

⓯ *The* **Add Behavior choices.**

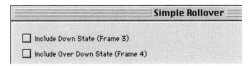

⓰ *The choices for a* **Simple Rollover.**

⓱ *A Simple Rollover as displayed in the Behaviors panel.*

Once you have created all the frames, you can assign the rollover behavior for the rollover area.

To assign a simple rollover behavior:

1. Select the object on one of the frames and choose **Insert** > **Slice.**

   or

   Use the Slice tool to create a slice that covers the image for the rollover ⓫.

   TIP The slice object needs to cover the entire object, including any glows or shadow effects.

2. Open the Behaviors panel by choosing **Window** > **Behaviors** ⓮.

3. With the slice object selected, click the Add Behavior button and choose Simple Rollover ⓯. The Rollover dialog box appears ⓰.

4. If needed, check the states for frames 3 and 4 and click OK. The behavior is listed in the Behaviors panel ⓱.

5. Use the Slice Object panel to set the URL links. *(For more information on working with slice objects for links, see Chapter 17, "Slices.")*

   TIP To check to see if the rollover is working correctly, use the Preview in Browser command *(see page 216).*

Often you need to create more than one simple rollover for a Web site. This is especially true when creating navigational bars that allow visitors to click to move to different areas of the Web site.

To create multiple rollovers:

1. Create the images and frames for all the rollovers.

2. Use the Slice tool or **Window > Insert Slice Object** command to create a slice object for each rollover area **⑱**.

3. Use the Behavior panel to apply the Simple Rollover command to each individual slice object.

⑱ *Create a slice object for each area when creating multiple rollovers.*

Behaviors assigned to objects can be edited or deleted at any time.

To edit a behavior:

1. Double-click the Behavior in the Behaviors panel. This reopens the dialog box for the behavior.

   or

   Choose Edit from the Behaviors panel menu **⑱**.

2. Make the changes in the Behavior dialog box and then click OK.

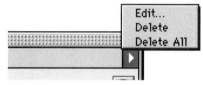

⑲ Delete or edit behaviors *using the Behaviors panel menu.*

To delete a behavior:

Click the Delete Behavior button or choose Delete from the Behavior panel menu **⑲**.

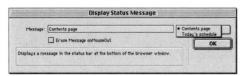

⓴ *The* **Display Status Message** *dialog box.*

㉑ *The* **Event choices** *in the Behaviors panel.*

In addition to rollovers, there are other behaviors you can assign to objects. The Display Status Message command lets you write a custom message that is displayed in the status bar of the browser.

To assign a Display Status Message behavior:

1. Select a hotspot or slice object.

2. Click the Add Behavior button and choose Display Status Message from the Behaviors list. The dialog box appears ⓴.

3. Type the message in the field.

4. Click Erase Message on MouseOut to delete the message when the cursor is moved away from the area and click OK.

5. Click the event in the Behaviors panel to change the event that triggers the behavior ㉑. The three choices are

- onMouseOver, which displays the message as the cursor is over the area of the object.

- onMouseOut, which displays the message after the cursor has first been over the area of the object and is then taken away.

- onClick, which displays the message as the mouse button is pressed over the area of the object.

TIP You can add more than one Display Status Message behavior to the same slice or hotspot object. This makes it possible to have one message as the cursor passes over the object and a different message as the cursor leaves the object.

TIP To check to see if the rollover is working correctly, use the Preview in Browser command *(see page 216)*.

A simple rollover changes only the image directly under the area of the slice object. Fireworks also lets you create a *swap-image* behavior. This means that moving the cursor over one area of the image triggers an action to show something elsewhere in the image ㉒–㉓.

You need to create certain elements in order to create a swap-image behavior. The order that you create these elements is also important.

To create the elements of a swap-image behavior:

1. Create the frames with different images under the area to be changed.

   or

   Create an external file, such as a GIF animation, which can be set to display under the area to be changed. *(For more information on creation GIF animations, see Chapter 19, "Animations.")*

2. Create a slice object (but not a hotspot) to define the area to be changed by the behavior *(see page 225)*.

3. Create a hotspot or slice object to define the area that triggers the behavior *(see page 225)*.

4. Assign a swap-image behavior to the hotspot or slice object *(see page 226)*.

To create the frames for the area to be changed:

1. Create a frame with the normal state for the image ㉔.

2. Duplicate this frame and create artwork for the changed area of the image ㉕.

3. If necessary, duplicate this frame and create artwork for any additional swap-image behaviors.

㉒ *When the cursor is outside an object, the image is displayed in its normal state.*

㉓ *When the cursor passes over the image, the* **Swap-image behavior** *changes the display of another part of the image.*

㉔ *Frame 1 displays the normal state of the image.*

㉕ *Frame 2 displays the second state of the image.*

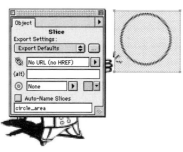

㉖ *The area to be changed in a swap-image behavior must be covered with a slice object.*

After you create the frames, you then need to add a slice object that defines the area to be changed.

To define the area to be changed:

1. Drag a slice object that completely covers the area to be changed **㉖**.

2. In the Slice Objects panel, set the Export Settings that for the area.

TIP Leave the Link to No URL (noHREF).

3. Give this slice a distinctive name.

TIP Although a distinctive name is not necessary, it will help as you assign the area for the Swap Image behavior.

㉗ *The area that triggers the change can be defined with either a hotspot or a slice object.*

You can use either a hotspot or slice object to define the area that triggers the swap-image behavior.

To define the area that triggers the change:

1. Select the path or object that triggers the change.

2. To create a hotspot area the same shape as the path, choose **Insert > Hotspot ㉗**.

   or

   Use any of the hotspot tools to define the area for the rollover.

TIP Using a hotspot object allows you to make a nonrectangular area.

   or

   To create a slice object that can trigger the change, choose **Insert > Slice**.

TIP Using a slice object to trigger the change allows you to have that area also change its appearance.

The final step in creating a swap-image behavior is to assign the behavior to the Hotspot or Slice that triggers the action.

To assign the swap-image behavior:

1. Select the hotspot or slice object that triggers the change.

2. Choose Swap Image from the Behaviors panel. The Swap Image dialog box appears.

3. Choose the name of the slice object that defines the area that triggers the change **28**.

   or

   Click the slice object in the slice area diagram **28**.

4. Choose the frame that is to be inserted into the area **29**.

   or

   Designate an image file that is to be inserted into the area **29**.

5. Click the Restore Image onMouseOut checkbox. This changes the area back to the original frame or image when the cursor leaves the trigger area.

6. Click OK to return to the document. The swap image behavior appears in the Behaviors panel **30**.

TIP To see if the swap image behavior is working correctly, use the Preview in Browser command *(see page 216)*.

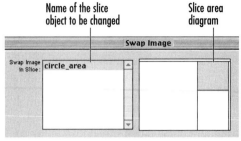

Name of the slice object to be changed / Slice area diagram

28 *The* Swap Image dialog box *lets you designate the area that is to be changed by the swap-image behavior.*

29 *Use the* Source of Swap *controls to choose the frame or external file that will display in the changed image area.*

30 *The* swap-image details *are listed in the Behaviors panel.*

31 *A* **toggle group** *lets you treat a group of buttons as a unit that displays different states.*

32 *Frame 2 (left) and frame 3 (right) of a* **toggle group.**

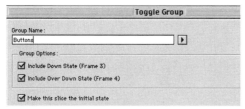

33 *The* **Toggle Group** *dialog box.*

The final behavior is a toggle group. A toggle group combines a series of rollovers so that when one rollover is triggered, the others in the group are also triggered **31**. For example, as one button is pressed, another botton pops up.

To create a toggle group:

1. Create the rollover states for all the objects in the group. Each state needs its own frame **32**.

2. Draw a slice object over each rollover area.

3. Assign rollover behaviors to the slice objects, as described on page 221.

4. Select a slice object and then choose Toggle Group from the Behaviors panel. This opens the Toggle Group dialog box **33**.

5. Enter a name for the toggle group or use the Group Name pop-up list.

TIP The Group Name pop-up list contains a list of all current group names in a file.

6. Check to include either the Down (Frame 3) or the Over Down (Frame 4) state, or both.

7. Check Make This Slice the Initial State to have the slice appear in its Down state when initially viewed.

8. Click OK to return to the document.

9. Repeat steps 4–8 for each slice in the group.

TIP To check to see if the toggle group is working correctly, use the Preview in Browser command *(see page 216).*

Toggle Group

The last step in working with behaviors is exporting them.

To export files with behaviors:

1. Set the slice object export options and Document Properties for the slice objects. *(See Chapter 17, "Slices," for more infomation on setting the export options for slice objects.)*

2. Choose File > **Export** and set the export options accordingly. *(See Chapter 15, "Basic Exporting," for more information on the export settings.)*

3. Click Next and name the file.

4. Choose the style of HTML code **34**. Use Dreamweaver 2 or Front Page if you are working with those programs. Use Generic for others. Use Dreamweaver Library to export as the library code that can be used within Dreamweaver.

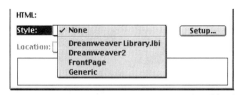

34 *The* **HTML Style** *choices in the Export dialog box.*

ANIMATIONS 19

I

t is hard to believe that just a few years ago, there were very few Web pages with animated images. Now, many Web images move, change from one shape to another, and perform other animations. Fireworks gives you all the tools you need to create these simple animations. (The GIF animations created in Fireworks are called simple animations to distinguish them from the more sophisticated animations created by programs such as Flash and Dreamweaver.)

In this chapter you will learn how to

Open the Frames panel.

Distribute objects onto frames.

Control frames in the Layer panel.

Share across frames.

Copy objects onto frames.

Distribute vector layers and pages onto frames.

Create symbols and instances.

Work with symbols and instances.

Tween objects.

Turn on and use onion skinning.

Use multi-frame editing.

Use the animation controls.

Set the animation export controls.

Set the timing and disposal of an animation.

Set the number of times an animation plays.

Specify which frames to export.

Any animation—cartoon, Web graphic, or motion picture—is basically a series of still images that appear in quick succession, giving the illusion of motion. (Just like the flip books you played with as a child.)

In Fireworks animations are controlled primarily by the Frames panel.

To open the Frames panel:

Choose **Windows** > **Frames**. The Frames panel appears **❶**.

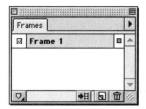

❶ *The* Frames *panel.*

If you have several different Fireworks objects you can easily put them on individual frames to create a simple animation.

To distribute objects onto frames:

1. Create a file with all the objects on Frame 1.

2. Select all the objects and choose Distribute to Frames from the Frames panel menu **❷**. New frames are created with each of the objects in the selection on its own frame **❸**.

TIP The number of objects determines the number of frames.

TIP The Distribute to Frames command does not work if objects are on shared layers *(see page 220)*.

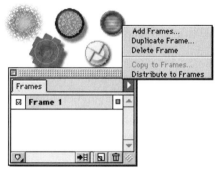

❷ *The* Distribute to Frames *command.*

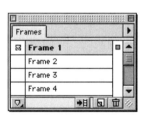

❸ *Choosing* Distribute to Frames *sends each of the original objects onto its own frame.*

Fireworks also gives you a shortcut in the Layers panel to move from frame to frame.

To control frames in the Layers panel:

1. Open the Layers panel.

2. Use the Frame pop-up list **❹** and choose the frame you want to move to.

TIP Use the animation controls to preview the animation *(see page 240).*

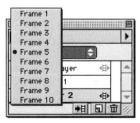

❹ *The* Frame *pop-up list.*

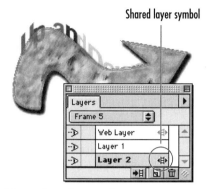

Shared layer symbol

❺ *A* layer *shared across frames.*

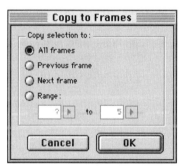

❻ *The* Copy to Frames *dialog box.*

When you create animations, you may need to put the same image on a series of frames. Fireworks offers two ways to add an object to multiple frames: shared layers and copying objects. Shared layers let you edit an object and have the changes appear on all frames. Copied objects are independent; changes you make to one object do not change the copies on other frames.

To share a layer across frames:

1. Place the element to be shared on its own layer.

2. Choose Share Layer from the Layers panel menu. The Shared Layer icon appears next to the layer name ❺. *(For more information on sharing a layer across frames, see page 220.)*

> **TIP** When a layer is shared across frames, editing the original object changes the object's appearance on all the frames.

To copy an object onto frames:

1. Create a file with multiple frames.

2. Create an object on one of the frames that you want to appear on all the frames.

3. With the object selected, choose Copy to Frames from the Frames panel menu. The Copy to Frames dialog box appears ❻.

4. Choose All Frames to copy the selected object onto all the frames of the image.

   or

   Use the other selections in the Copy to Frames dialog box to copy an object to a specific frame or a range of frames.

> **TIP** After you copy an object to frames, editing the object changes its appearance only on the frame where you work.

Although Fireworks has a robust set of drawing tools, you may find it easier to create artwork in programs such as Macromedia FreeHand or Adobe Illustrator ❼. This is especially true if you want to use the blend commands to make one shape turn into another.

Fireworks lets you distribute the artwork on layers onto frames.

TIP Use FreeHand's Release to Layers command to divide its blends onto layers.

To distribute vector layers onto frames:

1. Choose File>**Import** and find a vector file with objects on separate layers. This opens the Vector File Options dialog box.

2. Use the Layers pop-up list ❽ to assign objects on each layer to frames and then click the OK button.

You can also use FreeHand's multiple pages to create animations in Fireworks.

To distribute pages onto frames:

1. Choose File>**Import** and find a vector file with objects on separate pages. This opens the Vector File Options dialog box.

2. Use the Pages pop-up list ❾ to assign objects on each page to frames and then click the OK button.

❼ *Assigning a blend to layers in FreeHand and then importing the art into Fireworks allows you to* **create an animation** *of one letter turning into another.*

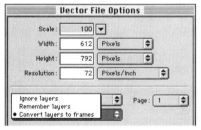

❽ *The* **Layers pop-up list** *lets you move objects in a vector file from layers to frames.*

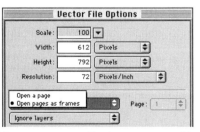

❾ *The* **Pages pop-up list** *lets you move objects from pages to frames.*

⑩ A **symbol,** *designated by the plus sign. Symbols are the "parents" that control instances; changing the symbol changes the instance.*

⑪ *An* **instance,** *designated by the arrow.*

Symbols are objects or groups of objects that have been given the power to control copies of themselves. The copies are called *instances.* Whatever changes are made to a symbol are automatically applied to the instance. Once you have created a symbol and instance, you can *tween* or create steps between them that can then be distributed to frames creating an animation. You cannot change the shape of paths of the artwork with tweening, but you can change the size, location, opacity, and rotation.

Any object, or group of objects, can be made into a symbol.

To create a symbol:

1. Select the object or objects that you want to be the symbol.

2. Choose **Insert** > **Symbols.** A plus sign appears in the bottom corner of the image **⑩** that indicates the object is a symbol.

There are several ways to create an instance based on a symbol.

To copy and paste an instance from a symbol:

1. Copy the symbol.

2. Paste. The instance covers the symbol. A small arrow in the corner of the object indicates it is an instance **⑪**.

TIP Instances can be copied from other instances.

To Option/Alt-drag an instance from a symbol:

1. Select the symbol

2. Hold the Option/Alt key as you drag the symbol. The copy created is an instance.

Once you have created a symbol with instances, you can modify the symbol to change the appearance of its instances.

To modify symbols and instances:

Select the symbol with the Subselection tool and change its appearance. All instances of that symbol change accordingly ⓬.

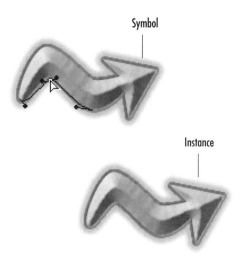

Symbol

Instance

To move both the symbol and instances:

Move the symbol with the Subselection tool. All instances of that symbol move accordingly.

⓬ *Changing the shape of the symbol changes the shape of the instance.*

To move only the symbol:

Move the symbol with the Pointer tool. The symbol moves without affecting the position of its instances.

TIP Moving an instance does not change the position of the symbol.

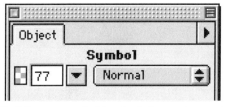

Almost all changes applied to the symbol are applied to its instances. However, you can adjust the opacity of the symbol without affecting the instances.

⓭ *When an **symbol is selected**, any changes to the opacity are applied on the the symbol, not any of its instances.*

To change the opacity of the symbol only:

1. Select the symbol with the Pointer tool. The Object panel lists the symbol ⓭.

2. Change the opacity setting. This only affects the symbol, not any instances

TIP If you select the symbol with the Subselection tool, the Object panel lists the path. You can then can change the opacity of both the symbol and its instances.

Symbols and Instances

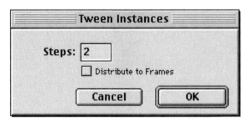

⓮ *The* Tween Instances *dialog box.*

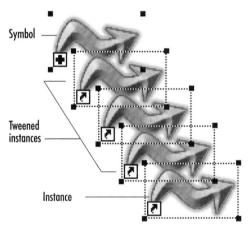

Symbol

Tweened
instances

Instance

⓯ Tweening *between the symbol (top) and the instance (bottom).*

Once you have a symbol and an instance, you can tween those objects to create a series of instances that move from the symbol to the instance. This creates the effect of one object moving to a second position.

To create motion by tweening:

1. Position the symbol where you want the move to start.

2. Position the instance where you want the move to end.

3. Select both the symbol and instance, and choose **Insert > Tween Instances**. The Tween Instances dialog box appears **⓮**.

TIP You can tween between the symbol and more than one instance so that the animation moves in different directions.

4. Set the number of new instances in the Steps field.

5. Click Distribute to Frames to automatically create new frames with each instance on its own frame.

TIP If you do not distribute the objects to frames using the dialog box, you can use the Distribute to Frames command *(see page 230)* later. This lets you first judge to see if you like the position of all the tweened objects.

6. Click OK. The new instances fill in the space between the original symbol and its instance **⓯**.

Although the actual shapes of the paths must be the same between symbols and instances, there are some things that can be changed independently. This allows you to tween so that the appearance of the one object changes as part of the animation.

To tween appearances:

1. Select the instance with the Pointer tool.

2. Apply any of the following changes:

- Lower the opacity. This fades one object into the other as they are tweened ⑯.

> **TIP** Use the Pointer tool to change the opacity of the symbol without changing the opacity of the instances.

- Change the size using the Scale tool. This makes one object shrink or grow into the other as they are tweened ⑰.

- Change the rotation using the Rotation tool. This makes one object twist into the position of the other as they are tweened ⑱.

3. Apply any additional changes to either the symbol or the instance. This creates multiple changes to the objects as they are tweened ⑲.

4. Choose **Insert > Tween Instances** to see the intermediate steps created.

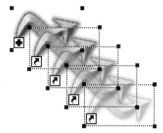

⑯ *Tweening between different opacities.*

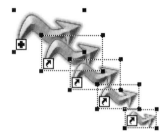

⑰ *Tweening between different sizes.*

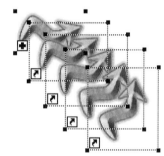

⑱ *Tweening between different rotations.*

⑲ *Tweening between different opacities, sizes, and rotations.*

Tween Appearances

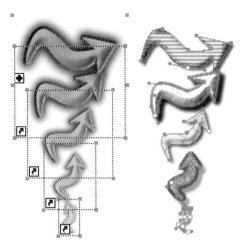

⑳ **Breaking the link** *between symbols and instances (left) allows you to make individual changes to the objects (right).*

Tweening is not a "live effect" such as the blends in Macromedia FreeHand or Adobe Illustrator. You must delete the original tweened objects to change the effect.

To alter a tweened image:

1. Delete the intermediate steps created by the Tween command.

2. Make whatever changes you want to the original symbol or instance.

3. If the tweened instances were distributed to frames, move the instance to the same frame as the symbol.

   or

   If the tweened instances were distributed to frames, turn on multi-frame editing *(see page 240)*.

4. Select the symbol and instance.

5. Choose **Insert > Tween Instances**. The instances are redistributed onto the empty frames.

You can also break the link between a symbol and its instances. This allows you to make changes to the individual elements of the tween.

To break the link between symbol and instances:

1. Select the instance from a symbol.

2. Choose **Insert > Symbol Options > Break Link**. The instance is released and appears as an ordinary object **⑳**.

You can also add an object to the symbol and have the object appear as part of all the tweened instances.

To add an object to a symbol:

1. Select the symbol and the object you want to add to it.

2. Choose **Insert** > **Symbol Options** > **Add to Symbol**. The object is added to all instances of the symbol **㉑**.

TIP If the instances have been altered by tweening, the object that is added will also be altered.

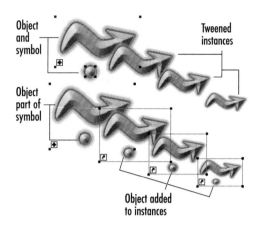

㉑ **Add an object to a symbol** *also adds the object to any instances of that symbol and tweens them accordingly.*

If you have many instances, it may be difficult to find the original symbol to make any changes to it. Fortunately, if you can find an instance, you can easily find the symbol.

To find the symbol an instance is based on:

1. Select an instance.

2. Choose **Insert** > **Symbol Options** > **Find Symbol**. The symbol is selected.

TIP The Find Symbol command works even if the instance is on one frame and the symbol is on another.

To delete all instances based on a symbol:

1. Select the symbol.

2. Choose **Insert** > **Symbol Options** > **Delete Instances**. All the instances based on that symbol are deleted.

TIP The Delete Instances command does not delete the frames that held the instances.

Add to a Symbol; Find Symbols

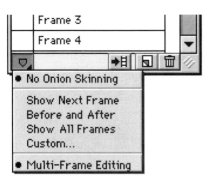

㉒ *The* **Onion Skinning controls** *in the Frames panel.*

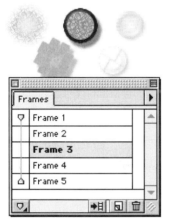

㉓ **Onion skinning** *lets you see the objects on the non-active frames.*

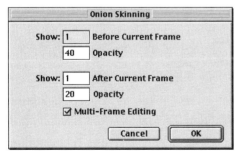

㉔ *The* **Onion Skinning** *dialog box.*

As you are working on animations, you may need to see how one object relates to others on different frames. Fireworks uses a technique called *onion skinning* which allows you to see the objects on the frames that are not selected. (The term comes from early film animators who used vellum sheets to plot their animations. When the sheets were layered, the artists could see through them like the layers of an onion.)

To turn on onion skinning:

1. Open the Onion Skinning controls in the Frames panel **㉒**.

2. Choose Show Next Frame to see the frame after the selected frame.

   or

   Choose Before and After to see the frames before and after the selected frame.

   or

   Choose Show All Frames to see all the frames in the document **㉓**.

TIP The opacity of frames viewed through onion-skinning is lowered so they are not as obvious as the selected frame.

You can also create your own custom settings for onion skinning.

To customize onion skinning:

1. Choose Custom from the Onion Skinning controls menu. The Onion Skinning dialog box appears **㉔**.

2. Change the number of frames that should be visible.

3. Change the opacity of the visible frames.

Onion Skinning

Multi-frame editing allows you to work with objects that are on different frames.

To use multi-frame editing:

1. Choose Multi-Frame Editing from the Onion Skinning controls menu or the Onion Skinning dialog box.

2. Make sure Onion Skinning is active.

3. Use the various selection methods to select objects on either the active frame or the visible onion-skinning frames **25**.

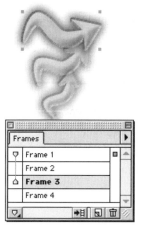

25 Multi-frame editing *allows you to select and manipulate objects on non-active frames.*

As you create animations, you may want to see how the frames look in sequence. Fireworks give you animation controls within the document window **26**.

To preview animation:

1. Click the next frame or previous frame buttons to move one frame at a time.

2. Click the first frame or last frame buttons to jump to the beginning or end of the animation.

3. Click the Play button to run the animation.

4. Click the Stop button to stop playing the animation.

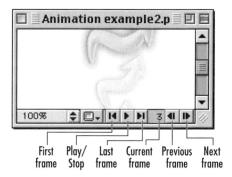

| First frame | Play/ Stop | Last frame | Current frame | Previous frame | Next frame |

26 *The* **Animation Controls** *in the document window.*

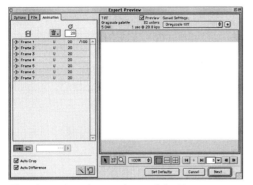

㉗ *The* **Animation options** *of the Export Preview.*

Frame-delay field

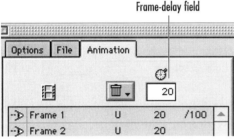

㉘ *Set the* **frame-time delay** *to control how long a frame is visible during an animation.*

After you have finished the frames of the animation, you use the Export controls to fine-tune the settings and export the file.

To set the animation export controls:

1. Choose **File > Export** to open the Export Preview window.

2. Choose Animated GIF from the Format list.

3. Set the GIF color and transparency options as desired *(see Chapter 15, "Basic Exporting").*

4. Click the Animation tab in the Export Preview window to open the animation options panel **㉗**.

5. Set the animation options as explained on the next two pages.

6. Click the Next button at the botttom of the Export window to export the file.

The animation options let you control the timing for each frame of the animation.

To set the duration for a frame:

1. Select a frame in the animation options panel of the Export Preview.

2. Enter a number in the frame-delay field **㉘**. This is set in hundredths of a second. The higher the number, the longer the frame remains visible.

TIP Use the Shift key to select more than one frame at a time.

You can also control how each frame blends between other frames and the background. Fireworks calls this the disposal of the frames.

To set the transition of the frames:

1. Select a frame in the animation options panel of the Export Preview.

2. Use the Disposal method list **29** to control how Fireworks treats the disposal of one frame to another.

- Choose **Unspecified** when the animation artwork is completely opaque. If you use Unspecified with artwork that is transparent, instead of each frame replacing each other, the new frame is added to the old one.

- Choose **None** to add some of the image in the next frame to the previous one.

- Choose **Restore to Background** when transparency is turned on so that each frame changes from one to another.

- Choose **Revert to Background** when moving objects appear over a larger frame created earlier in the animation. Revert to Background is not supported by all browsers.

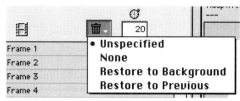

29 *The* **Disposal method** *list.*

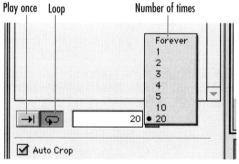

30 *The* **Loop controls**

To set the number of times the animation plays:

1. Set the Loop control **30** to either Play Once or Loop. (*Loop* means that the animation repeats.)

2. If you choose Loop, set how many times the animation is repeated.

- Choose a number to repeat the animation a finite number of times.

- Choose Forever to repeat the animation as long as the viewer stays on the page.

TIP The first time the animation plays is not counted in the Loop control. So to play the animation four times, set the loop number to three.

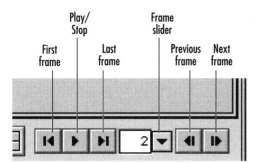

Play/
Stop

Frame
slider

First
frame

Last
frame

Previous
frame

Next
frame

31 *The* **player controls** *in the Export Preview dialog box.*

Visible
frame

Invisible
frame

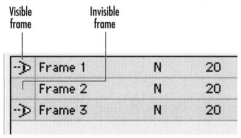

⠂ᗕ	Frame 1	N	20
	Frame 2	N	20
⠂ᗕ	Frame 3	N	20

32 *The* **visibility settings for frames.** *In this example, frames 1 and 3 are set to export, but frame 2 is not set to export.*

You can view the animation within the Export Preview dialog box **31**.

To preview animations with Export Preview:

1. Click the Play/Stop button to start the animation.

2. Click the Play/Stop button to stop an animation that is playing.

3. Click the First Frame button to rewind the animation.

4. Click the Last Frame button to skip to the end of the animation.

5. Click the Previous or Next Frame buttons to move one frame at a time.

6. Use the Frame slider to skip to a specific frame in the animation.

To specify which frames to export:

1. Click the Show/Hide icon in the Animation tab **32**. If the icon is visible, the frame exports. If the icon is not visible, the frame does not export.

2. Preview the animation and adjust which frames to export, if necessary.

DEFAULTS

As you have seen, Fireworks provides a great number of preset patterns, gradients, brushes, and effects that you can apply to objects. You can modify the default settings to create other effects. (Just remember the immortal words, "Defaults, dear Brutus, lie not in our stars, but in our software.")

This appendix shows the default settings for the presets. In each case, consider the defaults as just the start for creating your own looks.

In Appendix A you will see printouts of

The textures used for fills and brushes.

The patterns at their default settings.

The gradients at their default settings.

The brushes at their default settings.

The effects at their default settings.

Textures

The 26 textures can be applied to either fills or brushes. Once the textures are applied, they can then be adjusted using the opacity slider.

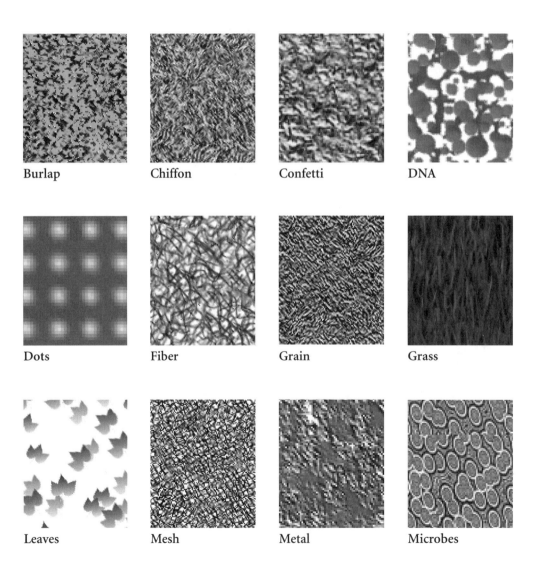

Burlap   Chiffon   Confetti   DNA

Dots   Fiber   Grain   Grass

Leaves   Mesh   Metal   Microbes

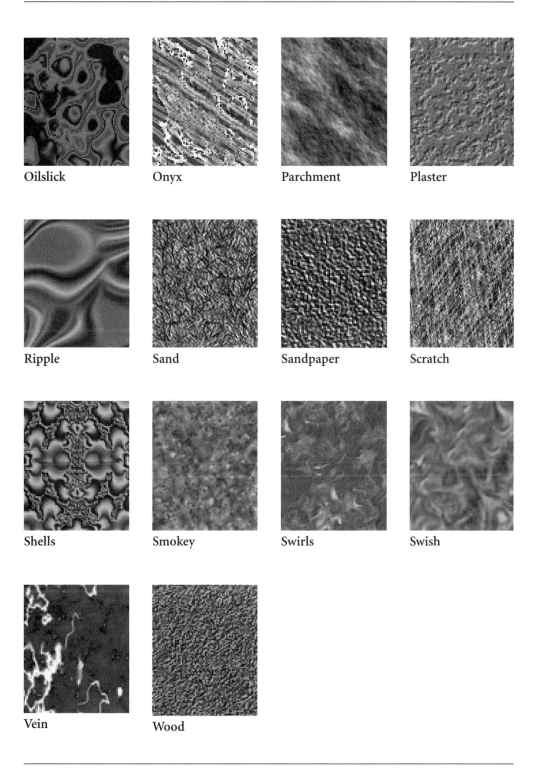

Oilslick   Onyx   Parchment   Plaster

Ripple   Sand   Sandpaper   Scratch

Shells   Smokey   Swirls   Swish

Vein   Wood

Textures

Patterns

The 14 patterns can be applied as fills. Once the patterns have been applied, they can then be adjusted using the Paint Bucket. These are the patterns in the order in which they appear in the patterns list.

Aggregate   Bark   Berber Rug   Blue Wave

Bricks—Small   Grass—Tiny   Illusion   Impressionist—Red

  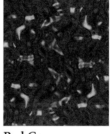 

Jeans   Leaves—Photinia   Red Goo   Tweed

 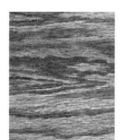

Weave   Wood—Light

Gradients

The 11 gradients can be applied as fills.
Once the gradients have been applied, you
can adjust them using the Paint Bucket.
These are the gradients in the order in
which they appear in the gradients list.

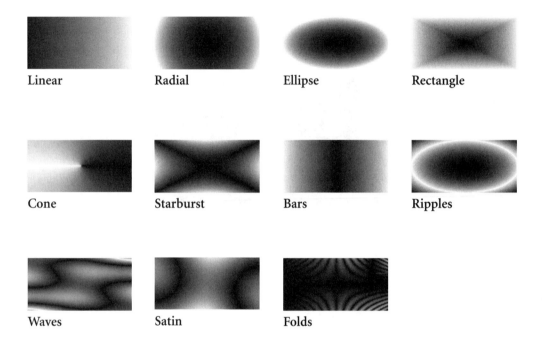

Linear	Radial	Ellipse	Rectangle
Cone	Starburst	Bars	Ripples
Waves	Satin	Folds	

Brushes

You can apply the 48 brushes to open or closed paths. Once the brushes have been applied, you can then adjust them using the Strokes panel.

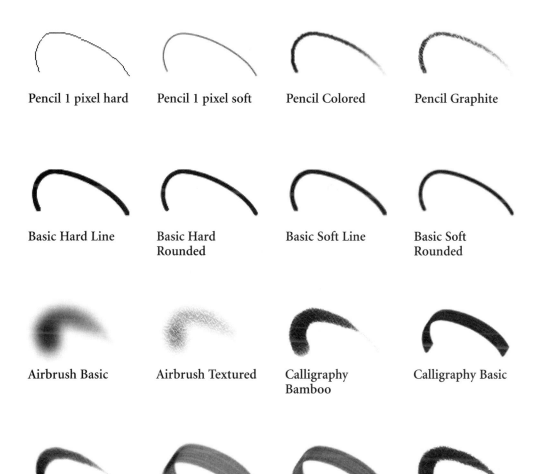

Pencil 1 pixel hard	Pencil 1 pixel soft	Pencil Colored	Pencil Graphite
Basic Hard Line	Basic Hard Rounded	Basic Soft Line	Basic Soft Rounded
Airbrush Basic	Airbrush Textured	Calligraphy Bamboo	Calligraphy Basic
Calligraphy Quill	Calligraphy Ribbon	Calligraphy Wet	Charcoal Creamy

Brushes *(continued)*

Charcoal Pastel   Charcoal Soft   Charcoal Textured   Crayon Basic

Crayon Rake   Crayon Thick   Felt Tip
Dark Marker   Felt Tip
Highlighter

Felt Tip
Light Marker   Felt Tip Thin   Oil Bristle   Oil Broad Splatter

Oil Splatter   Oil Strands   Oil Textured
Bristle   Watercolor Heavy

Brushes

Watercolor Thick

Watercolor Thin

Random Confetti

Random Dots

Random Fur

Random Squares

Random Yarn

Unnatural 3D

Unnatural 3D
Glow

Unnatural
Chameleon

Unnatural Fluid
Splatter

Unnatural Outline

Unnatural Paint
Splatter

Unnatural
Toothpaste

Unnatural Toxic
Waste

Unnatural Viscous
Alien Paint

Brushes

Effects

You can apply the 20 effects to vector objects or pixel images. Once the textures are applied, you can adjust them using the Effects panel. The effects shown here are in order as they appear in the Effect panel. They have been applied to the same object. Any differences in the sizes or are a result of applying the effects.

Effects

Inner Bevel Flat

Inner Bevel Frame 1

Inner Bevel Frame 2

Inner Bevel Ring

Inner Bevel Ruffle

Inner Bevel Sloped

Inner Bevel Smooth

Outer Bevel Flat

Outer Bevel Frame 1

Outer Bevel Frame 2

Outer Bevel Ring

Outer Bevel Ruffle

Outer Bevel Sloped

Outer Bevel Smooth

Drop Shadow Basic

Drop Shadow Soft

Embossed Inset

Embossed Raised

Glow Basic

Glow Halo

KEYBOARD SHORTCUTS B

As you become more familiar with the various Fireworks features, you should begin to use the keyboard shortcuts for the commands you use most often. For instance, rather than use the mouse to choose **File** > **Export**, it is much faster and easier to use the keyboard shortcut.

This appendix lists the shortcuts for Fireworks menu commands. Most of these shortcuts are also listed on the menus. So you do not have to use this list to find the shortcut for the commands you use the most. However, this list can make it easy to find a certain shortcut, or even to tell if a command has a shortcut assigned to it.

In Appendix B you have

A list of the keyboard shortcuts for Windows on pages 256–257.

A list of the keyboard shortcuts for the Macintosh on pages 258–259.

A list of the keyboard shortcuts to access the Toolbox features on page 260.

WINDOWS KEYBOARD SHORTCUTS

The following are the keyboard shortcuts for the Windows platform. These are the abbreviations used for the keys.

Ctrl. . . . . Ctrl key

Alt . . . . Alt key

Up. . . . . Up arrow key

Down . . . . Down arrow key

Left. . . . . Left arrow key

Right . . . . Right arrow key

Space . . . . Spacebar

File Menu (Win)

New . . . . Ctrl+N

Open . . . . Ctrl+O (oh)

Open Multiple . . . . . . Ctrl+Shift+O (oh)

Print . . . . Ctrl+P

Quit . . . . Ctrl+Q

Import. . . . . Ctrl+R

Close Window . . . . Ctrl+W

Export. . . . . Ctrl+Shift+R

Export Again. . . . . Ctrl+Shift+X

Save. . . . . Ctrl+S

Save As. . . . . Ctrl+Shift+S

Edit Menu (Win)

Cut . . . . Ctrl+X

Copy. . . . . Ctrl+C

Paste . . . . Ctrl+V

Ungroup . . . . Ctrl+U

Undo. . . . . Ctrl+Z

Redo. . . . . Ctrl+ Shift + Z

Paste Inside . . . . Ctrl+Shift+V

Paste Attributes . . . . . . Ctrl+Alt+Shift+V

Select All . . . . Ctrl+A

Deselect (Select None) . . . . Ctrl+D

Superselect . . . . Ctrl+Up

Subselect . . . . Ctrl+Down

Select Inverse . . . . Ctrl+Shift+I

Duplicate . . . . Ctrl+Alt+D

Clone . . . . Ctrl+Shift+C

Crop Selected Image. . . . . . . Ctrl+Alt+C

View Menu (Win)

Zoom In. . . . . Ctrl++

Zoom Out. . . . . Ctrl+-

Zoom In tool . . . . Ctrl+space

Zoom Out tool . . . . Ctrl+Alt+space

100% Magnification . . . . Ctrl+1

200% Magnification . . . . Ctrl+2

400% Magnification . . . . Ctrl+4

50% Magnification . . . . Ctrl+5

800% Magnification . . . . Ctrl+8

3200% Magnification . . . . Ctrl+3

6400% Magnification . . . . Ctrl+6

Fit Selection . . . . Ctrl+0 (zero)

Fit All . . . . Ctrl+Alt+0 (zero)

Full Display/Draft Toggle. . . . . . . Ctrl+K

Hide Selection . . . . Ctrl+M

Show All . . . . Ctrl+Shift+M

Hide Edges. . . . . Ctrl+H

Hide Panels . . . . Ctrl+Shift+H

Show/Hide Grid . . . . Ctrl+'

Snap to Grid . . . . Ctrl+Shift+'

Show/Hide Rulers. . . . . Ctrl+Alt+R

Edit Grid dialog. . . . . Ctrl+Alt+G

Guides . . . . Ctrl+;

Slice Guides . . . . Ctrl+Alt+Shift+;

Lock Guides. . . . . Ctrl+Alt+;

Snap to Guides . . . . Ctrl+Shift+;

Edit Guides dialog . . . . Ctrl+Alt+Shift+G

Insert Menu (Win)

Hotspot . . . . Ctrl+Shift+U
Image . . . . Ctrl+R
Symbol . . . . Ctrl+Alt+Shift+M
Tween Instance . . . . . . Ctrl+Alt+Shift+T
Create Empty Image (tool) . . . Ctrl+Alt+Y

Modify Menu (Win)

Stroke . . . . Ctrl+Alt+B
Fill . . . . Ctrl+Alt+F
Effect panel . . . . Ctrl+Alt+E
Image Object . . . . Ctrl+E
Edit Image Object . . . . Ctrl+Shift+O (oh)
Exit Image Edit . . . . Ctrl+Shift+D
Free Transform . . . . Ctrl+T
Numeric Transform . . . . . . Ctrl+Shift+T
Rotate 90° CW . . . . Ctrl+9
Rotate 90° CCW . . . . Ctrl+7
Bring to Front . . . . Ctrl+F
Bring Forward . . . . Ctrl+Shift+F
Send Backward . . . . Ctrl+Shift+B
Send to Back . . . . Ctrl+B
Align Objects Left . . . . Ctrl+Alt+1
Align Objects Center/Vert . . . Ctrl+Alt+2
Align Objects Right . . . . Ctrl+Alt+3
Align Objects Top . . . . Ctrl+Alt+4
Align Objects Center/Horiz . . . Ctrl+Alt+5
Align Objects Bottom . . . . . . Ctrl+Alt+6
Distribute Widths . . . . Ctrl+Alt+7
Distribute Heights . . . . Ctrl+Alt+9
Join . . . . Ctrl+J
Split . . . . Ctrl+Shift+J
Merge Images . . . . . . Ctrl+Alt+Shift+Z
Group . . . . Ctrl+G
Mask Group . . . . Ctrl+Shift+G
Ungroup . . . . Ctrl+U

Text Menu (Win)

Plain . . . . Ctrl+Alt+Shift+P
Bold . . . . Ctrl+Alt+Shift+B
Italic . . . . Ctrl+Alt+Shift+I
Underline . . . . Ctrl+Alt+Shift+U
Left Align Text . . . . . . Ctrl+Alt+Shift+L
Center Align Text . . . . . Ctrl+Alt+Shift+C
Right Align Text . . . . . Ctrl+Alt+Shift+R
Justify Text . . . . Ctrl+Alt+Shift+J
Stretch Justify Text . . . . Ctrl+Alt+Shift+S
Text Editor . . . . Ctrl+Shift+E
Convert to Paths . . . . . . Ctrl+Shift+P
Attach Text to Path . . . . . . Ctrl+Shift+Y

Xtras (Win)

Repeat Xtra . . . . Ctrl+Alt+Shift+X

Window Menu (Win)

New Window . . . . Ctrl+Alt+N
Toolbox . . . . Ctrl+Alt+T
Object Properties . . . . Ctrl+I
Stroke panel . . . . Ctrl+Alt+B
Fill panel . . . . Ctrl+Alt+F
Effect panel . . . . Ctrl+Alt+E
Info panel . . . . Ctrl+Alt+I
Tool Options panel . . . . Ctrl+Alt+O (oh)
Styles panel . . . . Ctrl+Alt+J
Color Mixer panel . . . . Ctrl+Alt+M
Swatches panel . . . . Ctrl+Alt+S
Layers panel . . . . Ctrl+Alt+L
Frames panel . . . . Ctrl+Alt+K
Behaviors panel . . . . Ctrl+Alt+H
URL Manager . . . . Ctrl+Alt+U

MACINTOSH KEYBOARD SHORTCUTS

The following are the keyboard shortcuts for the Macintosh platform. These are the abbreviations used for the keys.

Cmd . . . . Command key

Opt . . . . Option key

Up. . . . . Up arrow key

Down . . . . Down arrow key

Left. . . . . Left arrow key

Right . . . . Right arrow key

Space . . . . Spacebar

File Menu (Mac)

New. . . . . Cmd+N

Open. . . . . Cmd+O (oh)

Open Multiple . . . . . Cmd+Shift+O (oh)

Print . . . . Cmd+P

Quit . . . . Cmd+Q

Import . . . . Cmd+R

Close Window. . . . . Cmd+W

Export . . . . Cmd+Shift+R

Export Again . . . . Cmd+Shift+X

Save . . . . Cmd+S

Save As . . . . Cmd+Shift+S

Edit Menu (Mac)

Cut . . . . Cmd+X

Copy . . . . Cmd+C

Paste . . . . Cmd+V

Ungroup. . . . . Cmd+U

Undo . . . . Cmd+Z

Redo . . . . Cmd+ Shift + Z

Paste Inside . . . . Cmd+Shift+V

Paste Attributes. . . . . Cmd+Opt+Shift+V

Select All. . . . . Cmd+A

Deselect (Select None). . . . . Cmd+D

Superselect . . . . Cmd+Up

Subselect. . . . . Cmd+Down

Select Inverse . . . . Cmd+Shift+I

Duplicate. . . . . Cmd+Opt+D

Clone. . . . . Cmd+Shift+C

Crop Selected Image. . . . . Cmd+Opt+C

View Menu (Mac)

Zoom In . . . . Cmd++

Zoom Out . . . . Cmd+-

Zoom In tool . . . . Cmd+space

Zoom Out tool. . . . . . Cmd+Opt+space

100% Magnification. . . . . Cmd+1

200% Magnification. . . . . Cmd+2

400% Magnification. . . . . Cmd+4

50% Magnification . . . . Cmd+5

800% Magnification. . . . . Cmd+8

3200% Magnification. . . . . Cmd+3

6400% Magnification. . . . . Cmd+6

Fit Selection . . . . Cmd+0 (zero)

Fit All . . . . Cmd+Opt+0 (zero)

Full Display/Draft Toggle . . . . . . Cmd+K

Hide Selection . . . . Cmd+M

Show All . . . . Cmd+Shift+M

Hide Edges . . . . Cmd+H

Hide Panels. . . . . Cmd+Shift+H

Show/Hide Grid. . . . . Cmd+'

Snap to Grid . . . . Cmd+Shift+'

Show/Hide Rulers . . . . . . Cmd+Opt+R

Edit Grid dialog . . . . Cmd+Opt+G

Guides. . . . . Cmd+;

Slice Guides. . . . . . . Cmd+Opt+Shift+;

Lock Guides. . . . . Cmd+Opt+;

Snap to Guides . . . . Cmd+Shift+;

Edit Guides dialog. . . Cmd+Opt+Shift+G

Insert Menu (Mac)

Hotspot . . . . Cmd+Shift+U
Image. . . . . Cmd+R
Symbol. . . . . Cmd+Opt+Shift+M
Tween Instance . . . . . Cmd+Opt+Shift+T
Create Empty Image . . . . . . Cmd+Opt+Y

Modify Menu (Mac)

Stroke . . . . Cmd+Opt+B
Fill . . . . Cmd+Opt+F
Effect panel . . . . Cmd+Opt+E
Image Object . . . . Cmd+E
Edit Image Object . . . Cmd+Shift+O (oh)
Exit Image Edit . . . . Cmd+Shift+D
Free Transform. . . . . Cmd+T
Numeric Transform. . . . . . Cmd+Shift+T
Rotate 90° CW . . . . Cmd+9
Rotate 90° CCW . . . . Cmd+7
Bring to Front . . . . Cmd+F
Bring Forward . . . . Cmd+Shift+F
Send Backward. . . . . Cmd+Shift+B
Send to Back . . . . Cmd+B
Align Objects Left . . . . . . Cmd+Opt+1
Align Objects Center/Vert . . Cmd+Opt+2
Align Objects Right . . . . . . Cmd+Opt+3
Align Objects Top . . . . Cmd+Opt+4
Align Objects Center/Horiz . Cmd+Opt+5
Align Objects Bottom . . . . . Cmd+Opt+6
Distribute Widths. . . . . . . Cmd+Opt+7
Distribute Heights . . . . . . Cmd+Opt+9
Join. . . . . Cmd+J
Split . . . . Cmd+Shift+J
Merge Images . . . . . Cmd+Opt+Shift+Z
Group . . . . Cmd+G
Mask Group . . . . Cmd+Shift+G
Ungroup. . . . . Cmd+U

Text Menu (Mac)

Plain. . . . . Cmd+Opt+Shift+P
Bold . . . . Cmd+Opt+Shift+B
Italic . . . . Cmd+Opt+Shift+I
Underline . . . . Cmd+Opt+Shift+U
Left Align Text. . . . . Cmd+Opt+Shift+L
Center Align Text . . . Cmd+Opt+Shift+C
Right Align Text . . . . Cmd+Opt+Shift+R
Justify Text . . . . Cmd+Opt+Shift+J
Stretch Justify Text . . . Cmd+Opt+Shift+S
Text Editor . . . . Cmd+Shift+E
Convert to Paths. . . . . . . Cmd+Shift+P
Attach Text to Path . . . . . Cmd+Shift+Y

Xtras (Mac)

Repeat Xtra . . . . Cmd+Opt+Shift+X

Window Menu (Mac)

New Window . . . . Cmd+Opt+N
Toolbox. . . . . Cmd+Opt+T
Object Properties. . . . . Cmd+I
Stroke panel . . . . Cmd+Opt+B
Fill panel . . . . Cmd+Opt+F
Effect panel . . . . Cmd+Opt+E
Info panel. . . . . Cmd+Opt+I
Tool Options panel . . . Cmd+Opt+O (oh)
Styles panel. . . . . Cmd+Opt+J
Color Mixer panel. . . . . . . Cmd+Opt+M
Swatches panel . . . . Cmd+Opt+S
Layers panel . . . . Cmd+Opt+L
Frames panel . . . . Cmd+Opt+K
Behaviors panel . . . . Cmd+Opt+H
URL Manager. . . . . Cmd+Opt+U

TOOLBOX KEYBOARD SHORTCUTS

The following are the keys that are used to access the tools in the toolbox (*see page 18*). These keys are pressed without using any modifier keys such as Command or Ctrl. For instance, to choose the Rectangle tool, you press only the *R* key. If a letter is used for more than one tool, such as the *B* for Brush and Reshape Brush, it means that pressing the key again toggles between the tools.

Toolbox

A, 1	Subselection pointer
B	Brush
B	Reshape Path
C	Crop
D	Default Colors
E	Eraser
F	Freeform Reshape
F	Reshape Area
G	Polygon
H	Hand
I	Eyedropper
J	Export Area
K	Paint Bucket
K	Paint Bucket (Handles)
L	Lasso
L	Lasso (Polygon)
M	Marquee (Rectangle)
M	Marquee (Ellipse)
N	Line
P	Pen
Q	Transform tools
R	Rectangle
R	Ellipse
R	Hotspot Rectangle
R	Hotspot Circle
R	Slice
S	Rubber Stamp
T	Text
U	Path Scrubber (+)
U	Path Scrubber (-)
V, 0 (zero)	Pointer
V, 0 (zero)	Pointer (Pick Behind)
W	Magic Wand
X	Switch Fill and Stroke Colors
Y	Pencil
Z	Magnify

REGULAR EXPRESSIONS

C

The Find & Replace commands allow you to use Regular Expressions as part of the text and URL information. Regular expressions are special symbols that can be added to change how the Find & Replace commands work. They work like the special symbols and wildcard characters in word processing and page layout programs. There are hundreds of different regular expressions—many more than could be covered in this book. If you are interested in working with regular expressions, see *The Dreamweaver 2 Bible* by Joseph Lowery, published by IDG Books. You can also find information on regular expressions at *http://developer.netscape.com/docs/manuals/communicator/jsguide/regexp.htm*.

In Appendix C you have

A table of the basic regular expressions characters.

Character	Looks for	Example
∧	The beginning of the input or line.	∧H finds the H in **Help** but not **FreeHand**
$	The end of the input or line	s$ finds the s in **Fireworks** but not **wish**
*	The preceding characters that appears zero or more times	es* finds the es in **best** or the ess in **mess** or finds the e in **bet**
+	The preceding character that appears one or more times	es+ finds the es in **best** or the ess in **mess** but does not find the e in **bet**
?	The preceding character that appears zero or one times	st?on finds the **ston** in **Redstone** or the **son** in **Davidson** but does not find anything in **Littleton** or **Emerson**
.	Any single character except for the newsline character	.ealthy finds both **healthy** and **wealthy**
|	Either the characters before the | or the characters after the |	www|http finds both **www** or **http**
(n)	The preceding character when it occurs n number of times	e(2) finds ee in **sleep** or **keep** but not **kept**
(n,m)	The preceding character when it occurs at least n times but not more than m times	FF(2,4) finds FF in **FF0000**, **FFF000** or **FFFF00**
[abc]	Any of the characters in the brackets.	[abc] finds **a**, **b**, or **c**
[a-c]	Any of the characters in the range of the characters between the hyphen	[a-e] finds **a**, **b**, **c**, **d**, or **e**
[∧abc]	Any character not enclosed in the brackets	[∧aeiou] finds the d in **adapt** and the c in **ouch**
[∧a-c]	Any of the characters not in the range of characters between the hyphen	[a-s] finds the t in **text** or u in **ugly**, but not the a in **apple**
\d	Any numerical character from 0 to 9	\d finds the 2 in **H20** or the 7 in **7th Heaven**
\D	Any non-numerical character (same as [∧0-9])	\D finds the th in **7th** or the rd in **3rd**
\f	Form feed character	
\n	Line feed character	
\r	Carriage return	
\s	Any white space character such as a tab, form feed or line feed	\spress find the **press** in Peachpit **press** but not **depressed**
\S	Any single non–white-space character	\Spress finds the **press** in **depressed** but not Peachpit press
\t	A tab character	
\W	Any non-alphanumeric character	\W finds characters such as the & in **Big & Tall** or the @ in **@mindspring.com**

INDEX

A

Adaptive palette, 184
Add Files dialog box, 141
additive color, 32
Adobe Photoshop files, opening, 173
Aggregate pattern, 248
Airbrush brushes, 251
alignment
   commands for horizontal axis, 82
   commands for vertical axis, 82
   to grid, 26
   to guides, 26
   justified, 124
   stretch, 124
   text, 126
      horizontal, 124
      on path, 128
      vertical, 125
Align pop-up menu, 82–83
   illustrated, 83
   using, 82
alpha channel masks, 97
Alpha masks, 165
anchor points
   adding, 56
   connecting, 48
   creating, 48, 49, 50
   defined, 48
   deleting, 56
   moving, 59
   selected, 59
   viewing, 59
   See also control handles; paths
Animated GIF format, 193
Animation Controls, 240
animations, 229–243
   basics, 230–231
   with imported artwork, 232
   number of times played, 242
   options, 241
   previewing, 243
   running, 240
   stopping, 240
Arrange menu
   Bring Forward command, 83
   Bring to Front command, 83
   Send Backward command, 83
   Send to Back command, 83, 170
Auto-crop Images feature, 73
automation features, 131-144

batch processing, 142-144
Find & Replace commands, 136-140
Project Log, 141
styles, 132-135

B

Bark pattern, 248
Bars gradient, 250
baseline shift, 123
Basic brushes, 251
Batch Export dialog box, 143, 194
batch processing, 142-144
   export options, 194
   options, 143-144
   setting files for, 142
   settings, saving as script, 144
Batch Processing dialog box, 142, 194
Batch Replace dialog box, 143
behaviors, 217-228
   deleting, 222
   Display Status Message, 223
   editing, 222
   exporting files with, 228
   rollover, 221-222
   Swap Image, 224-226
   toggle group, 227
Behaviors panel
   Add Behavior choices, 221
   defined, 13
   detail listing, 226
   elements, 13
   Events choices, 223
   illustrated, 13, 221
   menu, 222
   opening, 221
   Swap Image option, 226
   See also behaviors
Berber Rug pattern, 248
bevel effects, 112-113
   applying, 112
   Button menu, 113
   color, changing, 113
   edge softness, 112
   light angle, 112
   light intensity, 112
   presets, 254
   size of, 112
   See also effects
Bevel effects panel, 112
blending modes, 98-101
   changing, 98

Color, 100
Darken, 99
Difference, 100
Erase, 101
Hue, 100
Invert, 101
Lighten, 99
Luminosity, 101
Multiply, 99
Normal, 99
Saturation, 100
Screen, 99
Tint, 101
Blue Wave pattern, 248
Blur More Xtra, 160
Blur Xtra, 160
BMP format, 193
Bricks—Small pattern, 248
brushes, 251–253
    Airbrush, 251
    Basic, 251
    Calligraphy, 251
    Charcoal, 251–252
    Crayon, 252
    Felt Tip, 252
    Oil, 252
    Pencil, 251
    Random, 253
    Unnatural, 253
    Watercolor, 252–253
Brush tool, 18
    Airbrush, 107
    black dot next to, 52
    Calligraphy, 107
    closed paths with, 52
    dragging, 104
    drawing straight segments with, 52
    drawing with, 52
    fills and, 106
    illustrated, 52, 104
    Option/Alt key with, 53
    path creation with, 104
    plus sign (+) next to, 52
    Shift key with, 52
Burlap texture, 246
Button menu, 113

C

Calligraphy brushes, 251
canvas
    color, 20, 23
    cropping, 22
    sizing, 22
Canvas Color dialog box, 23
Canvas Size dialog box, 22

Charcoal brushes, 251–252
Chiffon texture, 246
Circle Hotspot tool, 200
cloning objects, 67
closed paths
    with Brush tool, 52
    creating, 51
    defined, 51
    illustrated, 51
    See also paths
CMY mode, 11
    CMYK colors vs., 34
    color definition, 34
    color ramp, 34
    defined, 34
Color blending mode, 100
Color Export menu, 187
Coloring Web Graphics.2, 33
Color Mixer panel
    CMY mode, 34
    default colors icon, 40
    defined, 11, 32
    elements, 11
    fill mode, 88
    Grayscale mode, 36
    Hexadecimal mode, 33
    HSB mode, 35
    illustrated, 11, 32, 33, 34, 35, 36
    opening, 32
    RGB mode, 32
    swap colors icon, 40
    using, 32–36
color modes, 11
    choosing, 32
    CMY, 11, 34
    grayscale, 11, 36
    hexadecimal, 11, 33
    HSB, 11, 35
    RGB, 11, 32
    types of, 11
color palettes
    choosing, 180
    GIF, 184–187
    loading, 187
    saving, 187
color picker, 20, 26
colors, 31–42
    adding, to Swatches panel, 38
    arranging, 39
    attributes, in Find & Replace panel, 139
    bevel, 113
    canvas, 20, 23
    default, 18, 40
    defining, 38

deleting, from Swatches panel, 39
document grid, 27
drop shadow effect, 114
fill, 18
GIF palette, 186
glow effect, 116
guide, 26
highlight, 64
hotspot, 203
loading, 40
Macintosh System, 37
matte, 192
sampling, 41
saving, 40
slice, 210
stroke, 18, 104
Web-safe, 31, 37, 183
Windows System, 38
Color Well Swatches panel, 11
Combine menu
Crop command, 79
Intersect command, 78
objects created from, 79
Punch command, 79
Union command, 78
Cone gradient, 250
Confetti texture, 246
control handles
curves and, 49
defined, 48
extending, 50
retracting, 50
See also anchor points
Convert to Alpha Xtra, 165
copying
HTML code into Web pages, 216
instances, 233
objects, 66
objects, among layers, 86
symbols, 233
while moving objects, 67
Copy to Frames dialog box, 231
corner curves, 49
Crayon brushes, 252
cropping
canvas, 22
image objects, 147
overlapping objects, 79
Crop tool, 18
handles, 22
illustrated, 22
cross-platform issues, 3
CSI GradTone dialog box, 166
CSI HueSlider dialog box, 167

CSI Levels dialog box, 168
CSI MonoChrome dialog box, 167
CSI Negative dialog box, 168
CSI Noise dialog box, 168
CSI PhotoFilter dialog box, 167
CSI PhotoOptics filters, 166–168
defined, 166
GradTone, 166
HueSlider, 167
Levels, 168
MonoChrome, 167
Negative, 168
Noise, 168
PhotoFilter, 167
PseudoColor, 168
CSI PseudoColor dialog box, 168
cursors
Eraser tool, 77
four-headed arrow, 71
Hand, 181
icon, 18
precision, 18
curves, 49

D

Darken blending mode, 99
default colors, 18
changing, 41
defined, 40
working with, 40
See also colors
defaults
brush, 251–253
effect, 254
gradient, 250
pattern, 248–249
texture, 246–247
deleting
behaviors, 222
colors from Swatches panel, 39
files from Project Log, 141
GIF palette colors, 186
gradient control, 91
gradient fills, 92
guides, 26
layers, 85
points from paths, 56
from selection, 152
styles, 135
URL libraries, 204
URL links, 205
deselecting, 151
Designing Web Graphics.2, 4
Difference blending mode, 100
display modes, 29

Display Status Message dialog box, 223
distorting, 70
Distort tool, 18
   dragging with, 70
   illustrated, 70
DNA texture, 246
document grid
   aligning (snapping) to, 26
   color, 27
   editing, 27
   illustrated, 26
   showing/hiding, 27
   sizing, 27
   viewing, 26
Document Properties dialog box, 206
   Auto-Naming list, 214
   Slice Options, 213
   Table Shims list, 213
documents
   creating, 20
   detail, setting, 20
   displaying, 27
   dragging/dropping objects between, 67
   opening, as untitled, 23
   rulers, 24
   setting up, 19–30
   sizing, 21
   zero point, 24
document window
   Animation Controls, 240
   document info display area, 20
   illustrated, 20
Dots texture, 246
Draft Display mode, 29, 58
Draw Fill Over Brush setting, 110
The Dreamwear 2 Bible, 261
drop shadow effect
   color, 114
   light angle, 114
   presets, 114, 254
   transparency, 114
   See also effects
Drop Shadow effects panel, 114
Duplicate Frame dialog box, 219
duplicating objects, 67

E

editable text, 130
Edit Gradient dialog box, 91
editing
   behaviors, 222
   document grid, 27
   effects, 111
   colors in gradient fills, 91
   guides, 26

hotspot objects, 201
   instances, 234
   multi-frame, 240
   styles, 135
   symbols, 234
   URL links, 206
Edit menu
   Clear command, 98
   Clone command, 67
   Copy command, 66, 102
   Crop Selected Image command, 147
   Duplicate command, 67
   keyboard shortcuts, 256, 258
   Paste Attributes command, 102
   Paste command, 66
   Paste Inside command, 97
   Symbols submenu
      Make Symbol command, 233
      Tween Instances command, 235
Edit Stroke dialog box, 109
Edit Style dialog box, 132, 133, 135
Edit URL dialog box, 206
Effect panel
   Bevel, 112
   defined, 10
   Drop Shadow, 114
   elements, 10
   ellipse (...) button, 117
   Emboss, 115
   Expand button, 9
   Glow, 116
   illustrated, 10
   menu, 117
   Multiple, 117
   opening, 112
effects, 111–117
   bevel, 112–113
   drop shadow, 114
   editing, 111
   emboss, 115
   glow, 116
   multiple, applying, 117
   preset, 112, 254
   purpose, 111
   saving, 117
   See also Effect panel
Ellipse gradient, 250
ellipses, 45
Ellipse tool, 18
   illustrated, 18, 45
   Option/Alt key with, 45
   Shift key with, 45
   using, 45
Elliptical Marquee tool, 18

emboss effects
  appearance, changing, 115
  applying, 115
  defined, 115
  illustrated, 115
  light angle, 115
  light intensity, 115
  presets, 115, 254
  width/size of, 115
  See also effects
Emboss effects panel, 115
Erase blending mode, 101
Eraser, 18
  cursor, 77
  edge appearance, 156
  Erase-to-Transparent option, 156
  illustrated, 77, 156
  in Image Editing mode, 77
  size of, 156
  Tool Options, 156
  using, 77
expanding paths, 80
Expand Stroke dialog box, 80
export, specifying, 243
Export Area tool, 18
  in Export Preview, 195
  handles, 195
  illustrated, 195
  using, 195
Export dialog box, 215, 228
exporting, 179–198
  defaults, setting, 193
  files from Project Log, 141
  files in special formats, 198
  files with behaviors, 228
  frames, 243
  graphic format, 182
  images, 180
  options for batch processing, 194
  other file formats, 193
  portion of image, 195
  portion of image numerically, 196
  styles, 134
Export Preview window
  1-, 2-, and 4- icons, 190
  Animation tab, 241, 242
  Color Export menu, 187
  Disposal method list, 242
  Export Area tool, 19
  Export To Size Wizard button, 197
  Export Wizard button, 197
  File tab, 194, 196
  Hand cursor, 181
  illustrated, 180

Loop control, 242
  magnification controls, 181
  opening, 180, 181
  player controls, 243
  Pointer tool, 181
  Preview area, 190
  previewing animations in, 243
  Save Current Settings button, 192
  Save Defaults button, 193
  Show/Hide icon, 243
  Transparent GIF controls, 191
export settings
  comparing, 190
  Export Wizard and, 197
  list, 192
  saved, using, 192
  saving, 180, 192
Export to Size Wizard dialog box, 197
Export Wizard, 197
Eyedropper tool, 18
  defined, 157
  illustrated, 41, 157
  sampling colors with, 41
  for selecting transparent colors, 191
  Tool Options, 157
  using, 41, 157

F

feathering selections, 153
Feather Selection dialog box, 153
Felt Tip brushes, 252
Fiber texture, 246
file formats
  Animated GIF, 193
  BMP, 193
  choosing, 180, 182
  GIF, 182
  JPEG, 182
  PICT, 193
  PNG, 193
  TIFF, 193
  xRes LRG, 193
File menu
  Batch Process command, 142, 194
  Document Properties, 206, 213
  Export Again command, 196
  Export command, 180, 181, 192, 193, 197, 228, 241
  Export Special command, 198
  Import command, 147, 232
  keyboard shortcuts, 256, 258
  New command, 20
  Open command, 23, 146, 172, 173, 175
  Preferences command, 41, 64, 169, 177
  Preview in Browser commands, 216

Script command, 144
Fill panel
    defined, 10
    elements, 10
    Expand button, 9
    Fill category pop-up list, 88, 90, 94
    Fill-edge list, 89
    illustrated, 10, 88
    opening, 88
Fill panel menu
    Delete Gradient command, 92
    Edit command, 91
    Save Gradient As command, 92
fills, 87–102
    edges, changing, 89
    gradient, 90–94
    list of, 88, 90
    None setting, 88
    pattern, 94
    solid color, 88
    texture, 95
    Web dither, 89
    white, 88
    See also Fill panel
Find & Replace panel
    Attribute list, 137
    color attributes in, 139
    defined, 13
    elements, 13
    Find Next button, 137, 138, 139
    font attributes in, 138
    illustrated, 13, 136
    opening, 136
    Replace All button, 137, 138, 139
    Replace button, 137, 138, 139
    Search In pop-up menu, 136
    text attributes in, 137
    URL attributes in, 140
    See also searching
Find Edges Xtra, 164
Fireworks 2 Visual QuickStart Guide
    instructions, 2
    keyboard shortcuts, 2–3
    menu commands, 2
    modifier keys, 3
    organization, 2
    platform-specific features and, 3
    using, 2
Fireworks
    application icon, 8
    application in Start menu, 8
    basics, 5–18
    defined, 1
    installing, 8

launching, 8
learning, 4
uses for, 1
video, 4
The Fireworks Bible, 4
Folds gradient, 250
fonts
    attributes in Find & Replace panel, 138
    text, 121
frames
    controlling, in Layers panel, 230
    copying objects onto, 231
    creating, for rollover, 219
    distributing objects onto, 230
    distributing pages onto, 232
    modifying, for rollover, 220
    opacity, 239
    selecting, 241
    sharing elements across, 220
    sharing layers across, 231
    for swap-image behaviors, 224
    time duration of, 241
    transition of, 242
Frames panel
    defined, 9
    elements, 9
    illustrated, 9, 219, 230
    Onion Skinning controls, 239
    opening, 219, 230
    See also frames
Frames panel menu
    Copy to Frames command, 231
    Distribute to Frames command, 230
    Duplicate Frame command, 219
Freeform tool, 18
    defined, 74
    illustrated, 74
    Pull mode, 75
    Push mode, 75
    Tool Options panel, 74
    using, 75
Full Display mode, 29

G

Gaussian Blur dialog box, 161
Gaussian Blur Xtra, 161
GIF format
    choosing, 182
    JPEG format vs., 182
    options, 183
    transparent images, 191
    See also file formats
GIF palettes
    Adaptive, 184
    color control, 186

color deletion, 186
color locking, 186
color selection, 186
list, 183
loading, 187
options, 184
saving, 187
Web-safe, 183, 184
WebSnap Adaptive, 185
Glow effect panel, 116
glow effects
    applying, 116
    color, 116
    defined, 116
    presets, 254
    size of, 116
    softness, 116
    transparency, 116
    See also effects
Grabber tool, 18
    defined, 30
    illustrated, 30
    using, 30
gradient fills, 90–93
    appearance, changing, 93
    applying, 90
    defined, 90
    deleting, 92
    editing colors, 91
    end point, 93
    list of, 90
    preset, 90, 250
    rotation of, 93
    saving, 92
    start point, 93
    vector controls, 93
    See also fills
Grain texture, 246
Grass texture, 246
Grass—Tiny pattern, 248
grayscale colors (Swatches panel), 38
Grayscale mode, 11
    color definition, 36
    defined, 36
Grids and Guides dialog box
    Grids mode, 27
    Guides mode, 26
grouping objects, 62
groups
    adding objects to, 62
    nested, 63
    selecting objects within, 62
    toggle, 227
guides

aligning (snapping) to, 25
color, 26
creating, 25
deleting, 26
dragging, 25
editing, 26
horizontal, 25
locking, 26
positioning, 25
showing/hiding, 26
slice using, 208
vertical, 25
See also rulers

H

hard disk
    checking space with Macintosh, 6
    checking space with Windows, 7
    requirements, Macintosh, 6
    requirements, Windows, 7
hexadecimal mode, 11
    color definition, 33
    color ramp, 33
    defined, 33
Highlight color box, 64
highlights, 64
history list, 202
    adding to library, 205
    current, displaying, 210
    deleting URLs in, 205
Hotspot Object panel
    history list, 202
    Links field, 202
    menu, 201
    Shape menu, 201
hotspot objects, 200–201
    circular, 200
    color, 203
    converting, 201
    converting, shapes, 201
    converting objects to, 201
    defined, 199
    mixing slice objects with, 215
    moving/modifying, 201
    options, 203
    polygon, 200
    rectangular, 200
    showing/hiding, 200
    unlinked, 203
Hotspot tools, 18, 200
HSB mode, 11
    color definition, 35
    defined, 35
HTML code
    copying, into Web page, 216

for slices, 215
HTML for the World Wide Web Visual
   QuickStart Guide, 33
Hue blending mode, 100

I

icon cursors, 18
Illusion pattern, 248
Image Editing mode, 77
   indication, 148
   switching from, 146
   switching to, 146
image objects
   defined, 145
   importing scans as, 172
images
   appearing gradually, 189
   exported, scaling, 194
   exporting, 180
      portion of, 195
      portion of, numerically, 196
   interlaced, 189
   progressive, 189
   resampling, effects of, 21
   resizing, 21
   resolution of, 21
   scanned, 21, 172
   slicing, 207
   transparent, 191
Image Size dialog box, 21
importing, 171–177
   links, 204
   Photoshop files, 173
   pixel-based images, 147
   scans as image objects, 172
   styles, 134
   vector artwork, 174
Impressionist—Red pattern, 248
Info panel
   defined, 12
   elements, 12
   illustrated, 12
   menu, 42
   opening, 42
   using, 42, 66
Inner Bevel effects, 254
Insert menu
   Empty Image command, 146, 148
   Hotspot command, 201, 225
   keyboard shortcuts, 257, 258–259
   Slice command, 221, 225
   Symbol Options submenu
      Add to Symbol command, 238
      Break Link command, 237
      Delete Instances command, 238

Find Symbol command, 238
   Tween Instances command, 236, 237
Inset Path dialog box, 81
installation
   Fireworks, with Macintosh, 8
   Fireworks, with Windows, 8
instances
   copying/pasting, 233
   defined, 233
   deleting, 238
   editing, 234
   illustrated, 233
   symbol link, breaking, 237
   tweening, 235
   See also symbols
interface elements, 15
Invert Blending mode, 101
Invert Extra, 164

J

Jeans pattern, 249
joining objects, 96
JPEG format
   choosing, 182
   file size, 188
   GIF format vs., 182
   image edges, sharpening, 189
   image quality, lowering, 188
   matte color, 192
   options, setting, 188
   smoothing amount, 188
   See also file formats
justified alignment, 124

K

kerning, 122
keyboard shortcuts, 255–260
   learning, 3
   listings for, 2–3, 256–259
   Macintosh, 258–259
   modifier keys, 2, 3
   Toolbox tools, 18, 260
   Windows, 256–257

L

Lasso tool, 18
   deselecting with, 151
   illustrated, 150
   polygon mode, 150
   regular mode, 150
launching Fireworks, 8
layers
   adding, 85
   assigning blends to, 232
   default, 84

deleting, 85
displaying objects on, 85
duplicating, 85
hiding/showing, 84, 85
locking/unlocking, 84, 85
moving, 84
opening Photoshop files with, 147
shared, 220
sharing, across frames, 231
Web Layer, 84
Layers panel
defined, 9
elements, 9
Frame pop-up list, 230
illustrated, 9, 84
Option/Alt key with, 84
working with, 84
See also layers
Layers panel menu
Delete Layer command, 85
Duplicate Layer command, 85
Hide All/Show All commands, 85
illustrated, 85
Layer Options command, 85
Lock All/Unlock All commands, 85
New Layer command, 85
Share Layer command, 85, 220, 231
Single Layer Editing command, 86
leading, 123
Leaves—Photinia pattern, 249
Leaves texture, 246
Lighten blending mode, 99
Linear gradient, 250
lines
anti-alias, 54
constraining angle of, 51
creating, 51
erasing, 55
Line tool, 18
illustrated, 51
Shift key with, 51
using, 51
links
adding, to library, 205
applying, 202
deleting, 205
editing, 206
importing, 204
for slice objects, 210
See also URLs
lossy compression, 188
Luminosity blending mode, 101
Lowery, Joe, 4, 262

M
Mac Folders Preferences dialog box, 169
Macintosh
Fireworks installation, 8
hard disk space, checking, 6
launching Fireworks with, 8
memory, checking, 6
minimum system requirements, 6
Macintosh keyboard shortcuts, 258–259
Edit menu, 258
File menu, 258
Insert menu, 258–259
Modify menu, 259
Text menu, 259
View menu, 258
Window menu, 259
Xtras menu, 259
Macintosh System colors, 38
Magic Wand tool, 18
Control/Alt key with, 152
illustrated, 151
Shift key with, 152
Tolerance controls, 151
Tool Options, 151
using, 151
Magnification control menu, 27
Main toolbar (Win), 16
Marquee Options panel
Constraints list, 149
Edge list, 150
illustrated, 149
opening, 149
Marquee tool
constraints, 149
deselecting with, 151
edges, changing, 150
illustrated, 149
Option/Alt key with, 149
Shift key with, 149
Mask Groups
creating, 97
illustrated, 97
moving objects within, 98
releasing, 97
selecting, 97
selecting objects within, 98
masks
Alpha, 165
alpha channel, 97
defined, 97
moving objects within, 98
matte color, 192
memory
checking with Macintosh, 6

checking with Windows, 7
requirements, Macintosh, 6
requirements, Windows, 6
Mesh texture, 246
Metal texture, 246
Microbes texture, 246
modifier keys, 2, 3
Modify menu
  Align commands, 82
  Alter Path submenu
    Expand Stroke command, 80
    Inset command, 81
    Simplify command, 80
  Arrange submenu
    Bring Forward command, 83
    Bring to Front command, 83
    Send Backward command, 83
    Send to Back command, 83, 170
  Combine submenu
    Crop command, 79
    Intersect command, 78
    Punch command, 79
    Union command, 78
  Document submenu
    Canvas Color command, 23
    Canvas command, 22
    Image Size command, 21
  Exit Image Edit command, 146, 148
  Join command, 96
  keyboard shortcuts, 257, 259
  Mask Group command, 97, 165
  Merge Images command, 148
  Object Properties, 110, 127
  Split command, 96
  Transform submenu, 72
    command effects, 72
    Distort command, 70
    Numeric Transform command, 72
    Remove Transformations, 127
    Rotate 180 command, 72
    Scale command, 68
    Skew command, 69
  Ungroup command, 97
Modify toolbar (Win), 16
Mouse Highlight feature, 61
Move Guide dialog box, 25
moving
  anchor points, 59
  hotspot objects, 201
  layers, 84
  objects, 61, 66
    by eye, 66
    forward/backward in layer, 83
    between layers, 86

with Mask Group, 98
  numerically, 66
  in transformation mode, 71
  while copying, 67
symbol and instances, 234
symbol only, 234
multi-frame editing, 240
multiple effects, 117
Multiply blending mode, 99

N

nested groups
  creating, 63
  illustrated, 63
  working with original objects of, 63
  See also groups
New Document dialog box, 20
New Size dialog box, 22
New URL Library dialog box, 204, 205
The Non-Designer's Web Book, 4, 33
Numeric Transform dialog box, 72

O

Object panel
  Blending mode pop-up list, 98
  defined, 12
  elements, 12
  illustrated, 12
  Mask Group controls, 97
  Opacity slider, 96
  opening, 96
Object Properties dialog box, 66, 110
  Draw Fill Over Stroke box, 110
  illustrated, 110
  opening, 127, 129
  pop-up list, 110
  for text block, 127
  for text on path, 129
objects
  adding, to selection, 59
  adding, to symbols, 238
  applying styles to, 133
  blending mode, changing, 98
  cloning, 67
  converting, to hotspots, 201
  copying, 66, 67
    among layers, 86
    onto frames, 231
  deleting, 59, 60
  displaying, 27
  distorting, 70
  distributing, onto frames, 230
  dragging/dropping between documents, 67
  duplicating, 67
  filling, 41

flipping, 72
grouped, 62
grouping, 62
hotspot, 200–201
joining, 96
moving
   by eye, 66
   copying and, 67
   forward/backward in layer, 83
   between layers, 86
   with Mask Group, 98
   numerically, 66
   with Preview Drag option, 61
   in transformation mode, 71
opacity control, 12
order of, 83
overlapping, 61, 78–79
pasting, 66
pasting attributes between, 102
resizing, 72
rotating, 71, 72
scaling, 68, 72
selecting, 58
selecting, within groups, 62
sending, to front/back of layer, 83
skewing, 69
slice, 207–216
splitting, 96
transparency, 96
tweening, 235
ungrouping, 62
working with, 65–86
Oil brushes, 252
Oilslick texture, 247
onClick event, 223
onion skinning, 239
Onion Skinning dialog box, 239
onMouseOut event, 223
onMouseOver event, 223
Onyx texture, 247
opacity
   changing, 96
   control, 12, 96
   drop shadow, 114
   frame, 239
   glow effect, 116
   illustrations, 96
   object, 96
   symbol, changing, 234
   texture fill, 95
   tweening between, 236
   Open Multiple Files dialog box, 136, 141, 142
open paths
   converting to filled shape, 80

creating, 51
defined, 51
illustrated, 51
See also paths
Open Photoshop images, 147
Options panel
   defined, 12
   elements, 12
   illustrated, 12
   Mouse Highlight option, 61
   opening, 61
   Preview Drag option, 61
organization, this book, 2
orientation
   polygons, constraining, 46
   text on path, 129
Outer Bevel effects, 254
overlapping objects
   cropping, 79
   intersection of, 78
   punching holes in, 79
   uniting, 78

P

Paint Bucket tool, 18
   defined, 158
   edge options, 158
   filling objects with, 41
   illustrated, 41, 93, 158
   Tool Options, 158
   using, 158
panels
   grouping, 16
   tabs, 16
   ungrouping, 16
   See also specific panels
Parchment texture, 95, 247
paths
   adding points to, 56
   anti-aliasing, 54
   brush, modifying, 53
   brush position on, 110
   closed, 51
   deleting points from, 56
   elements of, 48
   erasing, 55
   expanding, 80
   finishing, 48, 49
   insetting, 81
   modifying, 53
   open, 51
   with series of curved segments, 49
   simplifying shape of, 80
   text conversion to, 130
   text on, 128–130

Index

See also segments
Path Scrubber tool, 18
   defined, 108
   effects, 108
   illustrated, 108
   Minus tool, 108
   using, 108
patterns
   adding, 94
   applying, to fill, 94
   defined, 94
   preset, 94, 248–249
   saving, as PNG format, 177
   See also fills
Pencil brushes, 251
Pencil tool, 18
   Anti-Aliasing option, 54
   Auto Erase option, 55
   dragging with, 55
   drawing with, 54
   fills and, 106
   illustrated, 54, 106
   lines, anti-alias, 54
   path creation with, 104
   preset settings, 106
   Stroke panel settings and, 106
   Tool Options, 54, 55
   using, 106
Pen tool, 18
   clicking with, 48
   dragging with, 49
   illustrated, 48
   Option/Alt key with, 49
   start icon, 48
PICT format, 193
pixel-based images
   combining, 148
   cropping, 147
   importing, 147
   rendering vector art into, 176
pixels, 145–158
   deselecting, 152
   selecting, 152
   swapping status of, 152
   see also, Sandee's cat Pixel
Plaster texture, 247
PNG files, 95
   exporting, 193
   saving textures/patterns as, 177
Pointer tool, 18
   dragging marquee with, 58
   Export Preview window, 181
   illustrated, 58
   Option/Alt key with, 62

Shift key with, 58
   temporary access to, 58
   using, 58
Polygon Hotspot tool, 200
Polygon Lasso tool, 18, 150
polygons, 46
Polygon tool, 18
   for creating stars, 47
   illustrated, 46
   Shift key with, 46
   Tool Options panel, 46, 47
   using, 46
precision cursors, 18
Preferences dialog box, 41, 64
   Additional Materials section, 169
   Macintosh, 177
   Windows, 169, 177
pressure-sensitive tablets
   Path Scrubber tool and, 108
   Reshape Area tool and, 76
   strokes and, 107
Preview Drag feature, 61
Project Log
   adding/deleting files to, 141
   defined, 141
   exporting files from, 141
   files in batch processing, 142
   updating, 143
Project Log panel
   defined, 14
   elements, 14
   illustrated, 14, 141
   menu, 141
   opening, 141
Pull Freeform tool, 75
Push Freeform tool, 75

R

Radial gradient, 250
Random brushes, 253
range kerning, 122, 124
Rectangle gradient, 250
Rectangle Hotspot tool, 200
rectangles
   constraining, 44
   creating, 44
   rounded-corner, 45
Rectangle tool, 18
   illustrated, 44
   Option/Alt key with, 44
   Shift key with, 44
   Tool Options, 45
   using, 44
Rectangular Marquee tool, 18
Red Goo pattern, 249

Redraw Path tool, 18
  illustrated, 53
  using, 53
regular expressions, 261–262
  defined, 261
  list of, 262
  resources, 261
Reshape Area tool, 18
  effects of, 77
  illustrated, 76
  precision amount, 76
  pressure-sensitive tablets and, 76
  strength, 76
  Tool Options panel, 76
  using, 77
resolution
  control, 174
  image, 21
RGB mode, 11
  color definition, 32
  defined, 32
Ripples gradient, 250
Ripple texture, 247
Rollover dialog box, 221
rollovers, 218–222
  assigning, 221
  behavior, assigning, 221
  defined, 218
  Down state, 218
  mouse passing over, 218
  multiple, creating, 222
  onClick state, 218
  Over state, 218
  plain image state, 218
  previewing, 221, 223, 226, 227
  state creation, 219
  See also behaviors
rotating
  with Auto-crop Images option, 73
  defined, 71
  with Numeric Transform dialog, 72
  objects, 71, 72
rounded-corner rectangles, 45
Rubber Stamp tool, 18
  brush size, 154
  defined, 154
  dragging, 155
  edge softness, 154
  illustrated, 154
  Option/Alt key with, 155
  Tool Options, 154
  using, 155
rulers
  displaying, 24

illustrated, 24
  See also guides

S

Sandpaper texture, 247
Sand texture, 247
Satin gradient, 250
Saturation blending mode, 100
Save As dialog box, 198
Save Backups dialog box, 144
Save Effect dialog box, 117
Save Gradient dialog box, 92
Save Stroke dialog box, 107
saving
  backups, 144
  batch process settings as script, 144
  colors, 40
  effects, 117
  export settings, 180, 192
  gradient fills, 92
  palettes, 187
  Stroke panel settings, 107
  textures/patterns as PNG formats, 177
Scale Attributes feature, 73
Scale tool, 18, 236
  dragging with, 68
  illustrated, 68
  Tool Options panel, 68
  Transform Options panel, 68
scaling
  defined, 68
  exported images, 194
  with Numeric Transform dialog, 72
  objects, 68, 72
  with Scale Attributes option, 73
scanned images, 21
  importing, 172
  opening, 172
Scratch texture, 247
Screen blending mode, 99
scripts, 144
searching
  by color attribute, 139
  by font attribute, 138
  by text attribute, 137
  by URL attribute, 140
  parameters, setting, 136
  See also Find & Replace panel
segments
  created by Eraser tool, 77
  curved, creating, 49
  defined, 48
  straight, creating, 48
  straight-line, with Brush tool, 52
Select Behind tool, 18

defined, 60
illustrated, 60
Option/Alt key with, 62
Shift key with, 60
using, 60
selections
changing shape of, 152
deleting from, 152
deselecting, 152
feathering, 153
similar, 153
Select menu
All command, 60, 152
Convert to Image command, 170
Feather command, 153
Group command, 62, 63
Inverse command, 152
None command, 60, 151, 152
Similar command, 153
Subselect command, 63
Superselect command, 63
Ungroup command, 62
shared layers, 220
Sharpen More Xtra, 162
Sharpen Xtra, 162
Shells texture, 247
shims, 213
Simplify dialog box, 80
skewing, 69
Skew tool, 18
dragging, 69
illustrated, 69
slice guides, 209
Slice object panel
Custom Name field, 214
Export list, 211
illustrated, 210
opening, 210
slices, 207–216
benefits of, 208, 211, 216
color, 210
creating, 209
custom naming, 214
defined, 207
defining, with ruler guides, 208
export options, 211
file names, 214
HTML code for, 215
illustrated, 208
mixing hotspots with, 215
multiple rollovers and, 222
options, 213
setting link for, 210
showing/hiding, 209

table shims, 213
text, 212
Slice tool, 18, 221
dragging, 209
illustrated, 209
sliders, 15
Smokey texture, 247
splitting objects, 96
Starburst gradient, 250
stars
acute-angled, 47
creating, 47
obtuse-angled, 47
stretch alignment, 124
Stroke Options dialog box, 109
Stroke panel
defined, 9
elements, 9
Expand button, 9
illustrated, 9, 104
opening, 104
Pencil tool settings and, 106
settings, saving, 107
size slider, 105
softness slider, 105
stroke category pop-up list, 104
Stroke panel menu
Edit Stroke command, 109
illustrated, 107
Save Stroke As command, 107
strokes, 103–110
angle, 109
appearance, 109
applying, 104
attributes, changing, 105
brush, 104
categories of, 105
changing, position on path, 110
color, 104
defined, 103, 104
edges, blurring, 105
edge softness, 109
fill meeting, 110
natural, 107
Option/Alt key and, 108
pausing effect on, 107
preset, 105
roundness, 109
sensitivity of, 109
shape, 109
sizing, 105, 109
textures, 106
width of, 107, 108
Stroke Sensitivity dialog box, 109

Stroke Shape dialog box, 109
styles, 132–135
    accessing, 134
    adjoining, selecting, 134
    applying, to objects, 133
    control properties, 132
    defined, 132
    defining, 132
    deleting, 135
    editing, 135
    exporting, 134
    importing, 134
    naming, 132, 133
    resetting, 135
    text, 133
    views, 135
Styles panel
    defined, 14
    Delete Style icon, 135
    elements, 14
    illustrated, 14, 132
    New Style button, 132
    opening, 132
    preview, 132, 133
    See also styles
Styles panel menu
    Delete Styles command, 135
    Edit Style command, 135
    Export Styles command, 134
    illustrated, 134
    Import Styles command, 134
    Large Icons command, 135
    Reset Styles command, 135
Subselection tool, 18
    dragging with, 59
    illustrated, 56, 59
    Option/Alt key with, 62
    using, 56, 59
subtractive color, 34
Swap Image behavior, 224–226
    assigning, 226
    changed area definition, 225
    defined, 224
    elements, creating, 224
    frame creation for, 224
    illustrated, 224
    trigger area definition, 225
    See also behaviors
Swap Image dialog box, 226
swatches
    choosing, 11
    grayscale, 38
    loading, 40
    Macintosh System, 37

    saving, 40
    sorting, 39
    Web 216 Palette, 37
    Windows System, 38
    See also color palettes; colors
Swatches panel
    adding colors to, 38
    arranging colors on, 39
    defined, 11
    deleting colors from, 39
    elements, 11
    illustrated, 11
    loading colors to, 40
    opening, 23
    saving colors in, 40
    using, 36–40
    See also swatches
Swatches panel menu
    Add Swatches command, 40
    Clear Swatches command, 39
    Grayscale command, 38
    illustrated, 36
    Macintosh System command, 37
    opening, 36
    Replace Swatches command, 40
    Save Swatches command, 40
    Sort by Color command, 39
    Web 216 Palette command, 37
    Windows System command, 38
Swirls texture, 247
Swish texture, 247
symbols
    adding objects to, 238
    creating, 233
    defined, 233
    dragging, with Option/Alt key, 233
    editing, 234
    finding, 238
    illustrated, 233
    instance link, breaking, 237
    moving, 234
    opacity, changing, 234
    See also instances
system requirements
    Macintosh, 6
    Windows, 7

T

text, 119–130
    accessing, 120
    aligning, 126
    attributes, applying, 121
    attributes in Find & Replace panel, 137
    baseline shift, 123
    conversion to paths, 130

editable, 130
flow, reversing, 125
fonts, 121
horizontal alignment, 124
horizontal scale, 124
kerning, 122
leading, 123
on path, 128–130
  alignment, changing, 128
  attaching, 128
  attributes, 130
  conversion to paths, 130
  direction, reversing, 130
  offset, 129
  orientation, 129
point size, 121
restoring, 127
sizing, 126
slice, 212
styles, 133
styling, 121, 126
in text blocks, 126–127
typeface, changing, 126
vertical alignment, 125
text blocks
  multiple, 126
  object properties for, 127
  text modification in, 126
  text transformation in, 127
Text Editor
  alignment controls, 124
  baseline shift controls, 123
  defined, 17
  elements, 17
  font list, 121
  horizontal scale controls, 124
  illustrated, 17, 120
  kerning controls, 122
  leading controls, 123
  opening, 120
  point size control, 121
  range kerning controls, 122
  reopening, 120
  styling controls, 121
  text flow controls, 125
  using, 120
  vertical alignment controls, 125
  See also text
Text menu
  Align command, 128
  Alignment command, 126, 128
  Attach to Path command, 128
  Convert to Paths command, 130
  Editor command, 120

keyboard shortcuts, 257, 259
Orientation command, 129
Reverse Direction command, 130
Size command, 126
Style command, 126
Text tool, 18, 120
textures
  adding, 95
  applying, to fill, 95
  applying, to stroke, 106
  defined, 95
  preset, 246–247
  saving as PNG format, 177
  transparent settings, 95
  See also patterns
TIFF format, 193
Tint blending mode, 101
Toggle Group dialog box, 227
toggle groups, 227
Toolbox
  Brush tool, 18, 52–53, 104, 107
  Circle Hotspot tool, 200
  Crop tool, 18, 22
  default colors icon, 40
  Distort tool, 18, 70
  Ellipse tool, 18, 45
  Elliptical Marquee tool, 18
  Export Area tool, 18, 195
  Eyedropper tool, 18, 41, 157
  Freeform tool, 18, 74–75
  Grabber tool, 18, 30
  illustrated, 18
  keyboard shortcuts, 18, 260
  Lasso tool, 18, 150–151
  Line tool, 18, 51
  Magic Wand tool, 18, 151–152
  Marquee tool, 149, 150–151
  Paint Bucket tool, 18, 41, 158
  Path Scrubber tool, 18, 108
  Pencil tool, 18, 54–55, 106
  Pen tool, 18, 48–49
  Pointer tool, 18, 58, 62, 181
  Polygon Hotspot tool, 200
  Polygon Lasso tool, 18, 150
  Polygon tool, 18, 46–47
  Pull Freeform tool, 75
  Push Freeform tool, 75
  Rectangle Hotspot tool, 200
  Rectangle Marquee tool, 18
  Rectangle tool, 18, 44–45
  Redraw Path tool, 18, 53
  Reshaping Area tool, 18, 76–77
  Rubber Stamp tool, 18, 154–155
  Scale tool, 18, 68, 236

Select Behind tool, 18, 60, 62
Skew tool, 18, 69
Slice tool, 18, 209, 221
Subselection tool, 18, 56, 59, 62
swap colors icon, 40
Text tool, 18, 120
tool illustrations, 18
Windows version, 18
Zoom tool, 18, 28, 181
transformation mode
  leaving, 68, 69, 70, 71
  moving objects in, 71
transformations
  Auto-crop Images option and, 73
  distortion, 70
  rotation, 71, 72
  Scale Attributes option and, 73
  scaling, 68, 72
  skewing, 69
  text block text, 127
Transform menu. See Modify menu
transparency. See opacity
transparent GIFs, 191
Tweed pattern, 249
tweening, 235–237
  appearances, 236
  defined, 235
  illustrated, 235
  images, altering, 237
  between opacities, 236
  between rotations, 236
  between sizes, 236
Tween Instances dialog box, 235

U

ungrouping objects, 62
Unnatural brushes, 253
Unsharp Mask dialog box, 163
Unsharp Mask Xtra, 163
URL libraries
  adding history list to, 205
  adding URL links to, 205
  creating, 204
  deleting, 204
  naming, 204
URL Manager menu
  Add History to Library command, 205
  Add URL command, 205
  Clear History command, 205
  Delete Link command, 205
  Edit URL command, 206
  illustrated, 205
URL Manager panel
  defined, 13
  elements, 13

illustrated, 13
  opening, 204
  options list, 204
URLs
  attributes, in Find & Replace panel, 140
  defined, 202
  link application, 202
  See also links

V

vector artwork, 174–176
  edge, setting, 176
  opening, 174
  pages, setting to open, 175
  rendering, into pixel images, 176
  setting layers of, 175
  setting size of, 174
Vector File Options dialog box, 174
  Anti-Aliased option, 176
  Height control, 174
  illustrated, 174
  Include Background Layers option, 175
  Include Invisible Layers option, 175
  Layer options, 175, 232
  Page options, 175, 232
  Remember Layers option, 175
  Render as Images options, 176
  Resolution control, 174
  Scale control, 174
  Width control, 174
vector objects
  applying Xtras to, 160
  converting to grayscale image, 165
  turning into image objects, 148
Vein texture, 247
View Controls toolbars, 14
View menu
  Draft Display command, 29
  Edit Guides command, 26
  Fit All command, 27
  Fit Selection command, 27
  Full Display command, 29
  Grid command, 26
  Hide Edges command, 64
  keyboard shortcuts, 256, 258
  Lock Guides command, 26
  Magnification command, 27
  Rulers command, 24
  Slice Guides command, 209
  Snap to Grid command, 26
  Snap to Guides command, 25
  Zoom In command, 27
  Zoom Out command, 27
Villarosa, Ray, 4

W

Watercolor brushes, 252–253
Waves gradient, 250
Weave pattern, 249
Web browsers, setting, 216
Web dither fill, 89
Web Layer, 84
Web-safe colors, 31, 37, 183
  defined, 37
  using, 37
  See also colors
Web-safe palette, 183, 184
WebSnap Adaptive palette, 185
  defined, 185
  options, setting, 185
  uses, 185
Weinman, Lynda, v, 4
Window menu
  Behaviors command, 221
  Color Mixer command, 32
  Effect command, 112
  Fill command, 88
  Find & Replace command, 136
  Frames command, 219, 230
  Info command, 42, 66
  Insert Slice Object command, 222
  keyboard shortcuts, 257, 259
  Layers command, 84
  Object command, 96, 210
  Project Log command, 141
  Stroke command, 104
  Styles command, 132
  Swatches command, 36
  URL Manager command, 204
Windows
  Fireworks installation, 8
  Hard Disk Properties display, 7
  hard disk space, checking, 7
  launching Fireworks with, 8
  memory, checking, 7
  minimum system requirements, 7
  System Properties display, 7
Windows keyboard shortcuts, 256–257
  Edit menu, 256
  File menu, 256
  Insert menu, 257
  Modify menu, 257
  Text menu, 257
  View menu, 256
  Window menu, 257
  Xtras menu, 257
Windows System colors, 38
Wood—Light pattern, 249
Wood texture, 247

X

xRes LRG format, 193
Xtras, 159–170
  adding, 169
  applying to vector objects, 160
  Blur, 160
  Blur More, 160
  Convert to Alpha, 165
  defined, 159
  Find Edges, 164
  Gaussian Blur, 161
  Invert, 164
  reapplying, 169
  Sharpen, 162
  Sharpen More, 162
  Unsharpen Mask, 163
Xtras menu
  Blur submenu
    Blur command, 160
    Blur More command, 160
    Gaussian Blur command, 161
  Invert command, 164
  keyboard shortcuts, 257, 259
  Other submenu
    Convert to Alpha command, 165
    Find Edges command, 164
  PhotoOptics commands, 166
  Repeat command, 169
  Sharpen submenu
    Sharpen command, 162
    Sharpen More command, 162
    Unsharp Mask command, 163

Z

zero point, 24
zooming, 28
  Export Preview window, 181
  to specific magnification, 27
Zoom tool, 18
  +/- icons and, 28
  Export Preview window, 181
  illustrated, 18, 28
  Option/Alt key with, 28
  using, 28